CW00739659

INDIA

A WOMAN'S GUIDE TO TRAVELING
IN NORTH AND WEST INDIA

Go! Girl Guides: India; First Edition
By Allison Sodha
Published by Go! Girl Travel LLC and its parent company, Inspired Holdings LLC.
©2022 All rights reserved.

Layout, Design & Illustration:
John H. Clark IV
Hop and Jaunt
www.hopandjaunt.com

ISBN: 978-0-9859122-5-3 (paperback)
       978-0-9859122-6-0 (digital)

ABOUT THE AUTHOR

Allison Sodha is the President of Sodha Travel, a company that specializes in sustainable and immersive travel to South Asia. As an India Destination Specialist, she has spent almost two decades exploring the country and writing for various publications. Allison has a passion for creating experiences fueled by a deeper understanding of local communities. When not traveling, you will find her dancing and creating globally-inspired sweet treats with her husband and three children. Learn more at www.sodhatravel.com.

TABLE OF CONTENTS

TABLE OF CONTENTS

TABLE OF CONTENTS

TABLE OF CONTENTS

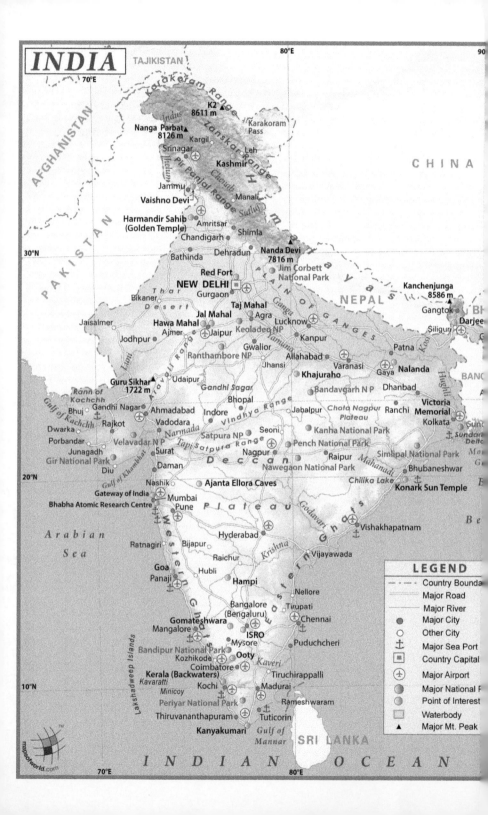

INDIA

TAJIKISTAN

80°E

90

70°E

AFGHANISTAN

Karakoram Range

Indus

Zanskar Range

K2
8611 m

Nanga Parbat
8126 m

Karakoram
Pass

Kargil

Leh

Srinagar

Jammu

Manali

Kashmir

CHINA

Jhelum

Pir Panjal Range

Chenab

Sutlej

Vaishno Devi

Harmandir Sahib
(Golden Temple)

Amritsar

Shimla

Chandigarh

30°N

PAKISTAN

Dehradun

Nanda Devi
7816 m

Jim Corbett
National Park

Kanchenjunga
8586 m

Bathinda

Red Fort

NEW DELHI

Gurgaon

Gangtok

Darjee

Bikaner

Thar

Desert

Jal Mahal

PLAIN OF GANGES

NEPAL

Siliguri

BH

Taj Mahal

Agra

Jaisalmer

Hawa Mahal

Ajmer

Jaipur

Keoladeo NP

Lucknow

Ganga

Patna

Jodhpur

Aravali Range

Gwalior

Kanpur

Yamuna

Kosi

Hughli

BANG

Ranthambore NP

Jhansi

Allahabad

Varanasi

Gaya

Nalanda

Luni

Udaipur

Guru Sikhar
1722 m

Rann of
Kachchh

Gandhi Sagar

Khajuraho

Bandavgarh N P

Dhanbad

Victoria
Memorial

Gulf of
Kachchh

Bhuj

Gandhi Nagar

Bhopal

Chota Nagpur
Plateau

Ranchi

Gandhi Nagar

Ahmadabad

Indore

Vindhya Range

Jabalpur

Kolkata

Sund

Dwarka

Rajkot

Vadodara

Narmada

Satpura NP

Seoni

Kanha National Park

Simlipal National Park

Sundar
Delta

Porbandar

Velavadar N P

Surat

Tapi

Satpura Range

Nagpur

Pench National Park

Raipur

Mahanadi

Mo

Junagadh

Gir National Park

Daman

Deccan

Nawegaon National Park

Bhubaneswar

Diu

Gulf of Khambhat

Nashik

Chilika Lake

Konark Sun Temple

20°N

Gateway of India

Ajanta Ellora Caves

B

Bhabha Atomic Research Centre

Mumbai

Pune

Plateau

Godavari

Western Ghats

Eastern Ghats

Vishakhapatnam

Be

Ratnagiri

Bijapur

Hyderabad

Arabian

Sea

Raichur

Krishna

Vijayawada

Goa

Panaji

Hubli

Hampi

Nellore

Bangalore
(Bengaluru)

Tirupati

Chennai

Gomateshwara

Mangalore

ISRO

Mysore

Puduchcheri

Bandipur National Park

Ooty

Kozhikode

Coimbatore

Kaveri

Tiruchirappalli

Kerala (Backwaters)

Kochi

Madurai

Rameshwaram

10°N

Lakshadweep Islands

Kavaratti

Minicoy

Periyar National Park

Thiruvananthapuram

Tuticorin

Kanyakumari

Gulf of
Mannar

SRI LANKA

70°E

80°E

INDIAN OCEAN

LEGEND

– – –	Country Bounda
	Major Road
	Major River
●	Major City
○	Other City
⚓	Major Sea Port
▣	Country Capital
⊕	Major Airport
◐	Major National F
◑	Point of Interest
▢	Waterbody
▲	Major Mt. Peak

mapsofworld.com

WELCOME
FROM KELLY & ALLISON

Namaste.

India is truly a sensory experience. It is a land of color, contrast, and community. Though transforming at such a rapid pace, the country fluently maintains its cultural, historical, and spiritual treasures. India offers something for everyone, including architecture, adventure, cuisine, ancient history, beaches, wildlife, backwaters, palaces, shopping, destination spas, festivals, music, dancing, and the majestic Himalayas - just to name a few.

Still yet, India can be an intimidating destination for the solo female traveler — which is why we've created this guide for you. In these pages, you'll find essential information on everything from cultural traditions to how to dress and pack.

India awaits. Enjoy the Journey!

Kelly Lewis and Allison Sodha

NOTE FROM ALLISON

Hello, travelers!

My love for India started even before I ever set foot in the country. Growing up in Atlanta, Georgia, I was exposed to various aspects of Indian culture - more than any other non-Indian I knew. When I was nine, my parents enrolled me in a Transcendental Meditation course. Our beach house was named Namaste. In high school, I wrote term papers about meditation, levitation, reincarnation, and polytheism. I attended seminars at the Deepak Chopra Center and read countless books on India's history. We had a Ganesha statue in our living room. My mother, a meditation instructor, would often discuss the benefits of Ayurveda.

During college, I studied Indian history and religion. My favorite courses were Hinduism, History of Modern India, Hindu Tantra, and Foundations of Buddhism. After graduating, I made my first trip to India and started researching and writing for various publications. My travels took me off the popular tourist routes and planted the seeds for my company, Sodha Travel.

My India expertise is not just from being well-traveled. It's a culmination of two decades of research, interviews, and insider access to local communities. This passion for India is what fuels me to create a guide for women.

Real talk.

We have all seen the bold headlines warning women about the dangers of traveling in India - staring, groping, assualt, and even rape. As a woman, travel professional, and India maven, I believe it is important to have an open dialogue and dispel any myths. In my opinion, there are many misconceptions about women traveling in India.

So here's my take.

India is a country of over 1.3 billion people. It is unfortunate but women will be the victims of senseless attacks. However, I strongly believe it is unfair to categorize an entire country under an umbrella of assaulters. The Indians I know are warm and welcoming and do not incite violence. I felt more threatened on a train from Rome to Prague and even when I lived in New York City.

India is my second home. I have traveled to the country countless times in various professional and personal capacities - solo, with groups, with family, and with friends. As a female, I can honestly say that I have never felt threatened. Uncomfortable? Sure, at times. I cannot speak for every woman, nor do I intend to minimize the experience of another, but it is sincerely possible and likely to have an enriching and engaging trip.

Vibrant. Chaotic. Crowded. Animated.

It is easy to become overwhelmed, and as a woman, traveling in India will likely require a heightened sense of awareness. As with any international travel, I advise being aware of your surroundings and also understanding basic social propriety. Common sense is key. Do I recommend booking services in advance and having a network available for assistance? I do. But does this mean if females travel independently they will be the victims of assault? Absolutely not.

Throughout this guide, I will offer recommendations that not only keep women safe but contribute to more enriching experiences. Use these resources to travel to India with an open mind and heart. Be cautious, but not anxious, and understand the difference between discomfort and danger.

I'll see you in India!

Cheers!

Allison

SAFETY

Don't be afraid to take on the world! Here at Go! Girl Guides, we believe that women should feel empowered, enthusiastic, and excited to explore the globe. We know you do, too. Why, then, does it seem like many of our well-meaning friends and family are opposed to the idea of us traveling solo - *especially* in India?

Perhaps it is because they don't understand:
Traveling solo does not mean you are alone.

These days, especially with the technological advances, it has become increasingly easier to connect with other like-minded travelers. In fact, you may find that you are very rarely *alone*. Especially in India, where personal space is at a minimum, you will find yourself in conversations with other travelers in trains, planes, boats, markets, restaurants, and beyond.

So, how can you reassure the critics that traveling solo is both safe and enriching?

Be informed, not influenced.

With the right resources and support system, we firmly believe it is not just possible but extremely likely to have a safe, comfortable, and enriching experience in India. It's important to do research and be informed (like with this guide!), but we also caution travelers from being emotionally influenced by the experiences of others.

Follow statistics, not sensationalism. Ask questions and connect with other women who have explored the same destinations. If there is a thread of commonality, ask the whats and whens and whos. Ultimately, the goal is for you to be confident in your traveling environment. It is our philosophy that when women are comfortable, they will be more open to new connections, conversations, and experiences.

What resists, persists.

Because India is an assault on the senses, it can be difficult to assimilate. The more you push back against the crowds, noise, and poverty, the more difficult it will be to enjoy the experience. Try to ease into the Indian rhythm sooner rather than later.

RESOURCES TO STAY SAFE
(TO BE DIALED FROM AN INDIAN SIM ONLY)

DEPARTMENT	NUMBER
Emergency Helpline Number	112
Covid 19 Helpline	1075
Police	100
Fire	101
Ambulance	102
Women Helpline	1091
Road Accident Emergency Service	1073
Railway Accident Emergency Service	1072
Air Accident	1071
Air Ambulance	9540161344

TRAVEL SAFE

For its size, India has a very low crime rate and is generally a safe country. Here are basic tips to keep you safe in India and beyond:

After Dark
Check with your accommodations about the safe and unsafe areas of town. Don't venture out solo at night. If you do go out after dark, don't walk! Pay a few bucks for a taxi.

Zip Up
Make sure your purse is zipped and wallets are in sealed pockets. The most common crime is pick-pockets at markets, train stations, and bus stations, so monitor your belongings at all times.

Travel Safe, Ride Alone

Ride Alone
Don't enter a taxi or rickshaw with other passengers, and don't allow a driver to pick-up additional passengers.

When in Doubt, Lie
Never share information on your travel plans or where you are staying. If you need to, lie.

Drink Responsibly
Enjoy a cocktail (or two) but don't lose your inhibitions. Being intoxicated may invite unwelcome behavior.

Respect Local Customs
Do your research and respect local laws and customs. This will help you avoid any unintentional cultural embarrassments or worse.

DEALING WITH CATCALLS / EVE TEASING

Eve Teasing is a form of sexual aggression toward women. Named after "Eve" in the bible, the harassment usually occurs in public spaces and can include teasing, flirtation, inappropriate comments, catcalls, and groping. Although serious instances are rare, as a foreigner and a female, you will naturally attract attention.

Get Comfortable with People Staring at You
It's common. Most of the time it's just out of curiosity, but it can feel uneasy. Do your best to ignore it.

Stay with the Ladies
If traveling by metro or urban train, try to sit in the woman-only compartment to avoid men pressing up against you. In public spaces like markets and train stations, try to stay by other women. If you are being followed, step into a restaurant or shop and ask for help.

Make a Scene
If you ever feel threatened, make a scene. Yell, push, and take out your cell phone to record. Indians avoid public shaming and other locals will step in to protect you. You can also dial 1091 from an Indian SIM to reach the Women Helpline.

Once, I was on a train from Delhi - Haridwar. As I was exiting the restroom, a man kept asking my name and blocked the door when I didn't respond. After asking him twice to move, unsuccessfully, I got in his face and started to yell. A few passengers quickly stood up to approach him as he started apologizing and sheepishly skulked away. "Sorry, Madam. Sorry, Madam. I'm so sorry, Madam. I never meant to upset you, Madam." Remember, don't try to be polite. Get loud and cause a riot!

HOW TO PROTECT YOUR BELONGINGS

Keep Cash in Different Places
Don't store all your cash in one wallet. Split up your bills so if the wallet is stolen, it won't be a (major) financial loss.

Password Protect It

Password Protect-It
Make sure all your devices are password protected. Erase your browsing history and clear your cache so no passwords are stored.

Choose Rooms with a Safe
Select accommodations with an in-room safe to store your passport and valuables. Unless you exchange money, book travel, or purchase a SIM card, you won't need your passport.

Secure Your Gear
Before you go, consider buying bags, backpacks, and wallets with anti-theft technology. Pacsafe is one company offering smart zipper security and cut resistant materials. Bonus: 74% of their products are made using recycled fabrics!

Keep Your Valuables Close
Sound obvious? Yes, but it's worth repeating. When outside your room, keep valuables close and not in open pockets or unsecure bags.

Don't Be Flashy

Unless you are attending a wedding or other formal event, don't wear expensive and extravagant jewelry in public. After visiting an ATM, put the cash away quickly and don't flash wads of Rupees.

COMMON SCAMS AND HOW TO AVOID THEM

In India, a foreigner means $$$ and local scammers are always ready to take advantage of unassuming travelers. Knowledge is power, and speaking from personal experience, understanding these common manipulations will keep you better prepared during your trip.

Airport Assistance

When you exit the airport, you will likely be swarmed by local drivers offering "assistance." It is an overwhelming cacophony of bargaining and opinions. The drivers will say anything to get a customer, much of it untrue. Do NOT reserve a pre-paid taxi, as the rates are sky high. Arrange airport transports in advance through your hotel or other reputable service provider.

Broken Meter, Madam

No, it's not a coincidence that you happen to flag down taxis and rickshaws with a "broken meter." Non-metered taxis are illegal in India. Drivers will offer a flat rate that magically doubles or triples when you reach your destination. Make sure you only enter a metered vehicle.

Distraction Scam
This is when someone (usually a local) will strike up a casual conversation to divert your attention while an accomplice swoops in to steal. It's common in crowded public spaces, including markets and train stations. Make sure no valuables are in your pockets and keep bags zipped in front of you.

SIM Card
Depending on your carrier and international plan, it may be cost effective to purchase a local SIM card when traveling. In India, passports, 2x2 photos, and documents are required. If approached by someone offering fast and cheap SIM cards, say no. Usually they are invalid or attached to another person's number - resulting in calls from random strangers. Take the time to visit an official mobile store and only load prepaid cards at licensed shops and kiosks.

The Bogus Blessing
Temples and sacred spaces are popular grounds for scammers. Locals dressed as priests and religious figures will offer a blessing, often with a small gift, and then act belligerent until you pay a large sum of money. Some men will also act as temple officials and repeatedly ask for a donation. Politely refuse and walk away.

Hotel or No-tel

Drivers will claim your hotel doesn't exist, moved, or shut down. They may also drive you to a hotel with a similar name, claiming they didn't understand English. Make sure you have the contact information of your property to reconfirm the address with the driver before you ride. If possible, arrange for transportation from the hotel directly.

Buying for Beggars

Fair warning: You will be approached by beggars. Millions of Indians live below the poverty line, earning less than $1.50 per day. Children, often coerced into working for a criminal gang, will ask you for food or toys instead of money. Women will also plead for milk for their babies. (Sadly, many of these babies are rented and drugged for the day.)

Well-intentioned travelers buy these items, thinking they are making a small difference. However, the scammers have deals with the shops and return the products after you leave. Some shop owners also inflate the prices and then split the difference with the offender. If you do feel compelled to give, bring candy, stickers, and small pens to distribute or inquire about reputable organizations.

Fake Luxury/Imports

No, a pack of plastic bangles from a local market does not cost 40 USD because the crystals were imported from Europe. A pashmina for 10 USD is not made of pure cashmere. Vendors will tell tall tales to make a sale, whether inflating the cost due to "import taxes" or selling a "luxury" item for ridiculously cheap. Either way, make sure you bargain! As a foreigner, your cost will start out 4x higher compared to a local.

Check your Change

Double check your change if paying by cash. The scammer may try to convince you that you paid with a smaller bill, resulting in an escalation. Since the demonetization of certain banknotes, some taxi drivers and vendors may claim the bill you provided is no longer in circulation. They may also try to return counterfeit bills, thinking you won't really be familiar with local currency.

Medical Care

If you become ill and require medical care, carefully check the bill. Although costs are relatively low compared to the United States, hospitals may "accidentally" add on additional services and medications, not expecting you to question the price or level of care. Also, some clinics may strongly recommend treatment that is not required, like x-rays or IV's. Purchase a travel insurance policy before your trip so any unexpected medical costs will be reimbursed.

Paying for Photos

Roadside attractions with people and animals will attract the crowds. The operators will smile and encourage photographs, only to follow you asking for a tip. If you refuse, they may become hostile. Click at your own risk!

I was once leading a women's tour in North India. After shopping in Jaipur's Old City, one of my guests excitedly came back on the bus with a bag filled with *jutti* (traditional Indian footwear). She showed us her colorful shoes and excitedly said, "All for only $250!" Unfortunately, the shopkeeper convinced her that these beautiful (yet common) shoes were made from premium leather and imported from Spain. The actual price of the footwear? Somewhere between $20-$25 for all four pairs. Shop wisely.

MODESTY IS THE BEST POLICY

Generally speaking, India is a conservative country. Don't attract unnecessary attention by wearing clothing that is too short, tight, or revealing.

Do's and Don'ts

Do wear tank tops. Just carry a wrap or shawl in your daypack if you need to cover your shoulders at a temple or religious site.

Do pack shorts and skirts, but make sure they are knee-length or longer.

Do wear crop tops. Showing the tummy is common in India (hello, saree!) but make sure the tops cover your chest.

Do dress more modestly outside of major cities and tourist spots.

Don't wear shirts that expose cleavage or have an open back with the bra showing.

Don't engage in excessive public displays of affection.

Don't walk around in a bikini or bathing suit. When not swimming or sunbathing, cover up!

U.S. EMBASSY AND CONSULATES

New Delhi: Embassy
Shantipath, Chanakyapuri
New Delhi - 110021
Phone: +91 11 2419 8000

Mumbai: Consulate
C-49, G-Block, Bandra Kurla Complex
Bandra East, Mumbai 400051
Phone: +91 22 2672 4000

Hyderabad: Consulate
Paigah Palace
1-8-323, Chiran Fort Lane
Begumpet, Secunderabad 500 003
Phone: +91 40 4625 8222; +91 12 0484 4644

Chennai: Consulate
Gemini Circle
Chennai 600 006
Phone: +91 044 2857 4000

Kolkata: Consulate
38A, J.L.Nehru Road,
Kolkata - 700 071,
West Bengal, India
Phone: +91 33 3984 6300

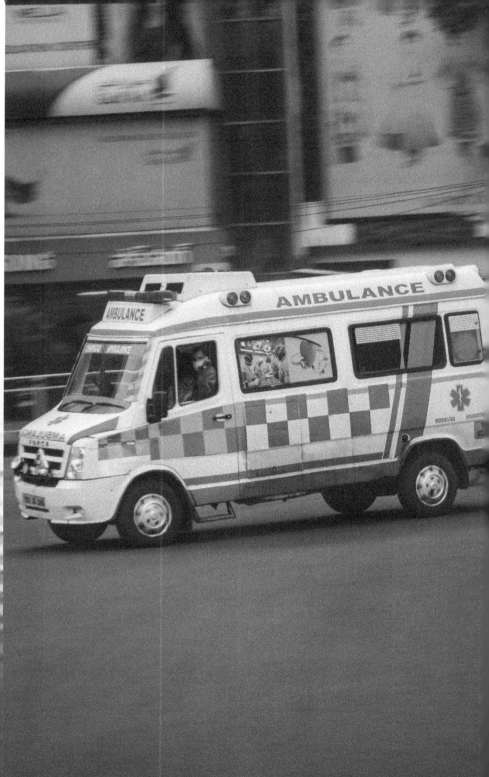

HEALTH

India has a universal healthcare model with both private and public (government) hospitals. Medical technology is quite advanced for a developing country, especially in larger cities. The lower cost of care has also made India a popular destination for medical tourism, especially related to cardiology, ophthalmology, fertility treatments, and plastic surgery. Healthcare is the responsibility of the state governments and not administered at the federal level.

Because India is the largest exporter of generic drugs, it has earned the title of "Pharmacy of the World." OTC and prescription drugs are very inexpensive. Many can even be prescribed at the pharmacy without a doctor's approval. Online pharmacies and chemists have also become popular platforms to order medicine and healthcare products. You can even request a consultation or diagnostic test. Unfortunately, India is not immune to the opioid crisis and painkillers have become the largest prescription drug on the black market.

You will find both Allopathy and Homeopathy in India. With Allopathic medicine, the cure differs from the cause. Doctors utilize modern, science-based treatments that may have side effects but work immediately. Homeopathic medicine uses the body's natural defenses to cure the disease (or dis-*ease*). Doctors believe the source that causes a symptom will also be the cure.

PRIVATE VS. PUBLIC HEALTHCARE

Public hospitals are free for Indian residents. Medical interns are required to volunteer as part of their academic process - otherwise most would opt to work in the private sector. Government hospitals have a reputation for long waits, irregular hours, and standard care. In many rural communities, however, they are the only option.

Almost 60% of India's hospitals are private. Compared to government facilities, they are known for having high-quality care. Private hospitals are also the least regulated, resulting in higher costs and malpractice claims. Over the years, I have had my fair share of visits to both government and private facilities. For general health concerns, either is fine. For a more serious illness and injury, try and find a private hospital instead.

LIST OF HOSPITALS

Here is a sample list of both private and government hospitals.

Delhi

Private - Indraprastha Apollo Hospital
Mathura Rd, New Delhi
Phone: +91 011 7179 1090
www.askapollo.com

Private - Max Super Specialty Hospital
1, 2, Press Enclave Marg, Saket Institutional Area, Saket, Delhi
Phone: +91 011 2651 5050
www.maxhealthcare.in

Private - BLK Super Specialty Hospital
Pusa Rd, Radha Soami Satsang, Rajendra Place, Delhi
Phone: +91 011 3040 3040
www.blkhospital.com

Government - All India Institute of Medical Sciences (AIIMS)
Sri Aurobindo Marg, Ansari Nagar, Ansari Nagar East, Delhi
Phone: +91 011 2658 8500
www.aims.edu

Government - Safdarjung Hospital
Ansari Nagar East, near to AIIMS Metro Station, Delhi
Phone: +91 011 2673 0000
www.vmmc-sjh.nic.in

Leh/Ladakh

Government - Sonam Norboo Memorial Hospital
Old Leh Road, Leh, Jammu and Kashmir
Phone: +91 19 8225 2014

Amritsar

Private - Fortis Escort
Majitha-Verka ByPass, Verka, Amritsar
Phone: +91 18 3503 2222
www.fortishealthcare.com

Private - Nayyar Hospital
3, Dasonda Singh Rd, Amritsar
Phone: +91 98 1499 9199
www.nayyarhospital.com

Government - Guru Nanek Dev Hospital
Majitha Rd, Medical Enclave, Amritsar
Phone: +91 18 3242 1050

Chandigarh

Private - Healing Hospital
SCO 16-17-18-19, Sub. City Center, Sector 34A, Sector 34, Chandigarh
Phone: +91 17 2508 8883
www.healinghospital.co.in

Private - Chaitanya Hospital and Gynecology
Hospital Site 1 And 2, 44C, Chandigarh
Phone: +91 17 2508 8088
www.chaitanyahospital.org

Government - Government Medical College and Hospital
Chandi Path, Sector 32B, 32B, Sector 32, Chandigarh
Phone: +91 17 2260 1023
www.gmch.gov.in

Haridwar and Rishikesh

Private - Metro Hospital and Heart Institute
Plot No. F - 1, Sector 6A, SIDCUL Sector 8A, Road, Integrated
Industrial Estate, BHEL Township, Haridwar
Phone: +91 81 9190 2600
www.metrohospitals.com

Government - All India Institute of Medical Science (AIIMS)
Virbhadra Road Shivaji Nagar, near Barrage, Sturida Colony, Rishikesh
Phone: +91 13 5246 2927
www.aiimsrishikesh.edu.in

Shimla

Private - Tenzin Hospital and Gynecology
NH-22, Bypass Rd Panthaghati, Kasumpti, Shimla
Phone: +91 17 7262 4663
www.tenzinhospital.com

Government - Indira Gandhi Medical College & Hospital
Ridge Sanjauli Rd, Lakkar Bazar, Shimla
Phone: +91 17 7265 4713
www.igmcshimla.edu.in

Dharamshala

Private - Fortis Hospital
Palampur - Dharamshala Rd, Adarsh nagar, Kangra
Phone: +91 18 9224 2555
www.fortishealthcare.com

Government - Dr. Rajendra Prasad Government Medical College
Tanda Hospital Rd, Pushp Vihar Colony, Kangra
Phone: +91 18 9224 2555
www.rpgmc.ac.in

Private - Heritage Hospitals
Lanka, Varanasi, Uttar Pradesh 221005
Phone: +91 54 2718 1911
www.heritagehospitals.com

Government - Institute of Medical Sciences BHU
Aurobindo Colony, Banaras Hindu University Campus, Varanasi
Phone: +91 54 2236 7568
www.bhu.ac.in

Ahmedabad

Private - Sterling Hospital
Sterling Hospital Road near Maharaja Agrasen Vidyalaya,
Memnagar, Ahmedabad
Phone: +91 79 4001 1111
www.sterlinghospitals.com

Private - Apollo Hospital International
Plot No, 1A, Gandhinagar - Ahmedabad Rd, GIDC Bhat, Bhat,
Ahmedabad
Phone: +91 79 6670 1800
www.ahmedabadapollohospitals.com

Government - Civil Hospital Campus
Address: D Block Asarwa, Haripura, Office of the Medical
Superintendent Civil Hospital Ahmedabad
Phone: +91 79 2268 3721

Vadodara

Private - Bankers Superspecialty Hospital
GIDC Rd, Opposite Mahalaxmi Party Plot Tulsidham GIDC Industrial
Area, Manjalpur, Vadodara
Phone: +91 26 5260 2602

Surat

Private - Asutosh Hospital Surat
Rajashri Hall Road, beside Kshetrapal Hanuman Temple, Majura
Gate, Surat, Gujarat
Phone: +91 93 2707 0000
www.asutoshindia.com

Lucknow

Private - Apollomedics Super Speciality Hospital
Kanpur - Lucknow Rd, Sector B, Bargawan, LDA Colony, Lucknow
Phone: +91 52 2678 8888
www.lucknow.apollohospitals.com

Private - Sahara Hospital
Sahara Hospital Rd, Viraj Khand - 1, Viraj Khand, Gomti Nagar,
Lucknow
Phone: +91 52 2678 0001
www.saharahospitals.com

Agra

Private - Global Rainbow Healthcare
Rainbow Hospitals, Maharishi Puram Colony, Agra
Phone: +91 81 9102 2444
www.rainbowhospitals.org

Private - Amit Jaggi Memorial Hospital
SECTOR-1, Vibhav Nagar, Tajganj, Agra
Phone: +91 56 2223 0515
www.ajmh.in

Jaipur

Private - Fortis Escorts Hospital
Jawahar Lal Nehru Marg, Sector 5, Malviya Nagar, Jaipur
Phone: +91 14 1254 7000
www.fortishealthcare.com

Government - Sawai Man Singh Hospital
Shop.44 Jain M M Emitra, near Sawai Mansingh Hospital ke Bhar,
Jaipur
Phone: +91 14 1251 8222

Jodhpur

Private - Goyal Hospital and Research Centre
961/3, Residency Rd, Shastri Nagar, Jodhpur
Phone: +91 87 6970 7913
www.goyalhospital.org

Government - All India Institute of Medical Sciences Jodhpur
Basni Industrial Area, MIA 2nd Phase, Basni, Jodhpur
Phone: +91 87 6450 5002
www.aiimsjodhpur.edu.in

Udaipur

Private - Aravali Hospital
332, Ambamata Scheme - A Rd, Ambamata, Udaipur
Phone: +91 29 4243 0222
www.aravalihospital.in

Private - GBH American Hospital
Meera Girls, 20-BHATT JI KI BARI, 101, College Road, Kothi Bagh,
Udaipur
Phone: +91 29 4353 5000
www.gbhamericanhospital.com

Jaisalmer

Private - Shri Maheshwari Hospital And Research Centre
Barmer Rd, Near Union Circle, Jaisalmer
Phone: +91 29 9225 0024
www.nhp.gov.in

Government - Shree Jawahar Hospital Jaisalmer
Jaisalmer, CVS Colony, Jaisalmer
www.nhp.gov.in

Mumbai

Private - Bombay Hospital and Medical Research Centre
12, Vitthaldas Thackersey Marg, Near to Liberty Cinema, New Marine Lines, Marine Lines, Mumbai
Phone: +91 22 2206 7676
www.bombayhospital.com

Private - Breach Candy Hospital Trust
60 A, Bhulabhai Desai Marg, Breach Candy, Cumballa Hill, Mumbai
Phone: +91 22 2366 7788
www.breachcandyhospital.org

Private - Lilavati Hospital and Research Centre
A-791, Bandra Reclamation Rd, General Arunkumar Vaidya Nagar, Bandra West, Mumbai
Phone: +91 22 2675 1000
www.lilavatihospital.com

Government - Grant Medical College
J J Marg, Nagpada, Mumbai Central, Mumbai
Phone: +91 22 2373 5555

Pune

Private - Columbia Asia Hospital
22, 2A, Mundhwa - Kharadi Rd, Near Nyati Empire, Santipur, Thite Nagar, Kharadi, Pune
Phone: +91 20 6165 6666
www.columbiaindiahospitals.com

Private - AIMS
AIMS (Aundh Institute of Medical Science) Hospital, Survey No.154, Near Aims Square, Near Parihas Chowk, Aundh, Pune
Phone: +91 20 6740 0100
www.aimspune.com

Aurangabad

Private - United CIIGMA Hospital
Plot no 6, 7, Darga Rd, Shahnoorwadi, Aurangabad, Maharashtra
Phone: +91 24 0667 6666
www.ciigmagroup.org

Government - Government Medical College Aurangabad
University Rd, Jubilee Park, Aurangabad
Phone: +91 24 0240 2412
www.gmcaurangabad.com

South Goa

Private - Victor Hospital
Old Station Rd, near Carmelite Monastery, Malbhat, Margao, Goa
Phone: +91 83 2672 8888
www.victorhospital.com

North Goa

Private - Galaxy Hospital
Mapusa - Duler - Camurlim Rd, Near S.P.G. Hall/Severina Gardens,
Xelpem, Duler, Mapusa, Goa
Phone: +91 83 2226 6666
www.galaxyhospitalgoa.com

Central Goa

Private - Manipal Hospital
Panaji, Dr E Borges Rd, Dona Paula, Goa
www.manipalhospitals.co.in

Government - Goa Medical College
N17, Bambolim, Goa
Phone: +91 83 2245 8727
www.gmc.goa.gov.in

VACCINATIONS AND REQUIRED MEDICINE

Immunizations are not required to visit India. (Exception: If you are traveling from an area affected with Yellow Fever, you must have a health certificate.) The recommended vaccinations and medications strongly vary depending on your region and season of travel. However, there are three we strongly encourage regardless of your travel plans: Covid- 19, Hepatitis A, and Tetanus. For more tropical destinations, like Goa or South India, consider a malaria preventative and typhoid vaccine.

Travel vaccinations are very personal. Some travelers want everything while others are more selective. Please speak with your physician or travel clinic about the pros and cons for each vaccine. You can also visit the CDC website for a comprehensive list of recommended India vaccinations: www.cdc.gov

MALARIA AND DENGUE FEVER

Malaria is a disease transmitted by the bites of infected mosquitos. Symptoms usually begin approximately two weeks after being bitten and include fever, vomiting, headaches, and exhaustion. If left untreated - and in more severe cases - it can cause yellow skin, seizures, and other serious complications. According to the World Malaria Report by the World Health Organization, India only represents 3% of global cases.

Malaria is NOT prevalent in all areas of India and the region and season of travel will determine the risk. For example, traveling during the monsoon season or visiting a tropical destination will avail a higher probability of contracting the disease. Prescription medication is available to prevent malaria, or you can purchase OTC tablets at Indian pharmacies. Depending on the medication, your doctor may advise starting the pills before your trip. Also, it is common for travelers to have adverse reactions to the medication, including strong hallucinations. Please speak to your physician about the options and side effects.

Dengue Fever is also a mosquito-borne viral disease. Symptoms include joint and muscle pain, high fever, and body rash. Although dengue can be incredibly painful, it's not often fatal. In more severe cases, hospitalization may be required. Unfortunately, there is no specific medicine to treat dengue; the best treatment is rest, fluids, and pain-relievers.

Dengue is highly seasonal and often occurs during the summer monsoon. Cases will spike from July - September and then drastically drop as the weather becomes cooler and dryer.

BIRTH CONTROL AND REPRODUCTIVE HEALTHCARE

With governmental efforts to educate the public about family planning, contraceptive use has more than tripled since the 1960's. Some Indian states have also adopted a two-child policy, mainly geared toward politicians to set an example to their constituents.

We asked Dr. Preeti Jobali, an OB-GYN in Mumbai, about reproductive health in India:

GGG: Is birth control available? How is it accessed?

Dr. Jobali: Commonly available and accepted methods of contraception are condoms, birth control pills, IUDs, emergency contraception pills, and contraceptive injections. Injections need to be administered by a healthcare professional after a medical history and examination. An IUD also needs to be inserted by a gynecologist. The others are available at pharmacies and don't need a prescription. Condoms are also inexpensive and available at big supermarket chains.

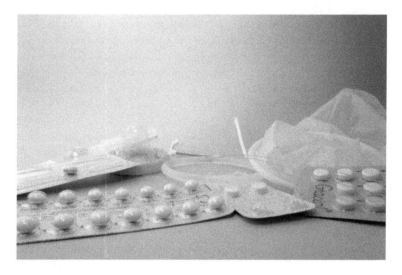

GGG: Are abortions legal?

Dr. Jobali: Yes, with the following guidelines: A pregnancy up to seven weeks can be terminated with oral medications; after seven weeks a surgical abortion is required. Both require a consultation with a gynecologist. While abortion pills may be available from secondhand sources, it is neither recommended nor legal to self-medicate with these pills as they may lead to serious life-threatening complications. Under no circumstances can a pregnancy beyond 20 weeks be terminated in India (barring a few exceptional cases which require prior court permission). A woman **must** approach a qualified gynecologist for any abortion related services.

A foreigner can undergo an abortion in India as long as all the Indian rules and regulations are followed. That being said, most gynecologists would be wary of taking on cases arising out of non-

consensual sex or one-night stands which usually have or may lead
to other legal implications in the future. In such cases, it is best to
approach a government hospital.

PREGNANCY

Surprise! I found out that I was pregnant with my third child on
day two of a 5-week trip across India. My family referred me to an
OBGYN clinic in Delhi (Gouri Clinic, Kamla Nagar) and I received
excellent care.

Interestingly, after the initial ultrasound, Dr. Gauri discovered that
although the pregnancy test was positive, no egg had developed. I was
only six weeks along, but she wanted to wait one more week until
administering any oral medications. One week later, I returned to
the clinic for my ultrasound. The technician turned up the volume
and said, "There is the heartbeat!" Yes, my little pumpkin was just
developing in her own time!

With almost five weeks of comprehensive care, including ultrasounds,
anti-nausea medication, and regular appointments, I paid $130 out of
pocket - all reimbursed by my travel insurance policy.

Unlike western hospitals, prices are often listed on the lobby board:
delivery (vaginal or cesarean; private or shared room; single or
multiples), daily hospital stay, IV fluids, ultrasounds, and other
specialized care.

If you are traveling while pregnant, it's advisable to stay close to
private hospitals for the best care. Dr. Jobali shares, "Most hospitals in
India have an in-house or at least a visiting gynaecologist so it is not
too hard to find one. However, in more remote locations there may be
some difficulty in locating one nearby."

SEXUALLY TRANSMITTED DISEASES

With 65% of India's population under the age of 35, it is incredibly
vulnerable to STDs. India has the third highest HIV infections in the
world, totaling more than 2.2 million cases.

There are approximataley 35 million annual cases of sexually transmitted diseases (STDs). The most common are Human papillomavirus (HPV), genital herpes, and syphilis. If you suspect that you have contracted an STD, visit a hospital for immediate consultation.

TAMPONS AND SANITARY SUPPLIES

I still remember paying $20 for a 10-pack of tampons! Fortunately, the cost of feminine hygiene products have decreased in recent years. Now you can buy period supplies at pharmacies, chain stores like Reliance and Big Bazaar, and online. Common sanitary pad brands include Whisper, Stayfree, Sofy, Peesafe, and WOW by Vwash. A 10-pack will cost approximately ₹75. Tampon brands include Sirona, OB SilkTouch, Vwash, and Peesafe with a box of ten averaging ₹200. Menstrual cups are an emerging product and mostly available online only.

Sanitary pads are definitely more common than tampons. There is still a cultural narrative that only women who have given birth can use tampons; otherwise, you will break your hymen, get an infection, and risk infertility. Because there is a strong taboo about menstruation, many Indian girls don't have access to the information they need about making an educated choice between different hygiene products.

Traveling to remote areas? Stock up!

Take it from someone who once spent half a day driving around rural Punjab looking for sanitary supplies. With a male driver. Who only spoke Punjabi. Finally I found a small shop, but it was a game of charades to communicate what I needed from the shopkeeper. (Have you ever tried to act out "period" or "menstruation" with only hand gestures?) If you are traveling to remote areas, make sure you have enough sanitary supplies. You *can* find products, but it's not always easy. Also, research the brands in advance so you can just name the product, regardless of the language barrier.

Watch: Period. End of Sentence.

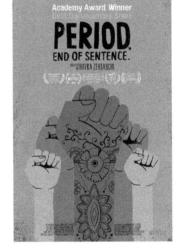

A period should end a sentence, not a girl's education. The 2018 documentary short film, directed by Rayka Zehtabchi, spotlights Indian women leading a quiet sexual revolution. Millions of girls in developing countries like India cannot afford or access sanitary pads, which means that when they get their period, they have to turn to unhealthy alternatives like dirty rags, leaves, or ashes.

In addition to the high risk of infection, every time their period comes, they have to miss school - and the more school they miss, the more likely they will fall too far behind and have to drop out entirely.

A man named Arunachalam Muruganantham from Tamil Nadu, India, created a machine that makes affordable, biodegradable pads from locally sourced materials. The machine does more than just supply girls with pads; it supplies a steady income to the women in the area who want to work on it.

EXERCISE AND FITNESS

Gyms and health clubs are gaining popularity in India. Most are on a monthly membership plan, though you can ask if the facility offers day or weekly passes. Many internationally-branded hotels and upmarket accommodations feature fitness centers with modern equipment. (Some don't have a gym on-site but partner with a nearby club.)

With crowds, traffic, unpaved streets, and pollution (not to mention the heat and humidity), it can be challenging to run outside. Try and find a large park or greenspace with trails/sidewalks and remember to stay covered. It's not appropriate to run in a sports bra or running shorts.

Download the Strava app or visit mapmyrun.com to discover routes in unfamiliar destinations.

TOILETS AND TOILET PAPER

Strengthen those quads! Yes, you will likely come across a squat toilet. Also, Indians rarely use toilet paper, instead preferring water from a spray hose. Water is cheap, accessible, and sustainable.

Definitely pack a roll (or two) of toilet paper or wet wipes.

If using a squat toilet, a bucket filled with water is used to "flush" the toilet. You can use toilet paper, but there are often signs posted to NOT throw it in the toilet. It's not designed for Indian plumbing. Instead, there is a small trash can to dispose of the paper.

Trains generally have two types of toilets: Indian and Western. The Western features a toilet while the Indian has a squat toilet. Both open directly to the train tracks below and toilet paper may or may not be available.

It's also worth noting that many Indian bathrooms don't have soap available. Remember to pack several travel-sized bottles of hand sanitizer.

BEFORE YOU GO

RUPEES

The Indian Rupee (sign: ₹/ code: INR) is the official currency of India. The issuance is controlled by the Reserve Bank of India. In November 2016, the Indian government announced the demonetization of ₹500 and ₹1,000 banknotes, making these notes invalid. A redesigned ₹500 banknote, in addition to a new denomination of ₹2,000 banknote, went into circulation while the ₹1,000 note was suspended.

In 2017, a new denomination of ₹200 banknote was added to the Indian currency; In 2018, the Reserve Bank of India released the redesigned series of ₹100 banknote.

> **Did you know?**
> Ancient India was one of the earliest issuers of coins in the world and the history of the Rupee traces back to the 6th century BCE.

MONEY AND ATMS

With a few exceptions, it is prohibited to carry Rupees in and out of India. Be prepared to exchange money upon arrival.

Many ATMs in India have a maximum withdrawal limit in a 24-hour period. It may be as low as INR 500 or as high as INR 25000. If you require a large sum of cash, be prepared to visit several machines over 2-3 days. Most debit cards connected to global payment systems are accepted, including Visa, Mastercard, Maestro, and Cirrus.

ATMs at ICICI, State Bank of India, Axis Bank, HDFC, HSBC, and Citibank accept foreign cards. ATMs are widely available in larger cities, like Delhi and Mumbai. However, hit up the ATM before you venture to remote destinations.

Currency Exchange and Cash

Currency exchange is available at banks or private money changers/ exchange bureaus. Rates at private facilities are usually higher but they are often open later than banking hours. Some hotels also exchange currency but at a premium rate. A passport is required to process the transaction.

Hold on to your money exchange receipt or encashment certificate, as you will need it to convert Rupees back to your home currency.

When receiving money or accepting change, do NOT accept torn or faded Rupees. The notes will not be welcomed by other merchants when you pay.

Smaller bills (₹10, ₹20 and ₹50 notes) are harder to find, so keep them for incidentals or gratuities.

Credit Cards/Debit Cards

Many hotels, guesthouses, shops, restaurants, and bars accept international credit and debit cards, including Visa, Mastercard, and American Express. You can also pay by card for train tickets and airfare. Be prepared to pay cash at small shops, markets, and stalls in rural communities. Also, a minimum purchase price may apply for card payments.

Cash advances are available at some banks with international credit cards.

Before you leave home:
- Contact your bank or set a travel alert so the debit or credit card is not blocked.

- Ask about the foreign transaction fees or ATM fees so you aren't hit with surprises.

- Keep a copy of your financial institution's emergency phone number in the event of loss or theft.

TIPPING & WHAT TO EXPECT

It is customary to tip guides, drivers, and porters, as well as anyone who provides a direct service. Be discreet when tipping in public.

Gratuities in Rupees is preferred. The following is standard:

Tour guides: INR 500/person per day
Private drivers: INR 300/person per day
Hotel, train, or airport porters: INR 60 per bag
Taxi driver: Round up to the next dollar
Spa therapists: 10% of the service

It is also appropriate to tip the person who watches your shoes at a temple or religious site, approximately INR 50.

Tipping in restaurants is customary but not required. If you are pleased with the service, you can tip 10% of the total. We recommended handing the money directly to the waiter. If it is added to a bill or left on the table, it may not be received. Some restaurants and bars charge a service fee in the final bill. This fee is not considered an inclusive gratuity.

HOW TO PROTECT YOUR MONEY

Always keep cash in separate locations. If your wallet is stolen, you'll have reserves.

Find a good daypack: A small, lightweight bag for carrying cash, cards, and other personal items.

If you do not plan to carry a daypack, consider a zippered pouch tucked under your clothes. The money belt can hold passports, cash, credit cards, and travel documents, without the risk of pickpockets.

Indian Currency

BUDGETING

Depending on your travel style, India can be a backpacker's paradise or a discerning destination. Are you prepared for basic accommodations and sleeper trains, or do you prefer a private driver and palace stays? Based on your spending, it's all possible.

The rates for travel services in India are greatly determined by the season. October - March are peak months across most of the country and prices are at a premium. Summer is monsoon season and rates are slashed. The estimates below are averages but may be higher or lower based on travel dates.

Note: You may find other resources estimating lower daily budgets, but as a woman, it is important to spend a little more money for safety and comfort. Budgets don't include personal expenses, cell phone bill, laundry, alcoholic beverages, incidentals, or gratuities. Also, the below estimates are based on a single room, not shared.

Budget / $20 - $50 per day
This is for basic, safe accommodations (think hostel or guesthouse), three meals, and public transportation. The range is determined by your destination - a small town will avail even cheaper rates while a larger city will be on the higher end.

Moderate / $50 - $110 per day
This is a comfortable budget for upgraded accommodations, local meals, public transportation, and some entrance fees. You will still need to be selective with the restaurants and activities.

Superior / $110 - $200 per day
Enjoy a boutique hotel, private driver, most entrance fees, and diversified dining options. There is still some frugality required but also room to play.

Luxury/ $200+ per day
For a splash of luxury, including stays at the best hotels and palaces in the world, expect to pay a premium. This budget will allow for private drivers, entrance fees, and fine dining. There are also premium luxury brands, like Oberoi, with some rooms starting at $500+ per night.

WHERE TO STAY

International Brands

Think Marriott, Hyatt, and Hilton. International chains offer the comfort and amenities of home but also create a barrier between you and the destination. Some travelers squirm at the thought of staying somewhere "just like home" while others appreciate the westernized facilities after spending the day immersed in India's cultural cacophony.

There are several international hotel brands in India:

Marriott/Courtyard by Marriott/JW Marriott/Crowne Plaza/Westin
Hilton/Hilton Garden Inn/Conrad/DoubleTree by Hilton
Holiday Inn/Holiday Inn Express
Hyatt/Hyatt Regency/Park Hyatt
Sheraton/Sheraton Grand
Ramada/Ramada Plaza/Travelodge

Even if you are opposed to the thought of a stark hotel room that could really be anywhere, there can be benefits. Those concerned about Delhi Belly or other gastro conditions will find the food is generally prepared to accommodate foreign tummies.

Also, chain hotels have back-up generators - a welcome amenity with India's frequent power outages.

LOCAL HOTEL CHAINS

Local Indian chain hotels range from budget to luxury. Although established in India, these properties *can* be owned and operated by a larger conglomerate. Certain chains, like Oyo and Treebo, cater to domestic tourists or Indians traveling throughout the country. Others, like Lemon Tree, ITC, CGH Earth, Taj Group, and Oberoi Group, are popular with foreigners.

Lemon Tree - India's largest hotel chain in the mid-range category. Fun fact: Lemon Tree is the largest corporate adopter of stray dogs in India. Each location adopts a pup and, based on the personality, assigns a "role" in the hotel.

Oberoi Udaivilas, Udaipur

Treebo - A premium-budget chain with over 600 hotels in 115+ cities across India. There are three sub-brands: Treebo Trip, offering basic comforts; Treebo Trend, the majority of properties; and Treebo Tryst, a premium stay.

Oyo - Oyo is a budget-chain mostly frequented by Indian tourists but it's starting to appeal to budget-conscious foreigners. The brand is not without controversy - Oyo has been accused of predatory pricing and was the site of several rape scandals. Not every hotel is created equal and some are very safe, but do your research before booking.

The Oberoi Group - A luxury brand that started in India in 1934. Although there are currently 32 hotels across Asia, the Middle East, and Africa, Oberoi is distinctly Indian. The Oberoi in Mumbai also features women butlers for solo female guests.

Boutique and Concept Hotels

Boutique and concept hotels are smaller and cater to a specific theme or interest. You may find yourself at a 300-year-old colonial bungalow, an eco-friendly beachside cottage, or an urban loft that doubles as an art gallery. There are generally three characteristics of a boutique hotel: size (smaller, with 10-100 rooms), service (very intimate and personalized), and style (loads of local character).

The staff at boutique and concept hotels are also known for their destination knowledge and can recommend more immersive experiences instead of big bus tours — a local shop owner instead of a handicraft emporium, for example. Also, the menu will reflect the property's unique location and specialize in local favorites.

Zostel, Goa

Hostels

Not long ago, hip hostels in safe neighborhoods were rare in India. Fortunately that has changed and you can now find cool spaces to connect with other travelers. What's common? Shared rooms, communal kitchens and lounges, free Wifi, laundry facilities, lockers, hot water, and yes - A/C! There are also properties that offer female-only dorm rooms, private rooms, and attached bathrooms.

Hostels cater to backpackers and the younger crowd. We recommend these well-established brands that are safe for women:

- Hoztel
- Zostel
- Moustache Hostel
- GoStops!
- The Hostel Crowd

There are also many independently-owned hostels outside these brands, but always check the location and neighborhood before reserving. (For example, Paharganj is a popular neighborhood for hostels in Delhi, but it's also known for prostitution and crime.)

Ashrams

Because India is a popular destination for spiritual seekers, ashrams abound. You will usually find the simplified lodging in pilgrimage and religious destinations, though they may also be located near a Guru's residence or at an energy vortex.

In North India, ashrams are common in Varanasi, Bodh Gaya, Haridwar, Rishikesh, and Dharamshala.

Many ashrams have a minimum night stay and require a form of service or long-term volunteer commitment. Also, you will likely be subjected to the ashram rules and activities, including meal times, spiritual practice/meditation, and education.

Ashrams can be free or low-cost, but usually range between $10-$30 per night for room, board, and programs. Some are with shared bathrooms and without A/C. Also, meals are almost always strictly vegetarian and no alcohol is allowed.

Coral Court, Agra

Guest House/Homestay

The thought of a homestay or guest house in India can ignite romantic images of cultural exchange. A comfortable room in a private residence, adorned with traditional fabrics and décor, can offer a warm contrast to a stark hotel room. Instead of room service, you can enjoy a homemade chai and paratha at the breakfast table while engaged in dynamic conversation with the owner.

A "guest house" or "home stay" is where a tourist rents a room from a local family. The idea is to offer a clean and affordable place to stay, usually with the intention of learning more about the community, language, and traditions. In India, the homeowner and his/her family reside at the property and rent out a minimum of one room and maximum of six rooms, or 12 beds. Remember, a "home" in India can be a detached structure or an apartment.

Licensed homestays and guest houses require all rooms to be clean, airy, and pest-free, with outside window/ventilation and a private attached bathroom. The property is also required to have 24-hour hot and cold running water with a proper sewage connection and a smoke-free, hygienic, and well-maintained kitchen. Optional amenities include a security guard, internet connection, luggage assistance, telephone service, washing machine, and heating/cooling in public spaces.

Havelis/Forts/Palaces/Heritage Hotels

We love havelis! A haveli is a grand house or mansion with architectural or historical significance that has been converted to accommodations. Often the proprietors are direct descendants of dignitaries, royals, and influential families, creating ample opportunities for historical narratives and lively storytelling. Haveli's can range from economical (3*) to luxury (5*) and almost always feature a central courtyard.

Forts and palaces are exactly as they sound - grand, historic sites that have been fully or partially converted to unique stays. Many have been awarded the top hotels in the world, including Taj Lake Palace in Udaipur and Umaid Bhawan Palace in Jodhpur. These palatial stays will be a higher price point but also a fun splurge. How often do you have the opportunity to live like royalty?

BrijRama Palace Varanasi

*Don't be fooled by a hotel with the word "palace" in the name. There are thousands of so-called palaces in India that are nothing more than a budget hotel with cold showers.

If a property was built before 1950, it is designated a **Heritage Hotel**. This can include havelis, forts, palaces, hunting lodges, or any other building with architectural detailing that is reminiscent of the area. To stay in a heritage hotel is to step back in time and experience the traditions of India's colorful past.

Yoga Retreats, Destination Spas, and Wellness Centers

Because Yoga and Ayurveda were developed in India, there are thousands of yoga retreats, destination spas, and wellness centers. Ayurveda focuses on balancing the emotional, mental, physical, and spiritual elements of life to create ultimate wellness.

The retreat center may require a minimum-night stay (3, 7, 10, and 14 are the most common) with a medical consultation on the first day. Based on your health and goals, the doctor will personalize a treatment plan that includes a Sattvic diet, therapeutic treatments, and yoga/meditation sessions.

The majority of destination spas are located in South India, but you

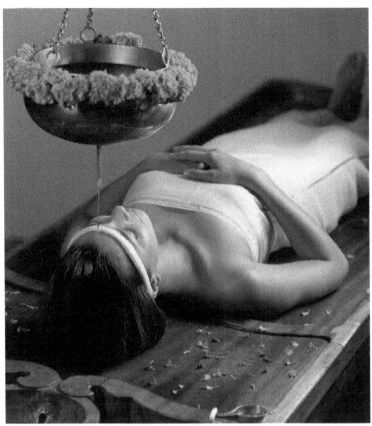

Ayurveda

will find some scattered in the north — Ananda in the Himalayas, outside Rishikesh, is one of the top ten spas in the world. I also love Sattva in Rishikesh (mid-range) and the Oberoi Sukhvilas in Chandigarh (luxury).

Rishikesh, in the foothills of the Himalayas, is often considered the birthplace of Yoga. With that designation, it's no surprise that the unassuming religious town is overflowing with multi-day yoga retreats. For more info, check out Destination: Rishikesh, **pages 129 - 141.**

Goa is a haven for wellness centers, yoga retreats, and overnight spas. For more info, check out Destination: Goa, **pages 371 - 390.**

Camping

Unless you are on a trekking program, skip the campgrounds. There are enough affordable options to rest your head instead of staying in a tent without a locked door. Also, never camp in city parks, recreation zones, or open spaces.

SS Goa

Vacation Rentals

The past decade has seen an upward trend in travelers reserving vacation homes across India. It's an affordable way to stay local for longer stays and integrate with the communities.

As a woman, try and find rentals that are hosted or managed by women. Read reviews thoroughly and always send your rental address to friends and family. Also, ask the following:

Is there lighting to/from the main door?
Do all windows have locks?
Is there an alarm? Security camera?

Check out:

- Home to Go
- Airbnb
- VRBO

Houseboat Kerala

Houseboats and River Cruises

Another enchanting option to rest your head is on water. River cruises have become more popular in recent years, with vessels gently sailing down the holy Ganges. Many of these feature the comforts of a 5-star hotel, including floor-to-ceiling glass doors, hand-painted murals, and spa-quality bath products.

Houseboats are centered in two areas: A kettuvallam, or traditional houseboat in Kerala, and a Shikara on Dal Lake in Srinagar. There are also luxury houseboats, like the Oberoi Vrinda, offering a touch of elegance to the traditional elements.

Couchsurfing

India has over 460,000 hosts on the Couchsurfing website offering a bed or couch for free. Not surprisingly, most of them are single males under 30.

DO NOT try to save money by staying with a stranger. Even if the accommodations claim to be "with a family" or "multi-generational," it isn't worth the risk.

TRANSPORTATION

It takes great time, patience, and determination to understand local transportation in India. There are many options available, including buses, cycle-rickshaws, auto-rickshaws, e-rickshaws, tempos, taxis, boats, tongas, metros, and urban trains. Traveling in India is embracing the adventure as it comes, no matter how fast or slow!

Auto Rickshaw

Auto Rickshaw, E-rickshaw, and Vikrams

The quintessential local transport of India is a tuk-tuk, a three-wheeled motorized vehicle with a tin or canvas roof. Also called an auto rickshaw, it is an inexpensive and fun way to zoom around town.

Generally green, yellow, or black in color, rickshaws have regulated metered fares and are a common fixture throughout the country. They are also the most convenient form of transport in urban areas. Some auto rickshaws run on meters; however, to avoid a hassle, agree on a price before you start your ride.

In some urban cities, you may find environmentally friendly rickshaws that are shared by passengers and comparatively cheaper. The e-rickshaws are called totos in the Northeast Indian states.

Vikrams are spacious outsized auto rickshaws that can accommodate more passengers with fixed routes and fares.

Sample Fare: Meter starts at INR 25, though many drivers prefer to set a flat rate.

Cycle Rickshaw

As the name suggests, the cycle rickshaw is the same as a regular rickshaw, but without the motor. They are powered by the driver, so the speed of your ride depends on the strength of their legs. While cycle rickshaws are not overly quick, they are a great option for sightseeing. The drivers earn a meager income compared to their counterparts who have proper autos and cars. Reserving a cycle rickshaw is an opportunity to support the locals as they skilfully navigate through the streets while sharing stories about the destination. Although banned in several cities for causing traffic congestion, they are still a feature in Delhi and provide a cheap mode of local transport. Establish the rate before you ride to avoid a disagreement later.

Sample Fare: INR 20 – INR 50

Taxi

Depending on the city/region, traditional taxis can be hired from stands or hailed from the street. They are required by law to be registered as commercial vehicles and have a fare-meter, though many drivers prefer to set a prepaid flat rate. Surcharges will apply for extra baggage, night rides, and tolls. Due to safety and convenience, taxis have become more popular in recent years.

Sample Fare: INR 15 – INR 25 per km

Private Vehicle for Hire

Private vehicles can be hired for the day or a proposed itinerary and offer more comfort and a flexible schedule. Depending on the destination and season, A/C or non-A/C vehicles are available.

Sample Fare: Dependent on itinerary, usually around INR 2500 for a licensed vehicle for 8 hours/80 km within city limits.

City Bus

City buses are generally government-owned and provide a convenient and cheap mode of public transportation. Until recently, buses were overcrowded, not air-conditioned, and offered limited access to the disabled. However, new features such as air-conditioning and low-floor lifts are being initiated in cities to improve the system and attract private car owners to decongest roads.

Sample Fare: INR 5 – INR 15 for a local ticket; INR 25 for an A/C bus

Intercity/Interstate/Overnight Bus

Let's break down the other bus options:

Intercity Bus - Travel between cities but stay in the same state

Interstate Bus - Travel to a different state

There are Intercity and Interstate busses traveling during the day and overnight, depending on the route.

At first, an overnight bus may appear advantageous. Not only do you save on accommodations, but you can conveniently travel at night while not wasting a day in transit to another destination. However, for safety and security, we do NOT recommend an overnight bus for women traveling in India. Spend the extra money to stay in a hotel or opt for an overnight train instead (1st A/C when possible).

Sample Fare: Depends on the route and distance

To reserve a bus ticket, please visit: www.redbus.in

Train

For many foreigners, experiencing India by train is an essential cultural experience. Visions loom of either luxury overnight trains, like Palace on Wheels, or overcrowded carriages with local's train surfing. There is something refreshingly charming when traveling by train, perhaps because the tradition is an integral part of the local transportation. The Indian rail system is the second largest in the world and serves nearly 20 million people at over 7,500 stations daily.

Traveling by train is a journey through (and with) a microcosm of the entire country. Families share food with other passengers while *chaiwallahs* traverse the train selling steaming cups of tea. Depending on the route and class of service, the journey can be intense, colourful, loud, and pungent – an experience that activates all the senses.

The Indian rail system is incredibly reliable. Your experience depends on the destination, how much you pay, and at what time you board the train. Timetables, seat availability, and live updates are available on apps like IRCTC, the official app of Indian Railways. Booking tickets online is beneficial as it removes the language barrier and is easy to use.

The train stations in India, particularly in large cities, are quite complex and can be overwhelming. If possible, hire a transfer representative to help you safely navigate entering/exiting the station. Please also keep a safe watch of your valuables. When we do hear of theft, it mainly occurs in or around train stations.

Trains are available for both day and overnight journeys. There are generally three classes of seating: 1st class A/C, 2nd class (A/C or non-A/C), and 3rd class (non – A/C). Most foreigners opt for 1st or 2nd class, where Western restroom facilities are available and seating is reserved. Depending on your itinerary and class of service, meals are delivered by a server or you may purchase food from a vendor.

For long-distance trips, reserve a higher class such as the AC1 or AC2. These compartments are air-conditioned and provide amenities like fold-down beds, pillows, and blankets. The doors are lockable and, depending on your group size, can convert to private cabins. They also have power points for charging electronic devices.

Taking an overnight train in India is NOT similar to European rail travel. (This refers to standard train travel, not luxury rail journeys including Palace on Wheels.) If you are particularly discerning, train travel can be a sensory overload.

To reserve a train, please visit: www.irctc.co.in

Sample Fare: Highly variable, based on distance; For local overnight trains, plan to spend INR 1400 in a 3rd class compartment; INR 1900 for 2nd A/C; and INR 2900 for 1st A/C

Plane

India has the third largest civil aviation network in the world, based on passengers. Flights are usually very reliable and inexpensive, with certain routes starting at just $19 one-way. The primary carriers are Air India, Vistara, SpiceJet, IndiGo, Go Air, and AirAsia.

At Indian airports, there are separate security lines for men and women. This is because passengers are individually patted down behind screens. (And yes, only female security personnel pat down female passengers.)

At check-in, don't forget to add a tag to each carry-on bag, including purses. After clearing security, the personnel will stamp your boarding pass and bag tag showing it was cleared. If your bag does not have a stamp, you will be denied boarding.

When traveling by air, pack lightly or be prepared to pay a hefty fee. Domestic airlines allow one carry-on bag weighing 7 kg (15 lbs) and one checked bag at 15 kg (33 lbs). Excess weight averages INR 400 per kilogram. Also, you will need to show your ticket and identification to security personnel before entering the airport. Only ticketed passengers are allowed inside.

One more thing: With the exception of chain restaurants like Subway and Burger King, skip the airport food. Even at chain establishments, try and eat veg.

Sample Fare: Depends on the route, but fares can be as low as $19 one-way

Ride-Sharing Services

Ola and Uber are the most popular ride-sharing apps. Compared to a taxi, they are cheaper and offer the benefit of entering the exact location of your destination without language barriers. You can also check the price before you ride and share your location with others for enhanced safety.

Suburban Rail System /Metro/ Rapid Transit System

Suburban Rail Systems in India are local trains (similar to the American commuter train) and currently operational in Mumbai, Delhi, Chennai, and Kolkata. The Mumbai Suburban Railway has the largest passenger density in the world, transporting over 6.4 million passengers daily.

In recent years, the Metro has become a popular means of mass rapid transit in India with an operational network of over 660 km across 12 cities. The metro is a safe, inexpensive, and efficient transport option. It has also integrated with Google India (through Google Transit) to provide train schedules and route information to mobile devices with Google Maps.

After being successfully implemented in the major metros, there are now 15 other cities in India with over 500 km of metro lines under different stages of implementation. The first carriage in the moving direction is always reserved for women and is depicted with pink signage at the station. The metro service is accessed through tokens and smart cards that are rechargeable and the facility is available across all metro stations.

We love the Delhi Metro, as it can take you to almost every tourist site, shopping mall, and neighborhood in India's vast capital.

The Delhi metro has the largest network with about 2.8 million people commuting daily. It was also the first Metro in the world to be certified for environmentally friendly construction. Route maps and station announcements are in Hindi and English, allowing for easy communication to foreigners.

Rapid Transit Systems are currently under construction in Chennai, Bangalore, Ahmedabad, Hyderabad, and Mumbai.

Sample Fare: Delhi Metro ticket is INR 10 – INR 60, dependent on distance traveled; Rail System tickets average INR 25 per ticket

Motorbikes and Scooters

Motorbikes are available for hire if you have ample time and wish to travel adventurously at your own pace. The chilly and mountainous destinations of North India like Ladakh and Spiti Valley are best explored on the cool Royal Enfields. Scooters can also be rented to explore destinations like Goa and Pushkar.

Boats

There are various kinds of local boats available in India. The Shikaras, beautifully decorated wooden boats, are an iconic part of Kashmir. Commonly used for sightseeing, fishing, and transportation, Shikaras are painted with bright colors and can also be reserved for overnight stays.

In Kerala, traditional houseboats offer travelers day and overnight trips on the backwaters. The kettuvallam or 'boat with knots' is held together with coir knots only — not a single nail is used during the construction.

Local boats are available on the Ganges River, providing sunrise and sunset views of the ghats and Aarti ceremony. Boutique luxury river cruisers also welcome guests for overnight or multi-day sailings on the Ganges.

CELL PHONES

You may have heard the saying: "Good, fast, cheap. Pick two. If it's good and fast, it won't be cheap. If it's fast and cheap, it won't be good. And if it's cheap and good, it won't be fast." This pretty much sums up the international cell phone experience in India.

Some mobile plans, like U.S.-based T-Mobile, are actually easy: they offer free international data, roaming, and even outgoing calls to hundreds of destinations. However, the speed can be very slow. Unless you add an international plan before your trip, it may take some time to connect in India.

First, the basics. India's network operates on the Global System for Mobiles (GSM). In the United States, GSM technology is used by T-Mobile and AT&T while Verizon and U.S. Cellular utilize Code Division Multiple Access (CDMA).

India, like most other countries, operates on GSM with frequency bands of 900/1800 megahertz. The primary mobile networks are Airtel, Idea-Vodafone, and Jio.

If you don't have a global phone that can be used on either GSM or CDMA networks, the best option is to use an unlocked GSM phone that will accept SIM cards from other carriers.

You can purchase pre-paid SIM cards at international airport kiosks or mobile stores. However, to activate a SIM you need documentation and identification: a passport photo, a copy of your passport, a copy of your India visa, and a local reference and address in India. It may also take a few days to activate. (Beware of the SIM card scam as outlined on pg. 11)

If you do not have access to an unlocked GSM phone, you can buy one before you leave or rent a local phone in India. Trabug is considered India's first travel phone, offering visitors a 4G smartphone compatible with all Indian networks OR a Wifi hotspot. Hotel delivery and pick-up is also available, making the process the closest you will find to cheap, good, AND fast! Bonus: The phones feature special apps with access to local information and resources, like currency exchange or taxi reservations. Rates start at $5.99/day for the travel phone and $3.99/day for the hotspot. www.trabug.com

You can also just use Wifi to connect, but service is spotty across India. The speeds and signals are not consistent and often unreliable.

EMERGENCY NUMBERS

DEPARTMENT	NUMBER
Single Emergency Helpline Number	112
Covid 19 Helpline	1075
Police	100
Fire	101
Ambulance	102
Women Helpline	1091
Road Accident Emergency Service	1073
Railway Accident Emergency Service	1072
Air Accident	1071
Air Ambulance	9540161344

CORDS AND WIRES

Electricity in India is 220 – 240 volts, alternating at 50 HZ. Outlets generally accept two kinds of plugs: two round pins or three round pins arranged in a triangular shape. If you choose to not bring a converter, you may usually borrow one from the hotel (if available) or purchase one at a local shop. If you intend on using your converter for laptops and digital cameras, we recommend a converter with surge protection.

Taj Mahal at Sunrise

WHEN TO GO

Much of India has a patchy climate with warm days and cooler evenings. Generally speaking, the best time to visit North and West India is from October - March. Less precipitation and humidity offer dry, sunny days. The weather becomes colder in December and January; dense fog can also blanket much of the region.

From October - March, the Himalayas will be cold but clear, allowing for brisk and beautiful views of the towering peaks. From late March - May, the spring flowers bloom across the valleys.

April - June is scorching hot. Temperatures can exceed 45° C in states like Rajasthan and Gujarat.

July - September is the monsoon season with heavy rains and high humidity. Depending on the destination, it may rain continuously or produce a daily downpour for a couple hours.

Some attractions, including national parks, are closed during the monsoon. Floods and landslides can also impact travel plans. However, this season also offers the cheapest rates.

LOCAL CLOTHING

India is a conservative country. Do not pack clothing that is too short, tight, or revealing. Unless you are traveling to a village or rural area, shorts, skirts, and dresses are acceptable. A light jacket or layering is best to sustain the varying temperatures.

If you feel comfortable, purchase local clothing. Besides being affordable, the fabrics are beautiful and generally made to accommodate and complement the local weather.

PACKING LIST

Clothing

Pack for the season. Traveling in summer? Maxi dresses, capri pants, sandals. Winter? Pants, jackets, gloves. Remember to pack a bathing suit!

Shoes: Comfortable for walking, with good traction. Sandals (preferably closed-toe) are a good option, but they still need to support your feet with good rubber soles for extensive walking on uneven surfaces. Leave your heels at home unless clubs, social events, or weddings are on the itinerary. Your shoes WILL get dirty, so be prepared for dusty, muddy footwear — and probably leave your new white Converse at home.

Scarf/Shawl: A head and leg cover may be required for women and men at certain sacred sites and places of worship.

Hat or Cap: Protection from the sun is essential in the region!

Toiletries and Personal Items

Medicine and Vitamins: If possible, keep medicine in original containers with legible labels.

Digestive Relief: Tums, Pepto Bismol, etc. Grapefruit seed extract is also a natural defense to unfamiliar bacteria, available at most natural food stores and vitamin shops.

Hand Sanitizer: Many public restrooms do not have soap available.

Flushable Wipes: For the public restrooms without toilet paper.

Tissues: Have a small pack available in your purse or daypack.

Plastic Bags: Bring a variety of sizes. The small sealable bags are good for carry-on liquids and items that become wet. Larger bags can hold laundry or be used as liners in your luggage.

Washcloth or Hand Towel: For public restrooms without paper towels or drying facilities. You can also use these to freshen up on long flights and overnight trains, or for minor spills.

Glasses/Contacts: Don't forget your contact solution!

Sunscreen + Mosquito Repellent: You can also purchase this at a local shop.

Convertor and Adapter: 220 – 240 volts, 50 Hz.

Personal Hygiene: Pack what you can from home.

Money and Travel Documents

Daypack: A small, lightweight bag is useful to carry sweaters, shawls, snacks, water bottles, guidebooks, cameras, etc. Make sure it has a zipper and/or a small lock.

Money Belt: If you do not plan to carry a daypack, consider a zippered pouch tucked under your clothes. The money belt can hold passports, cash, credit cards, and travel documents, without the risk of pickpockets.

Addresses: Fond of postcards? Don't forget a list of addresses!

Photocopies of Travel Documents: Remember to make copies of your passport and visa and keep them secure in a separate bag from where the original is stored. If the bag is lost or stolen, you will have a secondary copy available.

Optional Items

Snacks: Pack your favorite items for snacking on the go. We recommend granola bars, goldfish, trail mix, dried fruit, etc. Also, if you have a dietary restriction (Gluten Free, No-Dairy) be sure to pack essential items.

Portable Water Purifier: If your itinerary includes trekking/adventure activities or rural communities, bring a travel-sized device like the Steripen UV Water Purifier.

Batteries: If your electronic devices require specialty batteries, bring an extra set.

Gifts: If you will be the guest of local hosts, show your appreciation with small, unique souvenirs from your hometown. If you choose to bring items to distribute to the kids, we recommend candy (non-melting), pens, paper, stickers, puzzles and coloring books. Some of our clients have even bought the children ice cream cones or snacks.

Postcards/Photos: A collection of show-and-tell pictures (either digital or paper) is always a great conversation piece with locals you meet.

Hair Dryer: Most hotels 3* and above provide hair dryers, but consider packing it for homestays, hostels, ashrams, and other budget accommodations.

VISAS

India offers an electronic tourist visa on arrival (e-Visa). Applicants of the eligible countries (including the United States and Canada) may apply online a minimum of four days in advance of the date of arrival.

The process is fairly straightforward: enter your travel details and upload your passport and photo. You will then pay the fee (presently $25) and submit. The accepted visa is returned via email within 48-72 hours. Although it looks unofficial, this serves as your entry visa.

There is presently no visa on arrival in India and all applications must be approved before travel.

Upon arrival in India, proceed to the "E-Visa" line at customs for biometrics. For more information and to apply, visit the India Electronic Travel Authorization: indianvisaonline.gov.in

BORDERS

As the only democracy in the region, India shares borders with China, Pakistan, Bangladesh, Bhutan, and Nepal. The current border disputes center around Kashmir and the Northeastern states.

A visa is required to visit any neighboring country. For entry requirements, please visit the specific country's government websites or contact a visa processing center like Travisa: www.travisa.com

FESTIVALS AND HOLIDAYS

Owing to its rich amalgamation of ethnic backgrounds, languages, and religious sentiments, India is truly a land of festivals. Some of the most popular celebrations in north and west India include:

Holi Powder

Holi

The festival of colors represents the end of winter and start of spring, as well as the victory of good over evil. It is a day to meet others, laugh and play, repair broken relations, forgive, and throw colored powder! With no puja or religious ceremony, Holi is purely celebrated for enjoyment and entertainment.

Diwali

Diwali, or Deepavali, is the Hindu festival of lights. It spiritually signifies the victory of light over darkness, good over evil, knowledge over ignorance, and hope over despair. The dates change annually based on the lunar calendar, but generally the festivities occur in October or November. Families share sweets, light diyas, burst fireworks, and worship the deities Ganesha and Laxmi.

Navratri

Nava (nine) and Ratri (night) come together as Navratri, nine nights of festivities in the state of Gujarat. The celebration is in honor of the divine feminine form of the Hindu deity Goddess Durga. The Garba dance is performed in a circle around a lantern called "Garbha Deep" which means Womb Lamp. Celebrants twirl gracefully to the tunes of traditional folk songs, drums, and cymbals while donning colorful Gujarati costumes.

Diwali Lights

Ramadan and Eid-al-Fitr

Ramadan, also pronounced Ramzan, is the 9th month of the Islamic calendar and a time of fasting, prayer, and reflection. During the daily fast from dawn until dusk, Muslims refrain from eating, drinking, smoking, or engaging in any sexual activity. It is also a time of spiritual discipline by practicing self restraint, performing community service, and studying the Quran.

At the end of Ramadan is Eid-al-Fitr, a three-day festival that breaks the fast. Family and friends gather for a feast, rejoice with their loved ones, exchange gifts, and show gratitude to the Supreme Being for providing strength throughout Ramadan.

Ganesh Chaturthi

Ganesh Chaturthi

This ten-day Hindu festival celebrates the birth of Lord Ganesha, the elephant-headed God of new beginnings. The idols are worshipped every day with an Aarti celebration in the evening. The largest Ganesha statues on display to the public are immersed in water on the final day, Anant Chaturdashi. In Mumbai, more than 150,000 statues are immersed every year!

The exact dates rotate annually based on the lunar calendar, but the celebration generally falls in August or September.

With the innumerable communities honoring their respective cultures with different fairs and festivals, foreigners can almost always secure an invitation to a celebration. Expect an enthusiastic medley of singing, chanting, and dancing, and don't forget to always ask permission before photographing people, temples, and idols.

Raksha Bandhan

Celebrating the love between a brother and sister, Raksha Bandhan is a traditional Hindu festival that usually occurs in August. Sisters tie rakhi (or threads) on their brothers' wrists to protect against evil influences and pray for a long life. In return, the brothers promise to always watch over their sisters. With time the festival has become more symbolic, but it remains a popular bonding ritual between siblings.

There are three national holidays in India:

January 26: Republic Day

August 15: Independence Day

October 2: Gandhi Jayanta

Additionally, there are an average of 30 annual festivals in each Indian state and almost every week is marked by an important holiday that the country celebrates in unison.

Holi Woman

MEHNDI (HENNA)

Mehndi, or henna, is a traditional and temporary art made from dried leaves of the henna plant. It is generally applied during weddings, festivals, and special occasions, though its popularity now makes it a common cultural experience for visitors.

The use of mehndi is referenced in the ancient Hindu texts. Staining with *haldi* (turmeric) and mehndi are Vedic customs and represent the sun. In other regions, henna is applied to cool the body and also for ritualistic purposes. In India, the mehndi celebration is often one of the most important pre-wedding events. The designs are very intricate and can take hours to apply, with some brides even hiring professional artists to sketch the patterns.

Henna paste is applied to the skin using a brush or cone. As it dries, the paste will dry and crack. A mixture of lemon juice and sugar can be patted on the skin to moisten the area and intensify the color. Sometimes a wrap will be applied over the application, or it can dry openly.

Remember, it can take 1-2 hours for the mehndi to completely dry. (Use the restroom and hydrate in advance!) The application lasts between 5 - 14 days and the final color is determined by both skin type and exposure. Moisturizing with natural oils (olive, coconut) can also prolong the stain.

You will find henna artists everywhere in India, from malls to roadside booths. Some hotels also offer the service as a cultural element of the stay. The price is dependent on the design intricacy and artist's skill level.

BOOKS AND MEDIA
TO FUEL YOUR WANDERLUST

Movie Recommendations
Gandhi
Bombay
Water
Earth: 1947
Monsoon Wedding
Lagaan
Slumdog Millionaire
BBC Documentary Series: The Story of India
Looking for Comedy in the Muslim World

Suggested Reading
Travels through Sacred India by Roger Housden
Holy Cow: An Indian Adventure by Sarah MacDonald
Dreaming in Hindi by Katherine Russell Rich
The Mango Season by Amulya Malladi
Interpreter of Maladies by Jhumpa Lahiri
India: A History by John Keay
Midnight's Children by Salman Rushdie
The God of Small Things by Arundhati Roy
Out of India by Ruth Prawer Jhabvala
Shantaram by Gregory David Roberts

CULTURE
AND CUSTOMS

CULTURAL CURIOSITIES

From the holy cow to the Indian head nod, here are common cultural curiosities in India:

Eating with Hands

The practice of eating food with hands dates back centuries. In Indian culture, the practice is founded on Ayurvedic teachings. The Vedic communities believed that hands hold power and our bodies have a sacred connection with nature. In Ayurvedic text, each finger represents five different elements. The thumb, index finger, middle finger, ring finger, and pinky represent space, air, fire, water, and earth. That is why Mudras, symbolic and ritualistic gestures used in prayer or spiritual practices like Yoga, are performed with the hands and fingers. When food is eaten with the hands, the fingers should come together to touch. The practice is believed to increase awareness of our taste buds and creates both a physical and spiritual connection with the food.

Blessing the Elders

Adopted during the Vedic period, touching the feet of elders is a common practice in India. Also known as *Charan Sparsh*, it is a way to offer respect and seek blessings in return.

Elders can be considered parents, grandparents, siblings, teachers, priests, or other respected senior citizens. It is believed that when a person bows down to touch the feet of elders, the ego comes to an end. As an individual offers respect to an elder's wisdom, knowledge, age, and experience, they are blessed in return. Indians will touch the feet during many special and sacred occasions, including weddings, birthdays, an important exam, or journeying abroad.

The Indian Bromance

In the west, public displays of affection are often labeled as either heterosexual or homosexual. In India, however, it is common for heterosexual men to hold hands and wrap their arms around one another in public. This "Bromance" is different from same sex attraction. It is loving but not sexual. While there are differing theories as to how this public affection started, many believe it stems from gender segregation.

Traditionally, women would stay home while the men would work outside. The camaraderie would provide emotional nourishment among groups of men. While it is acceptable for males to show affection, the public display of intimacy between men and women is still widely considered inappropriate.

The head wobble is so inherent to Indian culture that locals hardly realize they are doing it. Foreigners have spent years attempting to decode the interpretation. Is it a clear yes? A kind no? A maybe? A sign of uncertainty? It all depends on the context, but usually it is to acknowledge someone's presence, to understand or agree, or to say "yes."

Without words accompanying the head nod it can be ambiguous, but usually the quicker the head wobbles, the more they understand you.

Holy Cow

The cow is sacred in Hinduism and associated with several deities, notably Shiva, Indra, and Krishna. It is a symbol of life and revered as the source of food (for its milk). Because cows are respected animals, they roam mostly unharmed and are familiar with the traffic and rhythms of the city.

Some animal scientists estimate there are two cows for every person in India — with a population topping 1.3 billion people, that means the country may share space with billions of bovines. Many millions of cows are now destroying crops and blocking traffic on already congested roads. Although the government and Hindu charities run shelters for aged and abandoned cows, they are too few to accommodate the millions of strays.

With western influences, beef is becoming more available but still considered uncommon. Visit an Indian McDonalds and you will not be able to order a beef burger — the menu includes more vegetarian options, like a Veg Maharaja Mac and McSpicy Paneer.

The Guest is God

Atithi Devo Bhava, meaning a guest is akin to god, is a Sanskrit verse from an ancient Hindu scripture that became part of the "code of conduct" for Indian society. It is a sacred guest-host relationship that often includes five key practices:

Fragrance, as that is the first element a guest notices upon entering a home
Lamp, to illuminate body language and create a positive interaction
Edibles, usually fruit or sweets, to share nourishment together
Rice, a symbol of being undivided
Flower, as a gesture of goodwill

The India tourism department has also adopted 'Atithi Devo Bhava' as a social awareness campaign to welcome incoming travelers. The concept of treating guests as God is also why India is globally renowned for remarkable hospitality.

The Indian Wedding

There are weddings...and then there are Indian weddings! A traditional Indian wedding averages three days and varies according to the region, religion, resources, and family preferences.

Allison's Wedding

A typical Hindu celebration starts with a puja, a ritual to offer blessings to deities or honor guests and relatives. The second day is reserved for mehndi, a celebration when female guests adorn their hands and feet with henna, followed by a festive dance and music filled sangeet. The third day consists of the ceremony and reception, often with the groom arriving on horseback to the venue.

Guest lists are often in the hundreds, if not thousands, and the festivities include elaborate costume changes, choreographed dances, extensive décor, and indulgent food stations. The ceremony can also be at unusual times – based on the couples astrology chart – and last for hours.

Arranged marriages have long been the norm in Indian society, where the families of the bride and groom select their respective partner. Recent studies suggest that fewer unions are now arranged without consent, though 80% of marriages are still considered arranged in some form.

Indian Family

FAMILY

In Indian society, the family is an institution and a symbol of collectivist culture. An especially important responsibility of the family is the transmission of beliefs and core values. Traditionally, a woman would leave her home after marriage and move-in with her husband and his family. Grandparents, aunts, uncles, cousins, and other relatives also often reside at home. However, with urbanization and western influence, the definition of a joint family has become more fluid.

Population studies across India are showing that in the past decade, joint families have decreased in rural areas and exponentially increased in larger cities. There is generally a socioeconomic or supportive purpose; as housing costs rise and more women work outside the home, there is a need to share resources and care for children and the elderly.

Indian Village

LOCALS

Indians are some of the friendliest people in the world. We encourage you to speak to the locals throughout your journey. They are usually excited to engage in delightful conversation with foreigners, and it will allow you to learn more about India's colorful culture.

The children of India are always charming. They will ask questions about your origin and frequently request hugs. If you choose to bring items to distribute to the kids, we recommend candy, pens, and paper. Some travelers also buy the children ice cream cones or snacks. Beggars are common. Many cities have homes that teach this craft as a scam, especially by manipulating children. If you feel compelled to give, we recommend donating money to a reputable charitable organization that will disperse the funds to the community.

Ganesha

RELIGION

The most common religion practiced in India is Hinduism:

Hindu - 80.5 %	Muslim - 13.4%	Christian - 2.3%
Sikh - 1.9%	Buddhist: 1.2%	Other – 0.7%

The Constitution of India declares that the country must support the right of its citizens to freely worship any religion. Separate personal law codes apply to Hindus, Muslims, and Christians. Although inter-religious marriage is not common, Indians are generally tolerant of all faiths.

THE CASTE SYSTEM

For generations, India's society has been defined by the caste system. The Hindu social stratification has determined acceptable jobs, relationships, marriages, and even lifestyle. From the outside, the caste system is an archaic form of discrimination and prejudice. The higher castes are the beneficiaries of more opportunities while the lowest rungs are subject to marginalization and even violence. Although the Indian Constitution banned caste discrimination in

1950, it remains a complex and controversial ingredient in the cultural melting pot.

First, let's touch briefly on the history of the caste system. In ancient Indian texts from Vedic society, the word "varna" was used for grouping people into classes. Scholars believe this was not intended for discrimination but instead a higher calling or a specific responsibility to society. There were four classes:

Brahmins
Priests and teachers of sacred knowledge. As leaders of society, they set the standard for social conduct. Within the varna framework, Brahmins can have everything, directly or indirectly.

Kshatriyas
Rulers, administrators, and warriors. This caste isn't considered "inferior" to the Brahmas, but instead expected to fight as respected warriors during conflict and govern in the time of peace. Approximately 20% of India's population are within this category.

Vaishyas
Merchants, traders, artisans, and farmers. Males were entitled to a rite of initiation during childhood while a "second birth" allowed them access to sacred knowledge and the ability to participate in

specified rituals. Their status also granted them the right to demand and receive menial services from the Shudras.

Shudras

Laborers who would serve the higher three castes. Although a lower designation, educated citizens of higher Varnas would always regard them as a respected and essential segment of society. After all, without the feet, the body can't stand. Shudras would obey the orders of their masters because they believed their loyalty would create moksha, or the liberation from death and rebirth.

Within the varnas there are thousands of sub-groups called *jati*, meaning birth. At some point a fifth classification arose for those entirely outside the scope of civilized society, called untouchables. They are also referenced as **scheduled caste or dalit** - the lowest of all castes. Meaning "ground," "suppressed" or "crushed" in Sanskrit, Dalits are typically associated with occupations regarded as ritually impure, such as those involving waste or corpses.

"Caste" is actually not an Indian word. According to the Oxford dictionary, it's a derivative of the Portuguese word casta, meaning race, lineage, and breed.

The modern-day caste system is largely the result of British colonialism. When the Mughal era collapsed, English men in positions of power aligned themselves with kings, priests, and others considered influential. The strict British class system profoundly influenced government operations and Indian caste categorizations. In 1860, the British Raj started hiring Christians and others from the higher castes for administrative and government jobs. Social unrest in the 1920's, including the rise of Mahatma Gandhi's popularity, sparked a rejection of a societal hierarchy.

In an attempt to correct historical injustice, the Indian government introduced a reservation system, similar to affirmative action. The policies and practices include quotas, or reserved spaces, in education and employment. With over a billion people vying for jobs and admission in higher education — especially in a country with *extraordinary* academic competition — the quota system has been contentious.

For centuries, inter-caste marriage was fiercely prohibited. This was to protect the idea that a lower caste would corrupt or contaminate the purity of a higher caste. Even today, many arranged marriages are only conducted within the same caste. Advertisements will specifically state the bride or groom's social lineage for spousal eligibility. This practice is slowly changing, but most Indian families still place importance on similar-caste relationships.

With westernization and a burgeoning middle class, customary ideas and practices, including social lineage, are being challenged. Also, the societal hierarchy is no longer a Hindu ideology as other religions have adopted similar practices. The caste system has become a human rights issue with economic inequality as a system of exploitation, especially for lower groups. There is also caste-related violence that is ignored or under-reported, particularly in rural communities.

GREETINGS

Namaste is a Sanskrit word and the common greeting in India. The literal translation means "I bow to you." The expression is accompanied by the gesture of joining two palms together and placing them at the heart level. Depending on the person (elder, teacher, priest), the greeting may also be accompanied by a slight nod or bow.

Because men and women rarely touch in public, *Namaste* is the safest way to greet members of the opposite sex.

HISTORY

Keeping it real, we could write several volumes about India's historical events and barely scratch the surface. Here is a summary of the timeline:

The Indus Valley civilization, dating back at least 5,000 years, is one of the oldest in the world. Additionally, India has always been rich in natural resources. Arab invasions started in the 8th century, followed by the Turkish in the 12th century and European traders in the late 15th century. By the 19th century, Britain had assumed political control of virtually all Indian lands.

Mohandas Gandhi led a nonviolent resistance to British colonialism, resulting in independence in 1947. The subcontinent was divided into the state of India and the smaller Muslim state of Pakistan. A third war between the two countries in 1971 resulted in East Pakistan becoming the separate nation of Bangladesh.

The current Republic of India is a unification of the states who rebelled against British colonialism. Think of India as Europe, where each state is a different country yet sharing similar democratic values. Each state also fiercely preserves its own regional languages, cuisine, attire, customs, and traditions.

CURRENT POLITICS

Present-day India is a democratic republic with a multi-party system. The latest publication from the Election Commission of India shows 2,598 registered parties: 8 national, 52 state, and 2,538 unrecognized. There are both national (federal) and regional (state) parties and each state has a Chief Minister and a Governor.

Indian Flag

The Prime Minister is the diplomatic figure who proposes and implements legislation, while the President is the head of the Armed Services and the final signing authority for any legislation.

Current political disputes are centered in two areas: Kashmir and the Northeastern states (Sino-Indian dispute).

FOOD AND WATER

Indian food is delicious — and spicy. Our bodies are not accustomed to the variety of Indian spices, so be cautious. Pack a digestive relief such as Pepto Bismol. To be safe, cautiously enjoy roadside stands or cafes, as the food may not be cleaned or cooked properly. Unfortunately, too many travelers get sick from a desire to eat "authentic" at these locations, and regret it later.

Indian restaurants are generally categorized as Veg (vegetarian) and Non-Veg (non-vegetarian). Remember, the cow is sacred in India and beef is rare.

To be safe, only drink bottled water during your journey and avoid ice. Opt for a cold bottle of soda or beer for the hot days. Always check the caps to make sure they are sealed. Although many hotels have their own water purification system, plan to use bottled water even for brushing your teeth and be cautious when ingesting water from the shower.

It is usually not necessary to bring iodine tablets unless camping, trekking, or staying at remote locations.

Our Top Tips for a Healthy Tummy:
- Pack a digestive relief: Tums, Pepto Bismol, etc.
- Grapefruit seed extract is a natural defense to unfamiliar bacteria. The extract is available at most natural food stores and nutrition/vitamin shops.
- As a precaution, request an antibiotic from your doctor prior to travel.
- Only eat fruits and vegetables that have a thick peel: bananas, mangoes, oranges, melons, squash, and eggplant. Avoid produce without a thick peel: apples, berries, and pears. Also, be cautious about salads. The lettuce is often washed in tap water.
- Only drink bottled water during your trip. Be sure to check for sealed and untampered caps.

Here is a sample list of common Indian dishes and ingredients:

Biryani: Steamed rice with fragrant fruit, nuts, meat, and/or vegetables

Roti (or Chapati): Unleavened wheat flatbread

Naan: Leavened, oven-baked flatbread that rises on one side

Chai: Traditional spiced black tea with milk and sugar

Tandoori: The tandoor is a clay oven. Tandoori is the preparation of food using the tandoor.

Dosa: A thin crepe made from rice and black lentils. It can also be stuffed with vegetables, meats, and spices.

Paneer: Cottage cheese

Dal: A preparation of lentils or dried beans

Ghee: Clarified butter

Lassi: A yogurt-based drink made with ice and spices

Curd (or Dahi): Yogurt

Thali: A selection of regional dishes served in bowls on a tray

Channa Masala: Chickpeas in a spicy sauce

Saag: Spinach

CHAI

In India, chai is more than a cup of spiced tea. It's a connection, a conversation, and a way of life. Although there is no standard preparation, there are generally four core ingredients: black tea, milk, spices, and sweetener. The spices vary depending on the region and personal tasting preferences, though the most common are cardamom, ginger, clove, and cinnamon. Other variations can include peppercorn, fennel, rose, and star anise.

A man drinking chai

Remember to simply call it chai. Chai means "tea" in Hindi, so if you order a chai tea, it translates to "tea tea."

PATRIARCHAL SOCIETY

Traditionally, Indian society has shown a preference toward males. From birth, girls are entitled to less than their brothers. A son is considered a blessing and a form of security while a daughter is a liability. Across the country, fathers and husbands are assumed the head of the household. As more women are educated and enter the workforce, the dynamic is slowly starting to shift. However, outside of larger cities, there remains a strong patriarchal preservation and women overwhelmingly face discrimination.

Feminist movements have added pressure for legislative changes regarding gender equality, including the right to healthcare and education, equal wages, and inheritance laws/land ownership. Many women do not take full advantage of their constitutional rights because they are simply not informed. The Indian government does not interfere with religious and personal laws, adding to the oppression in devout communities.

Unfortunately, statistics also show an increase in sex-selective abortion. Elective abortions and ultrasounds for gender determination are also illegal in India, but many doctors still covertly practice.

The female-to-male ratio is 933 to 1000, spotlighting considerably fewer women compared to men. Although illegal, female infanticides are still common in agricultural communities, as well as the practice of dowry. The hierarchical structures and familial traditions have been practiced for centuries, making the patriarchal society even more difficult to equalize.

SOCIAL ETIQUETTE

- Refrain from excessive public displays of affection

- Remove your shoes before entering a home, religious site, temple, or place of worship

- Unless otherwise posted, do not smoke in historical sites, places of worship, or sacred institutions

- Do not point at or touch items with your feet

- Dress modestly and conservatively

- Always ask permission if taking pictures of the locals (Also, it is best to ask permission to film a funeral procession and/ or at a religious site)

PHOTOGRAPHY AND VIDEOGRAPHY

Most historical and cultural sites allow you to photograph and record. Many times there is a fee associated with using cameras and video devices, so please check before entering. At certain sites the fee is included with the entrance fee, while at others it is a separate charge. This may include your cell phone, as well. Also, the fee will be different for locals and foreigners so be prepared to pay a higher cost.

If you are visiting a religious site, please ask if photography and videography are allowed.

SHOPPING

Jewelry, clothes, spices, tapestries, shoes, shawls, handicrafts, tea, rugs... shopping will soon become one of your favorite experiences in India! The shops and bazaars are overflowing with color and vitality.

An Indian Shopping Mall

Indian fabrics

Where to Shop?

Markets

In India, there are traditional markets, night markets, neighborhood markets, and street markets, just to name a few. Markets include chain and independent brands, may be indoor or outdoor, and can specialize in a product or theme — for example, a silver market or spice market. They can also be upmarket (like Khan Market in Delhi) or a bargainers paradise.

Government Emporiums

As the name suggests, government emporiums are owned by the respective state governments. Prices are fixed so there is (generally) no room for negotiation. The items are directly sourced from artisans and you often won't find the same pattern/workmanship at other shops. There is at least one government emporium in each tourist destination. In large cities like Delhi you will also find emporiums from other states. If you are not a fan of bargaining and appreciate quality workmanship, this is a fantastic option.

Private Showrooms and Emporiums

These shops are also government-approved; however, bargaining is welcome! The quality is similar to government emporiums and you will generally find at least 3-4 outlets in each tourist destination. For an additional cost, private emporiums can ship your bulky or fragile items overseas, so there is no hassle with carting your purchases around India.

*When it comes to emporiums (private or government), some travelers appreciate the quality and value while others feel they are overpriced and targeted for foreigners. Unlike markets and bazaars, the quality is guaranteed and there is recourse for returns and exchanges.

Bazaars

Traditionally, a bazaar was a bustling market with rows of stalls selling eclectic goods. It was also a place where bankers, merchants, and artisans would conduct business. Today, the words "bazaar" and "market" are often interchangeable, but bazaars remain places to shop, socialize, and catch up on the neighborhood gossip. Bring cash! Credit cards are rarely accepted.

Chor Bazaar

The "thief's market" is common in larger cities, including Delhi, Mumbai, Agra, and Jaipur. As the name suggests, the items are usually stolen, knock-offs, or second-hand, but you can also discover vintage and antique goods. You will find everything from automobile parts to sunglasses, but be prepared to rummage - think of it like a giant flea market. According to locals, if you lose an item you can likely buy it back...from the Chor Bazaar!

Malls

Indian malls are multi-floor and modern shopping venues. In addition to local and international brands, you will often find cinemas, restaurants, food courts, and entertainment. Malls may be sterile to some travelers, but it can be nice to pop in to the A/C on a super hot day.

Duty Free

Tax-exempt products can be purchased at airports by international passengers arriving and departing from India. A passport and boarding pass must be provided for all purchases, including liquor, makeup, perfume, and cigarettes. Presently, India limits each passenger to two liters of liquor and one carton of cigarettes. For the bargain hunters, it's important to note that duty-free does not always save money! Duty free can often be inflated compared to sale prices or outlets.

For a curated list of our recommended markets and emporiums in each city, please refer to Destination Inspiration, pages 101 - 390.

Bargain Bargain Bargain!

In some shops, like at malls, the price is fixed. For all others, bargaining is expected! If you are not used to this form of exchange, it can be uncomfortable. Try and remember that the practice is normal in India — a lively game that creates conversation.

Please be respectful during the bargaining process. The difference in Rupees amounts way more to a local shopkeeper than to you. Remember, the more you buy, the bigger the discount!

Bargaining Tips

Even if you are obsessed with an item, pretend to be only mildly interested. Shopkeepers won't be inclined to lower the price if they see a twinkle in your eye.

Don't bargain if you aren't willing to pay. If the seller accepts your price, buy the item/s. Don't change your mind or walk away.

Don't buy from the first stall you see. Many shopkeepers sell similar items, so browse the market before purchasing.

As a foreigner, your price will start around 3x higher than a local. A general rule is to not pay more than half the original asking price.

If the shopkeeper does not lower the price enough, casually walk away. Often this will prompt a deeper discount to retain your business. (If it doesn't, your price may be too low.)

Have fun! Bargaining is a part of India's cultural communication, so smile and ease into the process. Also, practice a few phrases in Hindi (or the regional language) before you hit the market.

SEX AND SEXUALITY

India may be the land of the Kama Sutra, but sex and sexuality are still taboo. Sex is considered a private, closed-door conversation. Public displays of affection are more common in larger cities and popular tourist destinations, especially with the younger generation. Foreigners may have a "pass" when it comes to PDA but India is still a conservative country, so refrain from any excessive public intimacy. I sometimes receive glares and stares from locals when holding hands with my husband (a Delhiite).

Historically, Indian entertainment has rarely portrayed any form of sexual contact, including kissing. Even in Bollywood, the world's largest film industry based on the number of annual productions, the idea of sex is romanticized by dance numbers in fields of wildflowers, loving gazes, and fully-clothed passionate embraces. Kissing and sex scenes are rare but slowly emerging in mainstream media.

Although prostitution is legal in India, the laws are vague. For example, brothels are technically illegal but operate fairly openly in specific districts like Sonapur in Mumbai and G.B. Road in Delhi. As long as a woman voluntarily uses her body in exchange for compensation or material benefit, it is allowed.

However, it is prohibited within 200 yards of a public place. Male prostitution is not recognized under Indian law. There is a growing movement to legalize brothels and stop the exploitation of sex workers, especially minors. It is also illegal to distribute or produce pornographic material, but accessing it privately is allowed.

POLICE

To reach the police, dial 100 from an Indian phone.

There is a strong underbelly of bribery and corruption within Indian law enforcement. Many policing practices are controversial and crimes are often "ignored" with compensation.

Through the years, I've had a few experiences with the police:

In Goa, I was pulled over for speeding on a scooter. My husband paid the police officer INR 1000 and he let us go without a ticket.

In Delhi, I was stopped at a sobriety checkpoint. Nobody was under the influence so we passed without incident. Note: checkpoints are common. Indian roads are challenging enough when sober. Never drive when intoxicated!

Again in Delhi, I was stopped after leaving a club with a few friends. Even though we had a designated driver, the police officer became harassing. My friends paid him and he left us alone.

This isn't to say that all police are corrupt and unwilling to ethically serve the public. Just know that these situations are not uncommon.

SMOKING/DRINKING

According to the World Health Organization, India is home to over 120 million smokers, more than any other country in the world. Far more men also smoke compared to women - 74% to 14% by recent estimates. Smokeless tobacco is generally more common compared to cigarettes. The legal smoking age is 18, though minors have access to tobacco much younger.

Since 2008, India has prohibited smoking in many public places. It is allowed in designated areas at airports, restaurants, and bars. Tobacco products can be purchased at convenience stores and cigarette/tobacco stands (often outside movie theaters, colleges, bus stops, office buildings, and ironically, hospitals).

Alcohol is available throughout India and the country has won international awards for its beer, rum and wine. The legal drinking ages are mandated by each state, and in certain states the drinking age depends on the type of liquor. Some states, like Delhi, have the oldest legal drinking age in the entire world: 25! In Rajasthan, it is 18. In Mumbai, the drinking age is 21 for beer and 25 for all other liquor. The younger population will find ways around these laws and many bars and restaurants will be more lenient for foreigners, but be mindful of local regulations.

Liquor is prohibited in the states of Gujarat, Bihar, Mizoram, Nagaland, and the union territory of Lakshadweep. However, tourists may obtain a liquor permit to purchase alcohol in government shops. Please respect the law and only consume liquor in a hotel room or private home.

In states where alcohol is permitted, there are two different types of liquor shops: Indian and English. Indian shops sell local variations similar to homebrews and moonshine. Leave these for the locals. English shops sell more international brands of beer, wine, and spirits. Purchase wisely and only drink in your hotel room, not in public.

DRUGS AND BHANG

All drugs, including Cannabis, are illegal in India. This often surprises foreigners, as many associate the slang "Ganga" with the Ganges and assume it's a cultural indulgence. Yes, marijuana is available and the smell permeates the air in many hill stations and religious destinations, but you can get arrested with possession and serve jail time.

Bhang is an edible cannabis preparation commonly used as an ingredient in cool drinks and sweets during the festivals of Holi and Shivratri. Using a mortar and pestle, the cannabis leaves are ground into a paste and added to foods. For beverages, the leaves are mixed with milk, filtered, and flavored with kusha grass, sugar, fruit, and various spices. The sale and consumption of bhang are permitted under Indian law; you can find it at government authorized bhang shops.

Hello obvious, but if you are approached with offers of hash or cannabis, politely decline and walk away. It's just not smart to accept drugs from an unknown source and it may be an undercover operation.

DESTINATION INSPIRATION

Let's explore where to stay, dine, shop, drink, tour, volunteer, and play!

Please note that this guide is NOT intended to cover every destination. Instead, we have thoughtfully selected 18 cities and five national parks to help guide your way across north and west India. Our curated lists of accommodations, restaurants, markets, bars, and attractions are a mix of highly rated experiences, popular landmarks, and personal favorites.

Contact information, hours, availability, and entrance fees are current at the time of publication and subject to change.

DELHI

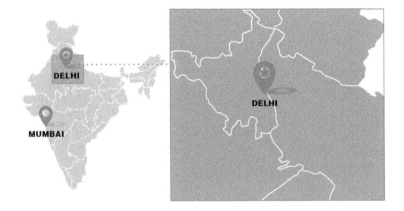

As the capital of India, Delhi is the political center of the country. With a population of 23+ million people, it is the world's second largest urban area. Historically the capital of multiple kingdoms and empires, the eclectic neighborhoods reflect a melting pot of ethnicities, heritages, and traditions. Delhi showcases India's unique ability to modernize at a rapid pace without casting aside its cultural, historical, and spiritual identity.

Is it called Delhi or New Delhi?

Delhi's official name is the National Capital Territory (NCT) of Delhi; New Delhi is the administrative district of Delhi that serves as the capital. Both names are interchangeable, though technically New Delhi serves as the capital. Delhi's urban area presently extends beyond the NCT boundaries and includes the neighboring cities of Gurgaon, Noida, Ghaziabad, and Faridabad in an area called the National Capital Region (NCR).

TRANSPORTATION HUBS

Delhi is bordered by the states of Haryana and Uttar Pradesh. The megacity joins Agra and Jaipur to form the popular Golden Triangle tourist circuit.

Indira Gandhi International Airport
www.newdelhiairport.in

As the capital of India, Delhi is very well connected by both domestic and international flights. Many international airlines have direct flights to the city.

New Delhi Railway Station (NDLS)
Bhavbhuti Marg, Ratan Lal Market, Kamla Market, Ajmeri Gate

Old Delhi Railway Station / Delhi Junction (DLI)
Near Chandani Chowk Metro Station, Mori Gate

Hazrat Nizamuddin Railway Station (NZM)
Nizamuddin, Nizamuddin East, New Delhi

Delhi Sarai Rohilla (DEE)
Guru Gobind Singh Marg, Railway Officers Colony, Sarai Rohilla, New Delhi

Delhi has 47+ rail stations to accommodate a population of over 23 million people. NDLS, DLI, NZN, and DEE service the more popular routes:

NDLS has trains operating to Agra, Jaipur, Haridwar, Amritsar, Varanasi, and Varanasi.

DLI has routes to Kathgodam (Nainital) and Ramnagar (Corbett).

NZN services the Gatimaan Express train to Agra.

DEE services the JP Double Decker to Jaipur.

Maharana Pratap ISBT Kashmere Gate
ISBT Anand Vihar, Kashmere Gate

As the oldest and one of the largest interstate bus terminals in India, ISBT has an extensive network throughout the country.

AREAS TO AVOID

Delhi is notoriously known as the most unsafe city in India, especially for women travelers. India's capital has two personalities during the day and night. After dark, avoid buses and rickshaws and instead opt for a rideshare, private car, or the metro. Also, don't venture out to the surrounding cities of Gurgaon or Noida at night.

In all my years of traveling to Delhi, I have never experienced or witnessed an assault, harassment, or other crime against women. Although the city has a questionable reputation when it comes to safety, I also believe it's not where you travel but how you travel. Schedule most activities during the day and be vigilant after dark.

LOCAL FESTIVALS

As the capital, people from across India migrate to Delhi for better opportunities. The assimilation and cultural diversity is evident in the multitude of festivals and celebrations. Please refer to pages 68 - 71.

The Republic Day parade on January 26th includes grand tableaus and cultural performances from all states of India.

WHERE TO STAY

Madpackers Delhi
A hip hostel with a rooftop garden in the trendy Hauz Khas neighborhood.
$ / www.madpackers.com / +91 88 0026 5725

Joey's Hostel
A dormitory-style property offering free breakfast and complimentary walking tours.
$ / www.joeyshostel.com / +91 98 1864 2824

Zostel Delhi
A basic yet budget friendly hostel in the backpacking hub of Paharganj.
$ / www.zostel.com / +91 22 4896 2267

Colonel's Retreat
An award-winning B&B in an exclusive, tree-lined neighborhood.
$$ / www.colonelsretreat.com / +91 11 4660 4927

Shanti Home
A boutique budget hotel with themed rooms located near the airport.
$$ / www.shantihome.com / +91 11 4157 3366

Maidens
A heritage hotel near Old Delhi with resident peacocks and a large pool.
$$$ / www.maidenshotel.com / +91 11 2388 5700

The Manor
A 12-room urban oasis set in a South Delhi secluded garden.
$$$ / www.themanordelhi.com / +91 11 4130 7777

Haveli Dharampura

A beautifully restored haveli with contemporary amenities in the heart of Old Delhi.

$$$ / www.havelidharampura.com / +91 11 2326 1000

Oberoi New Delhi

A luxury property with clean air technology offering the healthiest air in the city.

$$$$ / www.oberoihotels.com / +91 11 2436 3030

WHAT TO DO

India Gate

The India Gate is a war memorial built to commemorate the Indian soldiers who died in World War I. An imposing sandstone structure with four eternal flames sheltered at the base, India Gate is a stop for all tourists visiting Delhi. Surrounded by lush green lawns and a

boat club, it is the perfect picnic spot for locals who visit with their friends and family.

Entry: Free
Hours: 24/7

Lotus Temple
Shaped like a lotus, the Baha'i House of Worship is one of the most visited buildings in the world. Although it's called a Lotus Temple, there is no idol to be worshiped inside the temple. It follows the teachings of the Baha'i faith which believes in Oneness of God and religions. All are welcome to meditate inside the architectural marvel.

Entry: Free
Hours: Tuesday - Sunday from 9 am - 7 pm during summer; 9 am - 5:30 pm during winter. Closed on Mondays.

Qutub Minar and Mehrauli Complex
Built in 1193, the Qutub Minar is one of the most visited monuments in Delhi. With a towering spire stretching 238 feet into the sky, the red sandstone and marble mosque has the tallest minaret in India. Get an up-close look at the ornate exterior, which is covered in detailed

carvings of text from the Quran. Take a 15-minute walk to the nearby Mehrauli Archaeological Park where historical monuments and crumbling ruins will provide a unique look at the city's past. The park consists of various tombs, mosques, and stepwells, making it a unique heritage hub.

Entry: INR 600
Hours: 7 am - 6 pm daily

Raj Ghat

Located on the banks of the Yamuna River, Raj Ghat is a memorial dedicated to Mahatma Gandhi. The complex is designed to reflect the simplicity of his life. A black marble platform and eternal flame mark where the "Father of the Nation" was cremated after being assassinated in January 1948, less than six months after India gained independence from the British. There is also a museum with films of Gandhi's life and influence.

Entry: Free
Hours: 6:30 am - 6 pm daily; Every Friday there is a special prayer at 5:30 pm

Red Fort

The Red Fort served as the palace for Mughal emperor Shah Jahan when he shifted the capital from Agra to Delhi. The red sandstone structure and surrounding complex includes a mosque, geometrical gardens, and museums. Declared a UNESCO World Heritage site, the fort stands as a reminder of the power and glory of the Mughal empire. A sound and light show in the evening recreates the history connected with the fort.

Entry: INR 950
Hours: Open from Tuesday to Sunday from 9.30 am - 4.30 pm. Closed on Mondays.

Purana Qila (Old Fort)

As one of the oldest forts in Delhi, Purana Qila is a grand example of Mughal architecture. The fort was inhabited by a village until 1914 when it was cleared and became a site for temporary settlements during the Second World War and later during India's partition. Today, locals enjoy boating and other activities in the moat surrounding the fort. The museum at the entry depicts the history and features several artifacts.

Entry: INR 100
Hours: 9 am - 7 pm daily

Jama Masjid

Accommodating 25,000 devotees at one time, Jama Masjid is one of the largest mosques in India. With commanding views of Delhi, the entire structure stands on a high platform so its magnificent facade is visible from all sides. The mosque is located in Old Delhi and surrounded by bustling Chandni Chowk.

Entry: Free
Hours: 7 am - 12 pm and 1:30 pm - 6:30 pm daily

Humayun's Tomb

Humayun's Tomb is a grand mausoleum constructed for the Mughal Emperor, Humayun. Commissioned by his wife as a gesture of love and affection, the tomb became an inspiration for the Taj Mahal. The meticulously landscaped gardens and elevated design captures the architectural capabilities of the Mughal era.

Entry: INR 550; Children under 15 are free
Hours: 7 am - 6 pm daily

Lodhi (Lodi) Gardens

The 90-acre park is scattered with the domed tombs of the Lodi Dynasty. It is also a popular spot for Delhiites to enjoy morning walks. Lodi Gardens is protected by the Archaeological Survey of India, mainly because there is hardly any architecture from this period remaining in the country. Have a seat on a park bench with a good book, enjoy a stroll, or meander through architectural works from the 15th century.

Entry: Free
Hours: 5 am - 8 pm daily from April to September; 6 am - 8 pm daily from October - March

Jantar Mantar

Built by Maharaja Jai Singh of Jaipur, Jantar Mantar was built to measure the astronomical movements of the sun, moon, and planets. He went on to build such observatories in Jaipur, Ujjain, Varanasi, and Mathura. Located in the middle of the city, the various instruments in the complex are no longer in use as they cannot make accurate measurements due to the surrounding tall buildings. The red-colored monument stands out in the middle of the city and is a delight for people interested in astronomy.

Entry: INR 300
Hours: 7 am - 6 pm daily

Akshardham Temple

Explore 10,000 years of India's history, culture, architecture, and spirituality on over sixty acres of manicured grounds. Akshardham is an elaborate Swaminarayan temple complex that features an IMAX theater, musical fountains, sunken gardens, and the Mandir with over 20,000 statues of India's religious personalities. The main shrine of the temple houses the statue of Lord Swaminarayan. Be sure to experience the 12-minute boat ride that highlights India's heritage, including inventions, discoveries, and the world's first university of Takshashila.

Entry: Temple entry is free but the exhibitions have a ticket. The combined ticket for all shows and exhibitions is INR 220 for adults, INR 170 for senior citizens (60 years and above), and INR 120 for children ages 4-11. Children under 4 are free.
Hours: 10 am - 8 pm Tuesday - Sunday; Closed on Mondays

Gurudwara Bangla Sahib

Located in Old Delhi, the Gurudwara is a place of worship for the Sikh community. The complex includes the main Gurudwara with a golden dome, kitchen, large holy pond, school, and art gallery. The Sikhs are known for their generosity and their service to people in need. Anyone who visits will be fed a hot and hearty meal, regardless of religion, caste, or creed. In addition to the ideals of equality, the tradition of langar expresses the ethics of sharing, inclusiveness, and oneness.

Entry: Free
Hours: The Gurudwara is open 24/7; The langar timings are from 9 am - 3 pm and 7 pm - 10 pm

National Crafts Museum and Hastkala Academy

One of the largest craft museums in India, the National Crafts Museum displays tribal and rural art and artifacts. With over 35,000 pieces ranging from textiles to clay, the space is a welcoming community of artisans and art lovers. The museum was created over a 30-year period to preserve the sacred and traditional artistry of the region. Each month, approximately 50 craftspeople from across the country are invited to reside on the property and demonstrate their talents. Don't miss the Village Complex, an exhibition that displays village life from varying regions in India.

Entry: INR 200
Hours: 9:30 am - 6 pm daily; Closed on Mondays

Hauz Khas Village

One of the most popular hangouts in South Delhi is Hauz Khas Village (HKV). The artsy neighborhood is known for an eclectic mix of attractions, including a lake, deer park, boutique shops, restaurants, art galleries, and religious monuments dating back to the 14th century. From archaeology to designer clothes, you can easily spend an entire day browsing, eating, and shopping.

WHERE TO SHOP

In addition to the city's diverse historical and cultural identity, little compares to Delhi's shopping scene. From luxury brands in DLF Emporio to handicrafts and antiques in Sundar Nagar, India's capital is overflowing with markets, malls, and bazaars. Many travelers visit Dilli Haat, a paid-entrance open-air market and food plaza that features both permanent and transitional vendors. The space, designed to resemble a traditional village market, was created to showcase products from across India. Another popular spot is Paharganj, known locally as the *Hippie Market*. Located near the New Delhi Railway Station, Paharganj offers bargain-friendly bags, shoes, clothes, textiles, incense, jewelry, and more.

Janpath

Janpath is a marketplace that houses both government-approved shops and open-air stalls. Plan to visit soon after arriving in Delhi to grab a few local and traditional clothing items. Of course, there are hundreds of options: carpets, shoes, clothing, jewelry, handicrafts, textiles, accessories, paintings, and furniture. Be sure to have Rupees available. Most government-regulated shops accept credit cards, though cash is preferred, and the bazaar is cash only. Also, don't miss a cold coffee at De Paul's, famously served in a glass bottle with a straw.

Hours: Depends on the shop, but generally 10 am - 7 pm
Location: Near Connaught Place (CP)

Kamla Nagar

Kamla Nagar is one of the more traditional markets in Delhi. I have visited several times and rarely encounter other foreigners. Located in Old Delhi, Kamla Nagar is where the locals shop for everyday goods including bangles, stationery, clothes, and household items. It is also a prime area for mehendi (henna) and the artists sit on stools with picture books of designs.

Hours: Depends on the shops, but the market is usually lively between 10 am - 8 pm
Location: North Delhi

Khan Market

Although Khan Market is consistently ranked one of the most expensive commercial real estate locations in the world, don't let this deter you from visiting the collection of shops and restaurants. There are several moderately priced stores, like Fabindia (garments) and Amrapali (jewelry). My personal favorite is Forest Essentials, offering ayurvedic bath and body products. Stop for lunch at Big Chill Cafe, an Italian jaunt very popular with the locals. For easy accessibility and to avoid Delhi traffic, take the metro.

Hours: Depends on the individual shops and restaurants
Location: Rabindra Nagar, New Delhi

Chandni Chowk

Established by Mughal Emperor Shah Jahan in 1650 AD, Chandni Chowk is considered one of the oldest and busiest street markets in Old Delhi (Shahjahanabad). The street is positioned between two important historical sites: the Red Fort (Lal Qila) and Fatehpur Masjid, a 17th century mosque. Jama Masjid, the largest mosque in

Silks at Chandi Chowk Market

India, is also located within walking distance.

Chandni Chowk hosts an impressive mix of shops that specialize in silk, silver, crafts, spices, and leather goods. There are renowned restaurants, food stands, and sweet shops, including the original Haldiram's, Meghraj and Sons, Bikaner Sweet Shop, and Ghantewala Halwai. Nestled around Chandni Chowk are historic private residences and a labyrinth of small streets and neighborhoods. As a traveler, it is easy to become lost in the wondrous flurry of activity.

Please Note: Chandni Chowk has been termed *The Most Crowded Street in Asia*. The side streets are exceptionally narrow and personal space is rare. If you prefer less congestion, consider viewing the hustle and bustle from a distance or visiting an alternate marketplace.

Hours: 8 am - 8 pm; Most of Chandni Chowk is closed on Sundays
Location: Old Delhi

Lajpat Nagar, Central Market

Bargaining is expected at most local markets, but Central Market, Lajpat Nagar may take the gold. Just observing the Delhiites flaunt their negotiation skills is worth the visit. Haggling aside, the lanes are packed with jewelry, textiles, handbags, shoes, and accessories for all ages. My favorite stores include The Prakash Collection (be sure to explore the basement!) and shoe stalls (opposite KFC). Plan your visit in the mornings for smaller crowds and cooler weather.

Hours: 10 am - 8 pm; Closed on Mondays
Location: Southeast Delhi

Sundar Nagar

While many markets in Delhi offer endless rows of clothes, shoes, handbags, and accessories, Sundar Nagar specializes in handicrafts. Stroll the lanes to find both Indian and Nepali handicrafts, furniture, antiques, and silver jewelry. After shopping, order Silver Green Tea at Regalia Tea House or stroll through one of the art galleries in the neighborhood.

Hours: 10 am - 7 pm
Location: New Delhi District

Khari Baoli

Operating since the 17th century, Khari Baoli is Asia's largest wholesale spice market. In addition to finding overflowing mounds of cardamom, cinnamon, cumin, and chili powder, vendors also sell nuts, rice, herbs, and teas. With locals sipping chai and debating current events, and the air filled with aromatic spices, Khari Baoli is a feast for the senses.

Hours: 8 am - 5 pm; Closed on Sundays
Location: Western end of Chandni Chowk in Old Delhi

A warm thank you to my sister-in-law, Datri, for being my shopping companion, translator, and bargaining teacher the past 15 years!

WHERE TO EAT

Olive Bar and Kitchen

The Sunday Brunch at this popular Mediterranean eatery has been voted the best in the country.

One Style Mile, 6-8 Kalka Das Marg, Mehrauli

Indian Accent

Name the award and it has likely been presented to Indian Accent. The accolades are well supported by the innovative Indian food and renowned chefs.

The Lodhi, Lodhi Road, New Delhi

Bukhara

Bukhara is an icon in Delhi. The award-winning restaurant's specialty is tandoor-cooked cuisine prepared in a traditional clay oven. Come hungry and with clean hands — Bukhara is cutlery-free.

ITC Maurya, Sardar Patel Marg, Akhaura Block, Diplomatic Enclave, Chanakya Puri

Big Chill Cafe

Popular for its Italian menu and desserts, the Big Chill cafe attracts an eclectic crowd. With several locations across Delhi, the most visited and popular one still remains at Khan Market.

35 Khan Market, Rabindra Nagar

Hotel Saravana Bhavan

Dosas, thalis, and tiffins! Saravana Bhavan specializes in South Indian cuisine. Each dosa comes with unlimited sambar and three chutneys - the tomato chutney being the house favorite. Waits, especially on weekends, can be lengthy.

P-13, Connaught Circle, Connaught Place

Karim's

Love Kebabs? The original Karim's, located near Jama Masjid in Old

Delhi, is an institution. Order a few dishes to share, like Chicken Jahangiri, Rumali Roti, Chicken Seekh Kebabs, and Mutton Burra.
16 Gali Kababian, Jama Masjid

Barbeque Nation
With a live barbeque and grill on each table, and a staff who sings and dances, the meal becomes an experience. There are several locations of this eatery across India.
Munshilal building 2nd Floor N-19, Block N, Connaught Place

Rajdhani Thali
With over 72 rotating menus and several delicacies from Gujarat and Rajasthan, Rajdhani offers a wholesome unlimited thali vegetarian meal.
9 A, Atmaram Mansion, Scindia House, Connaught Place

WHERE TO DRINK

The Library Bar
Located in the exclusive Leela Palace Hotel, the Library Bar serves award-winning wines, top shelf spirits, and innovative cocktails.
The Lobby, Leela Palace Hotel, Delhi

Piano Man Jazz Club
A concept bar with live performances, jazz music, and a cozy lounge ambiance with a great drinks menu makes this place worth a visit.
Commercial Complex B 6/7-22 Opposite Deer Park, Safdarjung Enclave

Hauz Khas Social
Hidden in the bylanes of Hauz Khas Village, Hauz Khas Social is a place where people meet, work, and collaborate, all with good food

and drinks. It was one of the first bars in Delhi to introduce co-working space in their premises.

9A & 12, Hauz Khas Fort Rd, Deer Park

Ek Bar

A vintage bar with regionally inspired drinks and an innovative snack menu.

First Floor, Gali Number D17, Shiniwas Puri, Block D, Defence Colony

Depaul's

A trip to Janpath is not complete without having cold coffee at Depaul's, served in a classic glass bottle with a straw.

22 Janpath Bhawan, Delhi

Bille di Hatti

A lassi is a traditional yogurt-based drink often enjoyed during warmer weather. It can be served savory, with spices, or sweet with fruits and sugar. Located in Kamla Nagar, Bille di Hatti offers flavors like salted, mango, and rose.

72D Kamla Nagar, Delhi

Haveli Yoga

LOCAL TOURS AND EXPERIENCES

Old Delhi Rickshaw Tour
Join our friend Ritu for an interactive tour of Old Delhi's monuments, spice markets, and sacred spaces. The rickshaw (tricycle) tour is a comfortable way of navigating through the narrow bylanes of Old Delhi and witnessing life in the historical district.
http://www.wheninindia.com/old-delhi-rickshaw-tours

Walking Tour of Old Delhi
If you love to explore the city on foot, this tour will give you a close look at the rich culture and life of people in Old Delhi.
http://www.wheninindia.com/walking-tours

The Great Indian Wedding Tour
Indian weddings are a grand affair. Guest lists are often in the hundreds, if not thousands, and the festivities include elaborate costume changes, choreographed dances, and extensive décor. Learn about the matrimonial traditions as you execute a to-do list for the bride and groom!
https://www.nfpexplore.com/delhi/the-great-indian-wedding-tour/

Five Senses Tour of Delhi
Engage your senses with a tour through the city. View the Mughal architectural marvels, sample the local delicacies, listen to soothing music at a Gurudwara, smell the fragrance of locally handmade perfume, and engage with the community.
https://www.nfpexplore.com/delhi/5-senses-tour-of-delhi/

Old Delhi Food Photowalk
Join a professional photographer on an enriching culinary experience in Old Delhi. Watch your camera lens come alive with quintessential Shahjahanabad cuisines as the captivating subjects.
https://www.indiacitywalks.com/package/photowalking/

DAY TRIPS

Neemrana Fort Palace
Built in 1464 and restored as a luxurious resort in 1991, Neemrana is a popular weekend getaway from Delhi. Once you reach the palace, reserve a zipline tour, hire a vintage car, or immerse yourself in the history. Neemrana is a recommended day-trip or overnight getaway.

How to Reach: Direct buses are available from Delhi, or you can hire a private car for the two-hour (116 km) journey.

Mathura and Vrindavan
En-route from Delhi to Agra are the religious sister towns of Vrindavan and Mathura. Rediscovered in the 16th century, Vrindavan is considered the center of Krishna worship. It is also known as the "City of Widows" for the number of women who settled here after losing their husbands. (Historically, if a woman was widowed, she was exiled from the family and left on her own.) Several homes and organizations were established to offer resources, housing, and professional training.

Mathura is believed to be the birthplace of Krishna and therefore one of the seven cities considered holy by Hindus (Sapta Puri). It was also an important center of commerce and trade. Located on the Yamuna River, there are 25 ghats or bathing steps and several prominent temple complexes dedicated to Krishna.

How to Reach: Hire a private car or taxi from Delhi for the 2.5 hour journey on the Agra-Delhi National Highway.

GIVING BACK

Salaam Baalak Trust

SB Trust provides care and protection to street children through education, vocational training, nutrition, and health. Established in 1988, the NGO has been successfully running centers for boys and girls under the age of 18 who want to leave the streets and achieve something greater. Volunteering can be a life-changing experience as you witness the resolve of these young kids to fulfill their dreams.
https://www.salaambaalaktrust.com/

Katha

Launched in 1988, Katha focuses on quality education and literacy among the underserved communities and children from lower income households. The organization ensures holistic learning for children through their various initiatives like the I love Reading campaign, Katha Lab School, Katha's Slum Resurgence Initiative (SRI), Katha English Academy (KENGA), and Katha School of Entrepreneurship (KSE).
https://www.katha.org/

Helping Hand

Working for women's education and empowerment, Helping Hand India has been serving the community for the past decade. Through their education, healthcare, and livelihood programs, they have enabled and empowered women to become contributing members of their families and society.
https://helpinghandindiango.org/

INTERVIEW WITH A LOCAL

Vidyun Goel
Born and raised in India's capital, Vidyun is the Director of Haveli Dharampura, a 200-year-old restored mansion and boutique hotel in the heart of Old Delhi. She also leads The Toy Bank, a non-profit that successfully created 5,355 toy libraries impacting more than 500,000 children across India.

What do you love and loathe about the city?
I love Delhi's culinary scene, the people, heritage monuments, and abundance of gardens. I hate the traffic.

What experiences do you recommend?
Street-food and shopping, feeling the pulse of Old Delhi and walking through Lodhi Garden. Delhi is also THE place to be for festivals like Diwali and Holi.

Any areas for females to avoid?
I think it's best to stay indoors after 11 pm, except if you are visiting a crowded market or neighborhood.

What advice would you give when visiting Delhi?
Experience the city through all the senses. To really understand Delhi, open your eyes, ears, mouths, and hands - and especially your hearts.

Favorite local spots to dine and drink?
Yum Yum Cha, Khan Market for amazing Asian cuisine; Perch, Khan Market for casual cocktails; Bengali Market (near Connaught Place) for street food and Indian desserts; Lakhori, Haveli Dharampura for rooftop dining in 200-year-old restored haveli; and American Diner, India Habitat Centre for their all-day breakfast.

Favorite markets?

Chandni Chowk for traditional wear, jewelry, and food. Khan Market for chic shopping and great international dining like Big Chill Cafe.

What are your recommended day trips from Delhi?

Agra for the Taj Mahal and Fatehpur Sikri. I also love Shekhawati in Rajasthan for fresco paintings and restored havelis. It's a five-hour drive, so it's best for an overnight or weekend excursion. Both destinations are accessible by tourist cabs or you can take the express train to Agra.

Anything else you wish to share?

Generally, people come to Delhi for only a few days, but I feel they cannot really experience Delhi in such a short amount of time. Plan to spend at least five full days here - two in Old Delhi, one to shop and eat, and two in central and south Delhi. This city may be a large and bustling hub, but it's also incredibly special with unique neighborhoods to discover.

Connect with Vidyun:
www.havelidharampura.com
www.toybank.in

24 HOURS IN DELHI

Only have a day in Delhi? Here is an express itinerary to make the most of your stay.

8 am: Breakfast in Chandni Chowk

Start the morning in one of my favorite neighborhoods, Old Delhi. A visit to Chandni Chowk will surely activate your senses for the day ahead. It is an incredible experience to observe the unusual serenity at an otherwise chaotic marketplace. Try local dishes like Bedmi Poori, Nagori Halwa, Chole Kulche, Chole Bhature, and Lassi. Since the area is dominated by the Muslim community, I also recommend trying authentic Mughal breakfast dishes like Nihari and Paaya with traditional breads like Khameeri roti and Sheermal. Definitely save room for authentic Indian treats from one of the oldest sweet shops in India. Hop on a cycle rickshaw to reach Asia's biggest spice market while witnessing the architectural marvels and multicolored facades that line the historic alleys.

10 am: Jama Masjid

After a satisfying meal, visit one of the largest mosques in India, Jama Masjid. Its construction was started in 1644 and completed by Mughal emperor Shah Jahan. The courtyard of the mosque was constructed with red sandstone and can be accessed from the north, south, and east gates by flights of stairs that were once venues for house markets, food stalls, and entertainers. Climb to the top of one of the four towers for fantastic city views.

11 am: Gurudwara Bangla Sahib

This Sikh temple, with its glistening golden dome, is a quiet and serene spot amid the bustling marketplace. As you enter the sacred space, you will be enveloped in a sense of peace. After paying homage at the sanctum, where the holy book is kept, you can stroll along the tranquil pond in the Gurudwara. If you feel comfortable, I highly recommend volunteering in the community kitchen where free meals are offered to devotees. This practice of selfless service goes beyond the bounds of religion and serves to nourish the soul, creating a sense of unity and oneness.

12:30 pm: Janpath

Janpath is a bustling marketplace near Connaught Place that features carpets, shoes, clothing, jewelry, handicrafts, textiles, accessories, paintings, and furniture - just to name a few!

2 pm: Raj Ghat

After exploring Old Delhi, it is now time to visit New Delhi. Begin your exploration with a visit to the Raj Ghat, a memorial to Mahatma Gandhi. It was here where Mahatma Gandhi's last rites were

performed on January 31, 1948, one day after his death. His last words, 'Hey Ram,' are inscribed on the marble which is always adorned with flowers. The memorial was designed to reflect the simplicity of the Mahatma's life.

3:30 pm: Qutub Minar and Mehrauli Complex
Next is the Qutub Minar, a UNESCO world heritage site. With a towering spire stretching 238 feet into the sky, the red sandstone

and marble mosque has the tallest minaret in India. Get an up-close look at the ornate exterior, which is covered in detailed carvings of text from the Quran. Take a 15-minute walk to the nearby Mehrauli Archaeological Park where historical monuments and crumbling ruins will provide a unique look at the city's past. The park consists of various tombs, mosques, and stepwells, making it a unique heritage hub.

5:30 pm: India Gate

Although the India Gate is grand in any light, the site transforms at dusk when locals gather for picnics and social gatherings. Often you will be asked to join an impromptu cricket match or to enjoy a slice of birthday cake, all with the iconic archway as your backdrop. The emblematic monument resembles the Arc de Triomphe in Paris and commemorates the 71,000 soldiers who lost their lives in World War I. Stroll the grounds and stay until nightfall when the nearby fountains illuminate with colored lights.

7:30 pm: Hauz Khas

HKV (as it's known to the locals) is a lively commercial district featuring trendy restaurants, boutique shops, and art galleries. At night the area comes alive with rooftop bars and live music.

HARIDWAR/ RISHIKESH

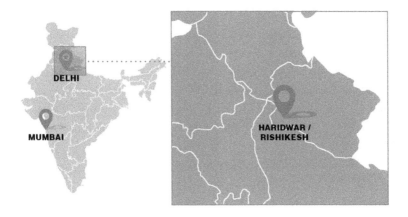

Sister Cities on the Ganges

Nestled in the foot hills of the Himalayas, Haridwar and Rishikesh are neighboring pilgrimage destinations on the Ganges River. Hilltop temples, sacred caves, and yoga ashrams cater to spiritual seekers while white water rafting, trekking, and bungee jumping invite the adventurers.

TRANSPORTATION HUBS

Haridwar and Rishikesh are located in the state of Uttarakhand, 240 km north of Delhi.

Dehradun Jolly Grant Airport (DED)
Airport Rd, Jauligrant, Uttarakhand

The closest airport is located in Dehradun, 1.5 hours from Rishikesh. Dehradun has daily flight connectivity to Delhi.

Haridwar Train Station (HW)
Purusharthi Market Road, Shikhu Pur, Devpura, Haridwar

The Haridwar train station serves both Haridwar and Rishikesh. Popular trains include Shatabdi Express, Jan Shatabdi, AC Special Express, and Mussoorie Express that link Haridwar to Delhi, Mumbai, Kolkata, Lucknow, and Varanasi. If traveling to Rishikesh, you can take a train to Haridwar and then continue by bus or taxi. The bus will take approximately 45 minutes; by taxi, 25-20 minutes.

ISBT Haridwar
Devpura, Haridwar

Located five minutes from the train station; signage in English is very limited. Buses operate to Delhi, Rishikesh, Dehradun, Mussorrie, and other towns in North India. Note that A/C buses are limited in the summer. https://utconline.uk.gov.in/

AREAS TO AVOID

Overall, Haridwar and Rishikesh are safe destinations. Hash and cannabis are common so be cautious of drug peddlers and don't accept unknown substances from locals. Also, be aware of fake sadhus who will offer "religious services" for unreasonable fees.

Kumbh Mela

LOCAL FESTIVALS

Kumbh Mela

The Kumbh Mela is often considered the world's most massive act
of faith. According to Hindu mythology, the Kumbh Mela started
during a war between demigods and demons for Amrita, the nectar of
immortality. While being carried in a pot by Lord Vishnu, a few drops
fell in the present day towns of Haridwar, Prayag (Allahabad), Ujjain,
and Nashik. The drops sprouted mystical powers in the respective
destinations; millions of believers from all stratas of society visit the
Kumbh Mela and take a dip in the holy river to wash away sins and
achieve liberation from the cycle of death and rebirth.

At any given place, the Kumbh Mela is held once every 12 years. There
is a difference of around three years between the Kumbh Melas in
Haridwar and Nashik; the fairs at Nashik and Ujjain are celebrated
in the same year or one year apart. The exact date is determined
according to a combination of zodiac positions of Jupiter, the Sun, and
the Moon.

Maha Shivaratri

Maha Shivaratri is an annual Hindu festival that celebrates Shiva.
Devotees chant prayers, fast, meditate, visit temples, and even make
a pilgrimage. Unlike most festivals that are celebrated during the day,
Maha Shivaratri is observed at night. Ardent devotees will remain
awake all night to overcome darkness and ignorance. It is celebrated
on the 14th day of the dark fortnight of Phalguna (February/March).

Ganga Dussehra

Also known as Gangavataran, the 10-day festival celebrates the
Ganges River descending from heaven to earth. In observance,
followers will bathe in the Ganges, attend the Aarti ceremony, and
offer prayers to Mother Ganga. Devotees believe that taking a dip
in Ganges will purify, heal any physical ailments, and wash away ten
lifetimes of sin. The annual dates are according to the Hindu calendar
and generally occur in June.

WHERE TO STAY

Bedhubs, Haridwar
A centrally located hostel near Ram Ghat and Har Ki Pauri Ghat.
$ / www.bedhubs.com / +91 82 7982 5933

Zostel, Rishikesh
A bohemian backpacker and activity-led hostel near the yoga hub.
$ / www.zostel.com/zostel/rishikesh / +91 22 4896 2265

Namaste by KarwaanLife, Rishikesh
An eclectic hostel near Lakshman Jula with female A/C dorms and
private rooms.
$ / www.karwaanlife.com / +91 76 1777 7456

Haveli Hari Ganga, Haridwar
A boutique heritage hotel with a private bathing ghat.
$$ / www.havelihariganga.com / +91 13 3422 6443

Aloha on the Ganges, Rishikesh
A mid-market hotel on the banks of Ganges surrounded by forested
hills.
$$ / www.alohaontheganges.com / +91 95 5508 8000

Sattva Retreat, Rishikesh
A wellness sanctuary with traditional and contemporary offerings.
$$$ / www.thesattva.com / +91 81 9105 5551

Taj Rishikesh
A luxury Himalayan retreat by the Ganges with a private beach.
$$$$ / www.tajhotels.com/en-in/taj/taj-rishikesh / +91 13 7835 0100

WHAT TO DO

Chandi Devi Temple, Haridwar

Chandi Devi is one of the most ancient temples in India. Devotees visit to receive blessings from the goddesses, most notably by Chandi, the presiding deity. Visitors can reach by a 3 km trek or ropeway service. Chandi Devi is one of three Peethas in Haridwar, or places of worship where prayers are answered; the other two are Mansa Devi Temple and Maya Devi Temple.

Entry: There is no entry fee to the temple, but the ropeway costs INR 650; leather accessories are prohibited
Hours: 5 am - 8 pm; temple hours may change during festivals, pujas, and religious observations

Har Ki Pauri Ghat, Haridwar

This revered ghat is believed to be the exact spot where the Ganges River exits the mountains and enters the plains. Literally translated, *Har* means God, *Ki* means of, and *Pauri* means steps. Every evening at sunset is the sacred Ganga Aarti with lighted lamps. The presiding Hindu priests stand on a *Chauki* (wooden stand) near the water. To the chant of Sanskrit mantras, and the clash of cymbals and drums, the river is worshipped with flowers, incense, sandalwood, milk, and vermilion.

Entry: None
Hours: Open 24/7

Kankhal Cremation Grounds, Haridwar

Hindus believe that for the soul to be reincarnated, it must be completely detached from the body (and the material world). Cremation offers a faster transition toward the next life, as the body is no longer needed to house the soul. Kankhal is where immersion rituals are held after a cremation. The "Sati Ghat" is where priests perform the last rites of the deceased.

Please remember that this is a highly emotional space of grief and bereavement. Be respectful and refrain from laughing, eating, or drinking; keep any discussions to a minimum and maintain a state of reverent observation.

Entry: Free
Hours: Though open 24/7, plan your visit during daylight hours

Shantikunj Ashram, Haridwar

Shantikunj is a world-renowned ashram and the headquarters of All World Gayatri Pariwar (AWGP). With a mission to provide cultural, ethical, moral, and social awakening, it is a popular center for spiritual seekers. Visitors can attend the morning prayers and evening meditation, but accommodations are only available for those participating in spiritual penance, training camps, or sacramental rites. Overnight visitors are also required to participate in all scheduled activities, starting at 3:30 am.

Entry: Free of cost, subject to availability

Ram Jhula and Lakshman Jhula, Rishikesh

The twin Jhulas are suspension bridges over the Ganges River. Named after mythical characters in the Ramayana, the bridges hang 70 feet above the water and are iconic symbols of the city. Because of deteriorating conditions, Lakshman Jhula is only open to pedestrians and will soon be closed permanently while a replacement bridge is constructed. Ram Jhula is open to both pedestrians and two-wheelers.

Entry: None
Hours: 24/7

Parmarth Ashram, Rishikesh

Nestled in the Himalayas on the Ganges River, Parmarth is the largest ashram in Rishikesh and "an abode dedicated to the welfare of all." Pilgrims come from all over the world for spiritual rejuvenation and restoration. Daily activities include yoga, meditation, kirtan, and Ayurvedic treatments. There are also intensive courses on Reiki, pranayama, acupressure, and other Indian sciences.

Fees: Depends on the Program

Chaurasi Kutia (The Beatles Ashram), Rishikesh

Although Chaurasi Kutia was closed for more than three decades, the complex became a jungle canvas for graffiti artists who sneaked into the property. The ashram was where the English band wrote an estimated 40 songs while practicing Transcendental Meditation under the spiritual direction of Maharishi Mahesh Yogi. Fortunately, the mystical space in Rajaji National Park reopened to the public in 2015.

Entry: INR 600
Hours: 8 am - 5 pm daily

WHERE TO SHOP

Ram Jhula Market and Lakshman Jhula Market, Rishikesh
These two popular markets sell everything from religious items to local spices. Shoppers will find jewelry, wooden idols, oils, clothes, precious stones, and sacred Rudraksha. Practice your bargaining skills!

Hours: 11 am - 9 pm
Location: Adjacent to the respective bridges

Moti Bazaar Market, Haridwar
Moti Bazaar is the primary market in Haridwar. The narrow lanes make for a very crowded shopping experience, but you can find local goods, housewares, jewelry, brass utensils, and decoratives. There are also great sweet shops and street eats. The bazaar is a fun place to browse, snack, and feel the vibe of a traditional market.

Hours: 11 am - 9 pm
Location: Between Har Ki Pauri and the Upper Road

WHERE TO EAT

Ira's Kitchen and Tea Room, Rishikesh
With a peaceful garden setting and delightful owners, Ira's Kitchen & Tea Room is a lovely spot to relax and stay awhile. Bring a book, journal, or make new friends while enjoying a crunchy bowl or steaming cup of lemon ginger tea.
Baba Balaknath Mandir Road, Upper Tapovan, Rishikesh / +91 90 5862 1247

Chotiwala, Rishikesh

It's not necessarily about the food at this Rishikesh establishment; instead, it's all about a selfie with a plump, face-painted Chotiwala. There are actually two adjacent restaurants by the same name; after the original owner died, a family feud led to a literal wall being built to split the eatery. There are now two (human) Chotiwala mascots who compete for customers at this simple eatery serving traditional Indian dishes.

Swarg Ashram, Rishikesh / +91 96 3949 0001

Sitting Elephant, Rishikesh

A Travellers' Choice winner, Sitting Elephant is a rooftop restaurant overlooking the Ganges River. Delicious food, sweeping views, and impeccable service make this a recommended dining experience.

Hotel EllBee Ganga View, 355, Haridwar Rd, Palika Nagar, Rishikesh / +91 88 8266 1577

Tulsi Restaurant, Rishikesh

Fresh food, lovely views, and thoughtful design touches make this simple restaurant a jewel in Rishikesh. Order the homemade banana nutella pancakes!

Ghugtyani Malli, Tapovan, Rishikesh / +91 95 3683 8181

Mohan Ji Puri Wale, Haridwar

This landmark eatery is known for local snacks and sweets, especially steaming puri's and fried potatoes. Good food brings the crowds and Mohan's stays packed until late evenings.

Shalesh Modi, Near Police Chowki, Har Ki Pauri, Haridwar

Mathura Walo Ki Pracheen Dukan, Haridwar

Indulge your sweet tooth at this popular spot frequented for generations. It's worth standing in line for the Peda and Gajar ka Halwa. There are also savory items like Aloo Puri Sabzi and Malai Samosa.

Moti Bazar Rd, near Thanda Kuan, Haridwar / +91 98 9760 6384

WHERE TO DRINK

Because Haridwar and Rishikesh are religious destinations, no alcohol is permitted. However, head to **Prakash Lok Lassi** in Haridwar for a delicious lassi (yogurt-based smoothie). *Upper Road, Ram Ghat, Haridwar*

Rishikesh Kirtan

LOCAL TOURS AND EXPERIENCES

Haridwar Heritage and Photography Walk

Just a few steps away from Har Ki Pauri is an intricate network of narrow streets brimming with local life. This walk starts in the afternoon and includes heritage buildings, local eateries, and neighborhood markets in the Old City, culminating with the Ganga Aarti.
https://rishikeshdaytour.com/haridwar-heritage-walk-photography-tour-itinerary.html

Bungee Jumping

India's first extreme adventure zone includes the country's highest bungee jump. At a height of 83 meters, the fixed platform structure was designed by experts from New Zealand.
http://jumpinheights.com/rishikesh

River Rafting

Originating in the Himalayas, the Ganges is an ideal river for rafting in India. Its many tributaries add to the volume of water while its step and pool make it one of the safest expeditions. Class: II, III, IV
https://www.redchilliadventure.com/collections/rafting-on-ganga-rishikesh

Mussoorie

DAY TRIPS

Kunjapuri Devi Temple

Rise and shine for a sunrise trek to Kunjapuri Temple, one of the 52 *Shakti Peethas* (power centers) in Uttarakhand. The morning air can be chilly at an elevation of 1,676 meters, but the views of the snow-clad Himalayas are well worth it. Dress warmly.

Location: 25 km from Rishikesh; Hire a local taxi from Haridwar or Rishikesh
Hours: Open daily from 5 am - 6 pm
Entry: None

Vashistha Cave

Vashistha Cave is dedicated to Vashistha, one of the seven great sages in ancient India. It is a beautiful place for reflection and many sages and sadhus visit to practice deep meditation. There is also a strong belief that Jesus Christ spent time here and in the surrounding caves during the Lost Years.

Location: 25 km from Rishikesh at Swami Purushottamananda Ashram; Hire a taxi from Haridwar or Rishikesh
Entry: None

Mussoorie

Nestled in the foothills of the Himalayas is the hill station of Mussoorie. With cooler summers and snowy winters, the town was developed as a resort for the British elite in the early 1800's. It remains a popular tourist destination for the mountain views and surrounding hiking trails, lakes, and waterfalls. There are also upmarket wellness centers like Vana Retreat offering yoga and Ayurveda treatments.

Location: 2 hours from Rishikesh; Hire a taxi or travel by bus from the Haridwar or Rishikesh stations

LEH/LADAKH

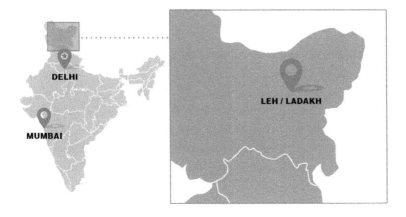

A Buddhist Abode

Commonly called *Little Tibet*, Ladakh is a remote region nestled between the Himalayan and Kunlun mountain ranges. Historically a Buddhist kingdom, Ladakh was strategically placed at the crossroads of major trading routes. Leh, the joint capital, is set at an elevation of over 11,500 feet.

Please note: It is advisable to allow two days at leisure for acclimation before beginning any touring activities.

TRANSPORTATION HUBS

Ladakh is a union territory that constitutes a part of the Kashmir region. Leh is the joint capital and largest town.

Leh Kushok Bakula Rimpochee Airport (IXL)
Ladakh, India

Domestic flights connect Leh to Delhi and Srinagar. Flights operate from March - October.

There is currently no rail service in Ladakh. Buses are available from Delhi, Manali, and Srinagar, but the journey takes 2+ days. Some travelers also rent a motorcycle for the journey over high mountain passes. Because of heavy snowfall, the roads are only accessible from May - October.

AREAS TO AVOID

Overall, Leh/Ladakh is a very safe destination for female travelers. There are very rare occurrences of crime or harassment.

LOCAL FESTIVALS

Hemis Festival
Marking the birth of Guru Padmasambhava, an Indian Buddhist mystic, the Hemis Festival is one of the most important monastic celebrations in Ladakh. The courtyards of the remote Hemis Gompa come alive with masked dances, music, vibrant brocade robes, and sacred rituals. The dates are based on the Tibetan calendar and rotate annually in June and July. During the event, giant thangkas (Buddhist

paintings) are revealed to the public; every 12th year, the largest thangka in Ladakh is unfurled at Hemis on the first day.

Sindhu Darshan Festival

The Sindhu Darshan Festival celebrates the Indus (Sindhu) River as an icon of communal harmony. During the celebration, devotees from across India bring water in an earthen pot from a river in their own state to offer to the Indus. The festival includes

Hemis Festival

cultural programs, pujas, and a reception where 50 lamas (monks) cite prayers in recognition of different religions. Although Sindhu Darshan was first celebrated in 1997, it became a grand affair from 2000 onward. The festivities are held annually in June at Shey Manla on the full moon day of Guru Purnima.

WHERE TO STAY

Zostel Leh

An activity-driven hostel centrally located near Leh Palace and the main market.

$ / www.zostel.com/zostel/leh / +91 22 4896 2268

Hotel Glacier View

A simple hotel constructed in traditional Ladakhi architecture with a lovely garden.

$$ / http://www.hotelglacierview.com / +91 94 1986 4417

Nubra Ecolodge

A family-operated ecotourism venture located near Sumur sand dunes in Nubra Valley.

$$ / +91 97 9798 3088

Saboo Resorts

15 luxury cottages with private verandahs near the quant Saboo Village.

$$$ / www.sabooresorts.com / +91 99 0627 1798

Nimmu House

A glamping and heritage retreat offering thematic tents and rooms.

$$$ / ladakh.nimmu-house.com / +91 84 4775 7517

The Grand Dragon

A luxury property decorated with handmade paintings by the first Ladakhi modern artist.

$$$ / www.thegranddragonladakh.com / +91 19 8225 7786

Stok Palace

A 200-year-old palace built by the rulers of the Namgyal Dynasty and converted into a heritage hotel.

$$$ / https://www.stokpalaceheritage.com / +91 98 9179 6671

WHAT TO DO

Shanti Stupa

Panoramic views await at this Buddhist white-domed stupa on a hill in Chanspa. Shanti Stupa was built by both Japanese and Ladakhi Buddhists in 1991 as part of the Peace Pagoda mission to inspire unity for all races. The base holds the relics of the Buddha, enshrined by the 14th Dalai

Lama, Tenzin Gyatso. Plan your visit in the early evening to catch the sunset views across the Indus Valley.

Entry: N/A
Hours: 5 am - 9 pm daily

Thikse Monastery
(Also known as Thiksey, Thiksay, and Tiksey)
With an exterior that resembles the Patola Palace in Lhasa, Thikse is a gompa (Tibetan monastery) located 19 km east of Leh. It also houses one of the only progressive nunneries in the region. Thikse's main feature is a two-story stucco statue of Maitreya Buddha seated on a lotus. The 12-story complex also houses eclectic Buddhist art and artifacts, including swords, paintings, statues, and stupas. If possible, try and arrive before 7 am to observe the monks gathered in the assembly hall for the morning prayer ceremony.

Entry: INR 20
Hours: 7 am - 7 pm daily

Stok Palace and Museum
The Stok Palace has an interesting story. Built in the early 1800's by the Namgyal Dynasty, it remains the summer home of the royal family of Ladakh. With blessings from His Holiness the Dalai Lama, the palace opened to the public in 1980. It has been converted to a heritage hotel but approximately 12 of the 80 rooms remain private for the family. If you enjoy viewing royal collections, definitely visit the Stok Museum featuring ceremonial dresses, jewelry, crowns, and imperial thangka paintings.

Entry: INR 100
Hours: 8 am - 5 pm daily

Alchi Monastery

Alchi Gompa is a monastic complex of temples in Alchi Village. The compound comprises four separate settlements in lower Ladakh with monuments dating to different periods, though Alchi is considered the oldest. The wall paintings are bold and bright, with intricate spiritual and artistic details of both Buddhist and Hindu kings. Alchi is renowned as one of the oldest Buddhist learning centers in North India and is also one of the few monasteries where guests can view the monk's personal spaces.

Entry: INR 50
Hours: 8 am - 6 pm daily

WHERE TO SHOP

Please remember that bargaining is encouraged in markets, but please do not bargain at government-operated craft emporiums in Leh.

Main Bazaar Road

Popular with both locals and tourists, Main Bazaar Road is lined with small shops selling Pashmina shawls, silver jewelry, handicrafts, handwoven rugs, and Buddhist ritual items. Stop by the Ladakh Environment and Health Organization (LEHO), an organization that promotes sustainable development by integrating holistic practices and traditional techniques.

Hours: Approximately 10 am - 8 pm
Location: Old Town Leh

Tibetan Market

True to its name, Tibetan refugees maintain this budget-friendly market near Leh Road. Savvy shoppers will find Tibetan handicrafts like shawls, carpets, and turquoise jewelry. Beware of fake antiques or precious stones and bargain hard!

Hours: Approximately 10 am - 8 pm
Location: Near Leh Road

Shar Market

If seeking traditional Ladakhi clothing, make a stop at Shar Market for Kuntop (colorful woolen robes for women), Perak (lambskin headgear adorned with semi-precious stones), and Goucha (thick woolen robes for men). You will also find stalls selling handicrafts and costume jewelry.

Hours: Approximately 10 am - 8 pm
Location: Opposite Main Bazaar Road in Leh

Ladakh Shopping

WHERE TO EAT

GGG Tip:
Ladakh is world renowned for apricots! Due to export restrictions, most of the fruit (known as *Chuli*) is only sold locally. Be sure to try the organic apricot jams, apricot momos, apricot juice, and dried apricots.

Alchi Kitchen
An unassuming yet authentic Ladakhi spot run by a woman-only team. Save room for dessert and order the apricot, walnut, or chocolate momos.
Alchi Choskhar, Leh / +91 94 1943 8642

De Khambir
Breakfast is served! Start your day with an egg and cheese Khambir sandwich, butter tea, and freshly squeezed apricot or sea buckthorn juice.
Hemis Zambala Complex 1st Floor Changspa Road near Moravian Church, Leh / +91 60 0624 3973

The Tibetan Kitchen
A cozy and popular eatery serving traditional Tibetan dishes. Try the mutton momos, chicken thukpa, and homemade currys, but be prepared for a wait during peak season!
Fort Road Near Hotel Ladakh Villa, Behind the Tibetan Handicrafts Market / +91 84 9291 1940

Bon Appetit
After a day exploring the Ladakh landscapes, refuel with a delicious pizza, glass of wine, or the honey chili potatoes. Come for the food but stay for the views!
Chang Spa Road Opposite Moravian Mission School, Leh / +91 19 8225 1533

WHERE TO DRINK

Lehchen Bar

A popular spot for live music, karaoke, brews, and cocktails. The food is hit or miss, so best to fuel up at another local eatery before getting your drink on.

Fort Road, Leh

Ladakh Prayer Flags

ADVENTURE AWAITS!

If time allows, take a 4.5 hour road trip from Leh to Kargil. From here you can explore the road less traveled with trekking, day hikes, river rafting, expeditions, and camping. We recommend **Roots Ladakh** for planning your adventure from Kargil. A few of our favorite experiences include:

Sham Valley Trek
A multi-day hike through "Apricot Valley" leads you through remote villages in Ladakh as you cross mountain passes, streams, shady willows and barley fields. Suitable for beginners.

Camping with Buddha
Hike to the village of Karste Khar and explore one of the few remaining 7th century rock-cut Buddha statues in the world. Pitch a tent by the river for picnics under the stars.

Cycling with the Moon
When the full moon rises, take a 3-5 hour bike ride on a picture-perfect trail and discover the nightscapes of Kargil.

Himalayan Brown Bear and Snow Leopard Lodge
Starting and ending in Leh, this exclusive 14-day trek is only available in April and November for the best wildlife sightings. Hike to the remote Brown Bear Lodge in western Ladakh and then to Snow Leopard Lodge in Ulley.

For more information, contact:

Roots Ladakh
www.rootsladakh.com
journeys@rootsladakh.in
+91 94 1988 7776

DAY TRIPS FROM LEH

Sangam

Located 35 km from Leh near the village of Nimmu, Sangam marks the confluence of the Indus and Zanskar Rivers. Ready for an adventure? Sangam offers the world's highest river rafting - or you can simply grab a cup of chai and enjoy the spectacular views of the multi-colored churning waters in the high desert. Nearby is Magnetic Hill where an "uphill" road is actually a downward slope, creating an optical illusion that objects and cars defy gravity.

How to Reach: Hire a private car or taxi for the 35 km drive on the Srinagar-Leh Highway.

Sangam

Tso Moriri Lake

With a driving distance of eight hours from Leh, Tso Moriri Lake is not a day trip. However, at 15,075 ft, it is the largest lake in the Trans-Himalayan region. In the local language, *Tsokar* translates to *Salty Lake*. Until 1959, salt was extracted from the lake for consumption by the locals. Because of recent threats to Tso Moriri, including road construction and the absence of garbage disposal, many conservation efforts have been initiated. It is an area rich in wildlife, vegetation, and natural beauty.

How to Reach: Hire a private car or motorbike for the multi-day trip.

A Ladakh Woman

GIVING BACK

Women Alliance of Ladakh

The alliance of 3,500 Ladakhi women was established to raise awareness of traditional agriculture, preserve the status of women, and create an alternative development model based on self-reliance. Visit the craft shop that was initiated to encourage the sale of handmade products and help boost the local economy. The WAL festival in August brings together Ladakhi exhibitors to demonstrate traditional skills and the preparation of local dishes, all accompanied by music and dancing.
http://waladakh.org

SECMOL

Founded in 1988 by a group of young Ladakhis, the Students Educational and Cultural Movement of Ladakh (SECMOL) aims to reform the educational system of Ladakh. Over time, the campus has developed into an eco-village where students, staff, and volunteers pursue practical, social, and environmental knowledge.
http://secmol.org

AMRITSAR

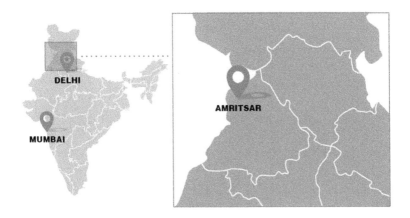

The Golden City

Amritsar, Punjab is an important seat of Sikh history and culture. Guru Ram Das, the fourth Sikh guru, is credited with founding the holy city that houses the Golden Temple. Amritsar is also a culinary paradise and known for its rich, hearty, ghee-laden cuisine.

TRANSPORTATION HUBS

Amritsar is located in the state of Punjab, 236 km from Chandigarh. It shares 553 km of international borders with Pakistan.

Sri Guru Ram Das Jee International Airport (ATQ)
Ajnala Road, Opposite Hotel Blue Radison, Raja Sansi, Punjab

ATQ services 160+ domestic and international flights daily, including direct flights to London, Dubai, Kuala Lumpur, and Doha.

Amritsar Junction Railway Station (ASR)
Guru Arjun Nagar, Amritsar, Punjab

ASR is the largest and busiest rail station in Punjab with connectivity to almost all major Indian cities. For reference, a train journey from Delhi - Amritsar takes approximately six hours.

Amritsar Bus Terminal (Shaheed Madan Lal Dhingra Interstate Bus Terminal)
Goal Bagh, Amritsar, Punjab

Amritsar is located on National Highway 1 and well connected by road. Daily government and private buses service Delhi, Chandigarh, Ambala, Patiala, and Jammu.

AREAS TO AVOID

Overall, Amritsar is a safe destination for female travelers. We do recommend being vigilant late at night by staying in livelier and well lit areas.

LOCAL FESTIVALS

Lohri

Lohri is a popular folk festival celebrated across North India on January 13th. With roots from Punjab, Lohri marks the passing of the winter solstice. It is a celebration of the final days of winter and welcoming of the new crop season. Indians of all faiths light bonfires, dance, sing songs, distribute gifts, and eat roasted corn and sugarcane from the new harvest.

Guru Nanak Gurpurab

Guru Nanak Gurpurab celebrates the birth of the first Sikh Guru and founder of Sikhism, Guru Nanak Dev. It is one of the most important festivals for followers of the Sikh faith. The celebration is generally similar for all Sikhs; only the hymns are different. On the day of the festival, typically held in November, a special community lunch is arranged at Gurdwaras (Sikh temples) by volunteers. Sikhs believe that everyone, irrespective of gender, caste, or creed, should be offered food in the spirit of seva, or service. The festival culminates with night prayer sessions.

Vaisakhi

Vaisakhi, also pronounced Baisakhi, is an ancient harvest festival celebrated annually on April 13th or 14th. For Sikhs, the festival recognizes important historical and religious events in Punjab; For Hindus, it celebrates the Solar New Year. Indians celebrate by hosting community fairs at pilgrimage sites, bathing in the Ganges River, holding kirtans, performing charity, socializing, and sharing traditional foods. Vaisakhi also marks the day of the Jallianwala Massacre in Amritsar.

WHERE TO STAY

Madpackers Amritsar

An award-winning youth hostel for backpackers, content creators, and digital nomads.

$ / https://madpackers.com/destinations/amritsar / +91 88 0026 5725

Bloom House B&B

A centrally located B&B with private bathrooms and delicious vegetarian breakfast.

$ / +91 98 8819 9911

Lemon Tree

A mid-range boutique chain with a fitness center, pool, and rooftop bar.

$$ / https://www.lemontreehotels.com/amritsar-hotels.aspx / +91 18 3524 5555

Ranjit Svaasa

A restored heritage colonial haveli restyled into an artistic culturally rich residence.

$$$ / https://www.svaasa.com / +91 98 7262 6618

Taj Swarna

A stylish and contemporary luxury hotel with pool and yoga deck.

$$$ - $$$$ / https://www.tajhotels.com/en-in/taj/taj-amritsar / +91 18 3665 8000

WHAT TO DO

Golden Temple (Harmandir Sahib)

The Golden Temple (also known as Harmandir Sahib) is the most sacred shrine of Sikhism. Shining in the morning light, the gilded splendor of its paneling, dome, and minarets illustrates spiritual transcendence. The gurdwara was built around a man-made pool that was completed in 1577 by the fourth Sikh Guru, Guru Ram Das. The temple is an open house of worship for men and women of all faiths. Adjacent to the complex is Langar Hall, the world's largest community kitchen offering free meals to all pilgrims irrespective of caste, creed, and religion.

Entry: Free
Hours: 24/7

Wagah Border Ceremony

Wagah Border runs along Grand Trunk Road between Amritsar in Punjab, India, and Punjab in Lahore, Pakistan. The Beating Retreat Ceremony, held daily before sunset, includes the closing of the international gates and the lowering of flags. It has been conducted by the Indian Border Security Force and Pakistan Rangers since 1959. Officially, the purpose of the ceremony is to formally close the border for the night and lower the national flag. However, it is an entertaining and patriotic display for the thousands of people who attend daily.

Entry: Free
Hours: 4:15 pm daily in winter / 5:15 pm daily in summer

Jallianwala Bagh

Jallianwala Bagh is the historic memorial site to the massacre in 1919 during the freedom struggle. Indians of all faiths had gathered in the garden to peacefully demonstrate the release of two popular Independence Movement leaders. A British General ordered troops of the Indian British Army to fire indiscriminately into the crowd of unarmed civilians. Hundreds were killed — both by gunfire and by jumping into the garden well — and thousands were injured. Many know this event as portrayed in the Oscar-winning movie Gandhi. The site now houses a garden and national monument.

Entry: Free
Hours: 6:30 am - 7:30 pm daily

Partition Museum

When independence was granted to India in 1947, it was partitioned into two countries - India (Hindu) and Pakistan (Muslim). What followed was the greatest forced migration with millions dead and displaced. The Partition of Punjab became one of the most violent acts in India's history. The "People's Museum" aims to showcase the 1947 partition as it was experienced by survivors and their families. It houses a collection of art, artifacts, multimedia displays, and oral histories.

Entry: INR 250
Hours: 10 am - 6 pm Tuesday - Sunday; Closed on Mondays

WHERE TO SHOP

Hall Bazaar

Located on the way to the Golden Temple, Hall Bazaar is popular with both locals and foreigners. This is a legit market with reasonable prices and a wide selection of goods - handicrafts, footwear, attire, lamps, and Phulkari, the folk embroidery of Punjab.

Hours: 9 am - 7 pm daily
Location: Katra Ahluwalia, Amritsar

Katra Jaimal Singh Bazaar

This is the place to shop for Pashmina shawls and original Phulkari attire, the folk embroidery of Punjab. Bargaining is expected but remember that the items are of a higher quality, so budget accordingly.

Hours: 11 am - 8 pm (Certain shops are closed on Sunday)
Location: Near Hall Bazaar

Shastri Market

Shastri Market houses many textile and apparel shops, but jewelry and gems are the stars of the show. You will often find the shops flooded with women looking to expand their gold collection.

Hours: 9 am - 9 pm daily
Location: Katra Ahluwalia, Amritsar

WHERE TO EAT

Kanha Sweets

A sweet shop for Kulchas? Don't let the name fool you, as Kanha Sweets has some of the best Kulcha (breakfast flatbread) in the city. Wash it down with a refreshing lassi.
Lawrence Road Opposite Bijli Pehalwan Mandir, Dayanand Nagar, Amritsar / +91 18 3222 2855

Bharawan da Dhaba

Try the Sarson ka Saag and Makki ki Roti at this family-friendly vegetarian establishment identified as one of the oldest restaurants in Amritsar.
Hall Bazar Rd. Town Hall, Amritsar / +91 18 3253 2575

Kulcha Land

Rise and shine for stuffed kulchas and chole at this popular breakfast spot. Go early to avoid the crowds.
DISTT Shopping Complex, Opposite M K Hotel, Center, B - Block, Ranjit Avenue, Amritsar / +91 98 1432 0652

Kesar da Dhaba

There's dal, and then there is slow-cooking-for-12-hours-dal from Kesar da Dhaba. This legendary spot opened in 1947 - the year of India's independence - offering a side of history with your lentils.
Hall Bazaar Road Town Hall, Amritsar / +91 18 3253 2575

Makhan Fish and Chicken Corner

What started as a fish eatery in the 1960's has evolved and expanded to include delectable non-veg dishes. Order the fried fish, tandoori chicken, and white butter chicken.
21A, Near Madaan Hospital Makhan Chowk, Majitha Rd, Amritsar / +91 98 1519 3241

Charming Chicken

Tandoori chicken, butter chicken, roasted chicken, kadai chicken, crispy chicken... all charming!
3 Janpath Market Shop No Majitha Road, Amritsar / +91 98 1409 6207

WHAT TO EAT IN AMRITSAR

Amritsar is a city where the joy of food is celebrated to its core, with iconic dishes to fill your bellies and hearts. With both veg and non-veg specialities, here is our list of the culinary delights to try when visiting Amritsar.

Amritsari Kulcha

Kulcha is a popular breakfast across India, proudly originating from Amritsar. It is similar to naan, a popular flatbread, but made with refined white flour. There are several varieties, including aloo kulcha, paneer kulcha, and masala kulcha - all layered with butter and served with chickpeas and spicy chutneys. An authentic Punjabi meal of Amritsari kulcha and Amritsari chole is a delicious delight on the plate and the palate.

Lassi

The Indian smoothie is a must try when in Amritsar. The lassis here are so creamy and thick with a dollop of butter that you need a spoon to scoop out. Apart from the refreshing elements of the drink, a Lassi is filled with Ayurvedic healing properties and provides a cooling and calming effect on the mind and body.

Amritsari Fish Tikka

Because Amritsar is located near the confluence of three rivers, there is an abundance of high-quality freshwater fish. The fish tikkas are seasoned, perfectly spiced, and sprinkled with masala. The secret lies in a handful of ingredients like carom seeds and gram flour, which adds a distinctive flavor.

Kulfa

Kulfa is the Amritsari cousin of the more familiar *kulfi*, a frozen dairy dessert often labeled THE traditional Indian ice cream. This dish includes a layer of phirni, a pudding prepared with sweetened milk and ground rice, and is topped with scoops of kulfi, falooda, and a dash of syrup and rose water. Finished with some rabri, or thick, sweet milk, Kulfa is indulgent and hits the sweet spot after a spicy meal.

Dal Makhani

The pride and delight non-vegetarians have over butter chicken is shared by vegetarians through dal makhani. Dal makhani might sound like a simple dish made from lentils, but there is a profound history and legacy. It was popularized in India following partition, when many people from Punjab migrated to the northern regions of India. Visit the legendary Kesar Da Dhaba, a celebrated vegetarian eatery that is over 100 years old and considered a pit stop for foodies across India and beyond.

Makki di Roti and Sarson da Saag

This is not just a customary dish of Punjab but also a seasonal dish, available in winter between October – March. When consumed with ghee, jaggery, or honey, this wholesome meal provides all the essential nutrients the body requires during winter. The ghee-soaked saag is made from farm-fresh mustard leaves and served with corn-flour rotis.

Chole Puri

Another breakfast staple is chole puri, a thin, crispy, and ghee-soaked puri served with chole (chickpeas) in a tangy potato curry. Head to Kanha Sweets for our favorite chole puri in the city.

Nutri Kulcha

Different from the other kulchas in Amritsar, nutri kulcha has its own loyal fan base. Made entirely of nutri (or Soya) and flatbreads with loads of butter, native herbs, and spices, the preparation is full of health benefits. The massive use of nutri chunks creates a distinct, thick consistency with a raw and rustic flavor.

WHERE TO DRINK

Ahuja Milk Bhandar

The locals say it best. "Heavenly Lassi!" "The best lassi ever!" "This is lassi heaven!" All the lassi's are creamy and dreamy, but definitely order the specialty kesar (saffron) lassi.
Near Hindu College, Amritsar / +91 85 4385 9000

Peddlers
A cozy bar and nightclub featuring live music, DJ sets, pool tables, sports screenings, and stand-up comedy.
Ranjeet Avenue, Amritsar / +91 70 8796 2021

Bar Exchange
A wall of vodka welcomes you to this casual bar and restaurant with excellent martinis and small plates.
District Shopping Center, GRD Tower, Basement Sco-108, Ranjit Avenue, Amritsar / +91 85 9000 0075

LOCAL TOURS AND EXPERIENCES

Amritsar Food Walk
A delicious (and convenient!) option for hitting the hot spots in a short amount of time. Enjoy jalebis, kulcha, chole bhature, and other street eats.
https://www.amritsarheritagewalk.com/amritsar-food-trail-walk

Family Cooking Session
Experience the best of Indian hospitality at a local family home. Learn the nuances of spices, make the perfect chai, and engage in lively conversation over a steaming bowl of curry.
https://www.roobaroowalks.com

Golden Temple Tour
Gain deeper insight into the historical, philosophical, and architectural keystones of Sikhism. Time is also included to volunteer at Langar Hall and visit the Akal Takhat, one of the five seats of power.
https://www.roobaroowalks.com

SHIMLA

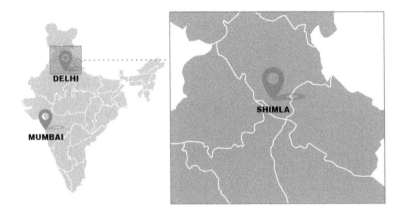

Queen of the Hills

Shimla, one of India's most popular hill stations, is both the capital and the largest city of Himachal Pradesh. Folklore states that the all-season retreat was named after Shyamal Devi, the fearless incarnation of Goddess Kali. With Himalayan vistas, pine forests, and Victorian-style architecture, Shimla is a postcard come alive.

TRANSPORTATION HUBS

Shimla is the capital of Himachal Pradesh, a north Indian state nestled in the Himalayas.

Shimla Airport (SLV)

Technically, Shimla does have an airport in Jubbarhatti, 23 km from the city. However, the high elevation and single runway contribute to only servicing unscheduled flights. The next nearest airport is Chandigarh (IXC), 120km from Shimla. From here you can hire a prepaid taxi to reach Shimla in 3-4 hours, enjoying the scenic beauty of the Kalka-Shimla highway.

Shimla Railway Station (SML)

The small railway station of Shimla, 3 km from the city center, is connected to Kalka by a narrow-gauge rail track. The track is actually listed in the Guinness Book of World Records for the steepest rise in altitude, covering 96 km in 5.5 hours. It is also a UNESCO World Heritage Site for accommodating the famous toy train.

To reach Shimla via train, first travel to Chandigarh. Many trains are available from Delhi to Chandigarh like Kalka Shatabdi; from Chandigarh, book a private cab to Kalka.

Want to reach Kalka by midday? Board the Kalka Shatabdi from New Delhi in the early morning.

Shimla Interstate Bus Terminal Tutikandi
Shimla Bypass, Tutikandi, Shimla

Reserve a deluxe bus ride to Shimla from New Delhi ISBT Kashmiri Gate. The ride is approximately eight hours, depending on traffic and weather conditions. If on a tight budget, book with Himachal Road Transport Corporation or utilize other private busses commuting between Shimla and other major cities in North India.

AREAS TO AVOID

Overall, Shimla is a safe destination. Stay in well lit areas at night and don't go outside the city limits without reliable transportation.

LOCAL FESTIVALS

Shimla Summer Festival

The Shimla Summer Festival is celebrated annually to thank God for a wonderful harvest and mark the arrival of a much-awaited summer. Started in 1960, the 5-day June extravaganza includes music, folk performances, local handicraft exhibitions, fashion shows, dog shows, and celebratory dishes.

Rhyali Festival

The Rhyali Festival is celebrated during the first day of the month of Shravana (July) to please the rain gods and mark the arrival of monsoon season. Ten days before the celebration, different seeds like wheat and barley are sown in a basket filled with earth. The ritual is performed by the head of the family or a priest. Additionally, a mock wedding is organized, symbolizing the holy marriage of Lord Shiva and Parvati.

Winter Carnival

The arrival of winter adds much cheer and excitement to Shimla. The annual winter carnival celebrates the snowfall and all the delights of cold weather. During the festival, you can enjoy activities like ice skating, skiing, snowman making, fashion shows, and dance performances.

WHERE TO STAY

Thira Shimla

A cozy hostel with private and shared rooms just ten minutes from Mall Road.

$ / +91 98 0555 8000

SunnyMead Homestay

A woman-owned homestay with a lovely garden located on the edge of the Reserve Forest.

$ / www.sunnymeadestate.com / +91 97 3658 4045

Chapslee

A heritage property from 1835 offering a library, card room, tennis court, and croquet lawn.

$ / +91 98 1664 4202

Suro Treehouse Resort

A luxury boutique resort set in a deodar pine and oak forest.

$$$ / www.suroresort.com / +91 98 1660 3700

The Oberoi Cecil

A luxury hotel featuring an outdoor jacuzzi with epic views of cedar forests and Himalayan peaks.

$$$$ / www.oberoihotels.com/hotels-in-shimla-cecil / +91 11 2389 0606

WHAT TO DO

Rashtrapati Niwas and Botanical Gardens

Formerly known as Viceregal Lodge, Rashtrapati Niwas was the former residence of the British Viceroy of India. It has since been converted to the Indian Institute of Advanced Study. Located on Observatory Hills and surrounded by well-maintained gardens, the facility houses articles, artifacts, and photographs dating back to British rule.

Entry: INR 50

Hours: 10 am to 5 pm

Shimla Church

The Ridge and Christ Church

The Ridge is considered the cultural hub of Shimla. Connected to Scandal Point and Lakkar Bazaar, it is also the site of the Shila Summer Festival. Christ Church is one of the most popular sites on the Ridge. Constructed in non-Gothic style in 1857, its silhouette is visible for many kilometres around the vicinity of Shimla. It is the second oldest church in North India after St John's Church in Meerut.

Entry: Free
Hours: 24/7

Jakhu Temple: Trek to the Summit

The 2.5 km trek takes you to the highest peak in Shimla. Dedicated to Lord Hanuman, the temple is at an altitude of 2455 meters. Beware of the mischievous monkeys who like to steal items from your pockets and purses!

Entry: Free
Hours: Sunrise - Sunset

Kalka Shimla Toy Train

Step back in time on the Kalka Shimla Toy Train. Gliding through tunnels, bridges, steep valleys, lush green meadows, and oak forests, the UNESCO World Heritage Site achieves a startling height of 2076

meters above sea level. During the 5-hour journey, pass through 20 railway stations, 103 tunnels, 800 bridges, and 900 curves.

WHERE TO SHOP

The Lakkar Bazaar

The shops at Lakkar Bazaar specialize in pashmina shawls, wool garments, wooden toys, and walking sticks, but you can also find daily goods and souvenirs. The narrow lanes can become crowded, especially in the evenings when locals come out to grab a bite and socialize.

Hours: 9 am - 7 pm
Location: Adjacent to The Ridge, Next to Mall Road

The Mall Road

As the primary shopping center in Shimla, Mall Road is filled with small stalls, shops, and upmarket showrooms. Popular with both locals and tourists, this is the place to see and be seen.
Shop for traditional jewelry, pop into a bookstore, dine al fresco, or

enjoy a pint at the pub.

Hours: Explore anytime, but many shops close at 9 pm

WHERE TO EAT

Cafe Under Tree

This is the highest place to dine in Shimla, located near Jakhu Temple at 8000 ft. The eatery serves vegetarian and vegan dishes from around the globe.

Jakhu Road Gian Estate, Highland, Near Jakhu Temple, Shimla / +91 92 1852 7773

Shimla Book Cafe

Enjoy your meal/coffee with the beautiful sight of Christ Church and Himalayan vistas. The cafe was previously run by prison inmates as a social experiment and gained immense popularity for the food and service.

Takka Bench, Ridge, The Mall, Shimla / +91 94 1881 7761

Wake & Bake

With bright yellow windows, this unassuming cafe has an extensive menu that includes waffles, crepes, pizza, salads, and surprisingly delicious Middle Eastern specialties. The inside of the centrally-located outlet is Instagram picture-worthy.

The Mall, 34/1, Mall Rd, Middle Bazar, The Mall, Shimla / +91 17 7281 3146

Cafe Simla Times

Cafe Simla Times is known for wood-fired oven pizzas, though we also recommend the small plates and banana nutella shake. In the evening, grab a cold beer and listen to live music.

Within Hotel Willow Banks Premises, Mall Road, Shimla / +91 17 7265 8125

Eighteen71 Cookhouse & Bar

This restaurant and bar derive its name from the year in which it was established. Serving classic pan-Indian cuisine, the unique decor is a combination of metal, wood, and leather.

Near Tourism Lift Hotel Willow Banks, The Mall, Shimla

WHERE TO DRINK

Sixteen 69 Lounge Bar

The in-house bar at Marina Hotel is in a popular location on Mall Road. With pop songs and fine liquor, it's the perfect balance of ambiance and offerings.

Mall Road, Kamla Nehru Hospital Road, Bemloi, Shimla

The Brew Estate

As the first microbrewery in the state of Himachal Pradesh, this rustic-industrial spot serves craft beers, pub staples, and elevated cocktails. All brewing ingredients are imported from western countries: malt from Germany; hops from the United Kingdom, United States, and Germany; and yeast from Belgium.

The Ridge Behind Christ Church, Shimla / +91 78 5100 0006

Rendezvous Bar and Restaurant

After a full day of strolling and sightseeing around Shimla, unwind with classic cocktails and crunchy appetizers. The ambience is complemented by perfectly loud Punjabi songs. Baile Baile!

Scandal Point, The Mall, Shimla / +91 98 8214 8366

LOCAL TOURS AND EXPERIENCES

As a hill station, Shimla is an ideal base for trekking, cycling, and other mountainside adventures. We recommend **Shimla Walks**, a team of writers, authors, naturalists, photographers, mountaineers, explorers, wanderers, and lovers of the Himalaya.

Shimla Walks
www.shimlawalks.com
shimlawalks@gmail.com
+91 94 5951 9620 / +91 98 1714 1099

DAY TRIPS FROM SHIMLA

Chail

Chail is a small, sleepy mountain village along hilly terrain with picturesque landscapes. It is popularly known as the world's highest cricket playground built in 1893. Glorious snow-capped Shivalik peaks surround the village orchards and sylvan pine valleys. Chail Wildlife Sanctuary also attracts a large number of green panthers and photographers.

How to Reach: Hire a private car or taxi for the 54 km drive from Shimla
Best time to visit: April to October

Kufri

Nestled at the feet of the Himalayas, Kufri is surrounded by snow-capped mountains and home to the world's highest amusement park (Kufri Fun World). In the winter, snow bunnies flock to a ski track; the town also has a Himalayan wildlife zoo with rare antelopes, felines, and birds.

How to Reach: Hire a private car or taxi for the 14 km drive from Shimla
Best time to visit: December to February and April to June

Solan

Solan derives its name from Goddess Shoolini Devi, the deity of
the region. Solan is also known as the "Mushroom Capital of India"
and "City of Red Gold" for the wide production of tomatoes in
the vicinity. Places of interest include Gurkha Fort, Shoolini Mata
Temple, and Yungdrung Tibetan Monastery.

Solan is also home to one of the oldest breweries, Mohan Meakin's
Brewery. Folklore states that the cave near the summit of Karol Peak
is where the Pandavas resided during their banishment.

How to Reach: Hire a taxi or private car for the 46 km drive from
Shimla
Best time to visit: March to November

Fagu

Fagu is a secluded retreat that serves as basecamp for trekking and
camping. With valleys of apple orchards and draping cedars, the town
is often covered by snow or mist. Plan a sunrise or sunset trek from
Fagu to Chharabra via Tattapani stream for epic views or simply enjoy
the laid-back vibe of India's "secret" hill station.

How to Reach: Hire a taxi or private car for the 22 km drive from
Shimla
Best time to visit: April to June and October to December

DHARAMSHALA

Land of the Lamas

Nestled in the Dhauladhar range of the Himalayas is Dharamshala, the spiritual sanctuary of the Lamas. It is most commonly known as the residence of His Holiness The Dalai Lama and the Tibetan government-in-exile; the suburb of McLeod Ganj is a Tibetan settlement affectionately termed "Little Lhasa." Draped in cedar forests, Dharamshala offers Buddhist monasteries, trekking, tea plantations, and restorative retreats.

TRANSPORTATION HUBS

Dharamshala is located in Himachal Pradesh, a north Indian state nestled in the Himalayas.

Gaggal Airport (DHM)
National Highway 154, Gaggal, Himachal Pradesh

The nearest airport is located 14 km away in Kangra. Flights operate daily from Delhi. Upon arrival, book a taxi to reach the city.

Pathankot Junction Railway Station (PTK)
2nd outgate of railway station, Punjab

Pathankot Junction in the neighboring state of Punjab is the closest railway station, 25 km from the city. Overnight trains are available from Delhi. Upon arrival, hire a private car or taxi to reach Dharamshala.

Interstate Bus Terminal
MDR45, Sudhir, Dharamshala, Himachal Pradesh

You can reach Dharamshala by taking an overnight bus from ISBT Kashmiri Gate New Delhi. The journey takes approximately ten hours, depending on the roadblocks and the weather conditions.

Dharamshala is connected to Chandigarh by NH503, the same as New Delhi. You can take a private or government bus from the Chandigarh ISBN station and the journey takes about six hours. You can also hire a private taxi or cab.

AREAS TO AVOID

Overall, Dharamshala is a safe destination for female travelers.

LOCAL FESTIVALS

TIPA Festival (Tibetan Institute of Performing Arts)

The Tibetan Institute of Performing Arts (TIPA), established by the 14th Dalai Lama Tenzin Gyatso, preserves and promotes Tibet's unique art and culture. The annual 10-day festival is celebrated in April with dancing, folk songs, and recreational activities.

Haldi Festival

Also known as the Halda Festival, the *Festival of Light* is celebrated on a full moon night in January when it coincides with Magh Poornima. Dedicated to Shiskar Apa, the Goddess of Wealth, the celebration marks the beginning of the new year. As part of the ritual, locals gather at a commonplace selected by the Lamas and throw lit cedar twigs in a burning bonfire.

Dharamshala Film Festival

Started in 2012 by two filmmakers, Ritu Sarin and Tenzing Sonam, the festival promotes contemporary cinema and independent art media. It aims to promote local filmmaking and provide a platform for young talent. The festival also started a fellowship program in 2014 to support upcoming filmmakers from the region. It is held annually in October/November.

International Himalayan Festival Dharamshala

The International Himalayan Festival honors the day when His Holiness the 14th Dalai Lama was awarded the Nobel Peace Prize in 1985. During the 3-day extravaganza in December, activities are organized that reinforce the harmony and community ties between the locals and Tibetan settlers. Artisans, performers, and students host exhibitions and cultural shows that showcase Tibetan traditions.

Losar Festival

Losar is a 15-day Tibetan New Year celebration in February or March, based on lunar dates. It's a time to enjoy dumpling soup, yak butter tea, and a local barley liquor called chang. There are several days of traditions, from cleaning the house to making elaborate butter altars. Families also worship, exchange gifts, and visit monasteries to pay respects to the Lamas.

WHERE TO STAY

The Unmad
A contemporary B&B located in the neighborhood of Upper Dharamkot.
$ / www.theunmad.com / +91 95 8231 5984

Hotel Norbu House
A peaceful budget hotel perched on a ridge facing the Dalai Lama's Temple.
$$ / +91 75 5970 0887

Chonor House
An 11-room property featuring traditional Tibetan and 21st-century art near the Thekchen Choling Temple.
$$$ / +91 83 5281 6561

Junglaat Ecorganic Stays
A luxury and rustic boutique lodge nestled among Himalayan cedars.
$$$ / +91 98 9114 9380

WHAT TO DO

The Norbulingka Institute

Founded in 1988, the institute aims to preserve and showcase Tibetan culture, artifacts, and literature. It was named after the summer home of the Dalai Lamas in Lhasa, Tibet. Norbulingka features 1173 murals of Buddha and drawings from the life of the 14th Dalai Lama.

Entry: INR 110
Hours: 9 am - 5:30 pm

Namgyal Monastery

Originally founded in Lhasa by the Second Dalai Lama in 16th century Tibet, the monastery was relocated to Dharamshala after the uprising in 1959. As a center for education per the Buddhist treatises, Namgyal serves to assist the Lamas in public affairs and ritual performance. The resident monks have a rigorous schedule including hours of meditation and the study of philosophy and traditional art.

Entry: Free
Hours: 4:30 am - 8:30 pm

Gyuto Monastery

Founded in Tibet by the disciple of the First Dalai Lama in 1474, the monastery was also relocated to Dharamshala in 1959. The Gyuto monks study various tantric text forms like Chakrasamvara, Yamantaka and Guhyasamaja. They are also renowned worldwide for their overtone singing or "chordal chanting."

Entry: Free
Hours: 5 am - 6 pm

Triund Trek

At the foothills of the Dhauladhar range is Triund, a pleasant settlement at an altitude of 2828 meters in Kangra Valley. The short but steep climb through rhododendron and oak trees offers epic views. It's a moderate and popular expedition that also is recommended for birdwatching.

Hours: Sunrise to Sunset

Bhagsunath Temple and Bhagsu Falls

Dedicated to Lord Shiva, the Bhagsunath Temple is surrounded by freshwater springs that are believed to heal with sacred medicinal properties. Cascading into a rocky pool, Bhagsu Falls are particularly stunning during the monsoon season and also considered an important spot for Hindu pilgrimage.

Hours: Sunrise to Sunset

St. John Church

Constructed in non-Gothic architecture in 1852, the church is dedicated to John the Baptist. Also known as St. John in the Wilderness, the Anglican church is located between Mcleodganj and Forsythganj. The deodar forest setting and Belgian stained-glass windows add to the beauty of this secluded house of worship.

Entry: Free
Hours: 9 am - 6 pm; 10:30 am - 11:30 am on Sunday

WHERE TO SHOP

Semshook Tibetan Handicrafts

Italy meets Tibet at this popular shop selling leather purses, designer skirts, handicrafts, and Thangka paintings. The Tibetan artifacts have a spiritual meaning and the artisans enjoy sharing stories about the cultural inspiration.

Hours: 9 am - 5 pm daily; Closed on Sunday
Location: McLeod Ganj, Dharamshala

Jogiwara Road Bazaar

The Tibetan mini market stays busy all day with shops and stalls lining both sides of Jogiwara Road. You will mostly find Tibetan handicrafts, shawls, woolen clothes, hand carved jewelry, and the favorite Chamba slippers.

Hours: 9 am - 9 pm
Location: Jogiwara Road, McLeod Ganj

Kotwali Bazaar

Considered the main market of the city, Kotwali Bazaar sells everything from handicrafts to housewares, including embroidered shawls, exotic paintings, and miniature Buddha statues. It's also a popular spot for street food and local snacks — you can never have too many momos!

Hours: 9 am - 9 pm
Location: Chandigarh-Chintpurni-Dharamshala Road, Sudher, Dharamshala

WHERE TO EAT

Tibet Kitchen

Tibet Kitchen is a simple eatery that serves traditional Tibetan favorites like *thukpa* (noodle soup), momos (dumplings), and yak butter tea.

Jogiwara Road, Main Square, McLeod Ganj, Dharamshala / +91 78 0741 9692

Morgan's Place

Head to the rooftop terrace and order a clay-oven pizza from the cozy, Italian-inspired cafe. Located near the Tushita Meditation Center, it's also a popular spot for breakfast and brews.

Dharamkot Village, Tushita Meditation Center, Dharamshala /
+91 86 2693 9538

Norling Hummingbird Cafe

Grab a seat in the outdoor rock garden at this cozy cafe at Norbulingka Institute. The vegetarian lunch buffet (12 pm - 2:30 pm daily except Sunday) serves 5-6 mains, breads, rice, and sweets.
Mohli Lahrandi, Himachal Pradesh / +91 18 9224 6405

Nick's Italian Kitchen

Nick's Italian Kitchen serves the best pizza, gnocchi, and risotto in town. Come hungry to the buffet brunch (daily except Sunday) with views of the snow-capped mountains from the open terrace.
Bhagsu Road, McleodGanj, Dharamshala / +91 18 9222 1180

Illiterati Cafe

As one of the most-talked-about spaces in Himachal Pradesh, Illiterati doesn't disappoint. The unique bookshop-turned-cafe features an impressive collection of books and a menu with family recipes.
Lower Jogiwara Road, Dharamshala, India

WHERE TO DRINK

Labooze Cafe Bar Lounge

One of our favorites in Dharamshala. Order the Absolute pitcher.
Hotel Surya Road, Off Dolma Chowk, Mcleodganj, Dharamshala / +91 88 9478 8981

McLlo Resto and Bar

Located on the main square in Dharamshala, McLlo's is what you need when you need it - a cold beer and live music in a convenient spot to close out your day.
Jogiwara Road, City Centre, McLeod Ganj, Dharamsala

The Cliff Rooftop Bar and Restaurant
As the name suggests, the drinks here come with a side of elevated views.
Blossoms Village Resort, Khanyara Road, Sidhpur, Dharamshala /
+91 86 2896 6338

LOCAL TOURS AND EXPERIENCES

Tibetan Pottery Session
Visit Dharamkot Studio, a co-working and learning space for earthenware and Himalayan black pottery. The artists are kind, the vibe is positive, and the views spark creativity.

www.dharamkotstudio.com

Guided Meditation and Buddhism Courses at Tushita
The renowned Tushita Meditation Centre offers daily drop-in meditation sessions (9 am daily except Sunday) led by experienced students. It's free to attend but a donation is appreciated. Guests can also visit the library or practice meditation privately in a vacant gompa. If seeking a more extensive program, Tushita offers group retreats and a variety of Buddhism courses ranging from beginner to advanced.

http://tushita.info/

Cooking Session at Lhamo's Kitchen
Reserve an interactive and informative cooking class on traditional Tibetan dishes. The teacher, Lhamo, fled Tibet at the age of 16 and settled in McLeod Ganj (his mother was a chef in Lhasa and the

inspiration for his recipes.) The menu includes breads, soups, and momos! +91 981 646 8719

DAY TRIPS

Bir-Billing
The neighboring towns of Bir and Billing are known for ecotourism, adventure activities, and spiritual studies. Activities include mountain biking, hang gliding, riding the toy train, and meditating at Tibetan Buddhist monasteries. Bir-Billing is also considered one of the best (and safest!) paragliding sites in Asia; the town hosted the Paragliding World Cup in 2015 and continues to host international competitions.

How to Reach: From Dharamshala, you can reach Bir by local bus leaving at 6 am and 2 pm; you can also rent a taxi for approximately 1500 INR. The drive takes two hours each way.

Palampur Cooperative Tea Factory
Unlike in other states, the tea gardens near Dharamshala are not spread over vast acres of land; It is one of the smallest tea-growing regions of India known for premium and fragrant leaves. Located at an altitude of 4780 feet, the shadow of the Dhauladhar Mountains adds to the panoramic vistas as you stroll through the narrow paths. At Palampur Cooperative Tea Factory, observe the plucking and processing, chat with the planters, and sample the varieties of Kangra Tea. The gardens capture the essence of simplicity and sustainability.

How to Reach: Hire a taxi or private car for the 35 km drive from Dharamshala. The factory is generally open from 9 am - 6 pm.

Kangra Fort
The Kangra Fort is such an important fortification in Indian culture that it was mentioned in the epic *Mahabharata*. It is the largest fort in the Himalayas and the 8th largest fort in the country. It's a climb to the top, but well worth it for the commanding views.

How to Reach: From Dharamshala, hire a private car or taxi for the 50-minute drive.

GIVING BACK

LHA Social Work

Launched in 1997, LHA is an award-winning charitable trust working to provide necessary resources to the local Tibetan refugees. The NGO has an active volunteer community of more than 7k people in 43 different countries. Projects include the Clear Vision Project, HIV & AIDS Initiative Project, and Clean Water Project.
www.lhasocialwork.org

Dharmalaya Institute for Compassionate Living

Established in 2010 by a team of educators, artists, and environmentalists, Dharmalaya has four foundation principles: Ahimsa (Non-harming), Maitri (Love and Kindness), Karuna (Compassion), and Seva (Service). The organization runs various educational and charitable programs covering experimental education, green vocational training, economic self-sufficiency, and community service.
https://dharmalaya.in/

AHMEDABAD

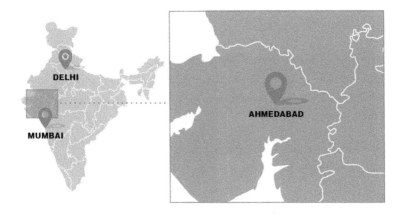

The Manchester of India

As the second largest producer of cotton in the country, Ahmedabad is affectionately called the "Manchester of India." Located on the Sabarmati River, Ahmedabad was a major base camp during the Indian freedom struggle. The city is a unique fusion of textiles, contemporary architecture, and non-violent philosophy. Ahmedabad is presently one of the most industrialized cities in India while the historic city was also declared India's first UNESCO World Heritage City.

TRANSPORTATION HUBS

Ahmedabad is located in the western state of Gujarat.

Sardar Vallabhai Patel International Airport (AMD)
Hansol, Ahmedabad, Gujarat 380003
www.ahmedabadairport.com

Ahmedabad has excellent flight connectivity to most major domestic cities, including Delhi, Mumbai, Kochi, Bangalore, Hyderabad, and Chennai. The airport also services international flights to Dubai and Doha, among others.

Ahmedabad Junction Railway Station (ADI)
Kalupur Railway Station Rd, Sakar Bazar, Kalupur

Daily trains connect Ahmedabad to all major cities such as New Delhi, Mumbai, Goa, Hyderabad, Patna, Jaipur, and Bangalore.

Geeta Mandir Bus Station
Gita Mandir Road, Ahmedabad

The Ahmedabad station has intercity and interstate buses connecting to all towns within Gujarat and major cities in neighboring states.

AREAS TO AVOID

Overall, Ahmedabad is a very safe destination for female travelers.

LOCAL FESTIVALS

Navratri

Nava (nine) and *Ratri* (night) come together as Navratri, nine nights
of festivities in October/November. The celebration is in honor of
the divine feminine form of the Hindu deity Goddess Durga. The
Garba dance is performed in a circle around a lantern called "Garbha
Deep" which means "Womb Light." Celebrants twirl gracefully to the
tunes of traditional folk songs, drums, and cymbals donning colorful
Gujarati costumes.

Rann Utsav

Rann Utsav is an annual festival celebrated in the Great Rann of
Kutch (white salt desert) from November through to February. The
best time to visit is during the full moon night when you can view the
vast salt desert in its full glory. Enjoy folk dances and music, sample
Gujarati cuisine, and shop for traditional crafts directly from the
artisans. Rann Utsav is a true representation of Gujarati folk culture.

Uttarayan

The festival of Makar Sankranti is celebrated as Uttarayan in Gujarat. According to the Indian calendar, the festival marks the beginning of summer or the harvest season. Occuring on the 14th and 15th January, Uttarayan is celebrated by flying kites or *patangs*. The city skyline is filled with color as people of all ages gather on the rooftops.

At the other end of the city, on the banks of Sabarmati, the Ministry of Tourism organizes the International Kite Festival. People from across the world participate in various competitions and showcase their beautiful kites.

WHERE TO STAY

Charyana Hotel AC Dormitory

A clean and functional hostel offering female-only bunk rooms.
$ / +91 73 8300 8521

French Haveli

A 150-year-old, artistically restored heritage home in the Old City.
$$ / https://frenchhaveli.com / +91 98 9861 8396

Dodhia Haveli

A classically restored heritage house and the sister property to French Haveli.
$$ / https://frenchhaveli.com / +91 98 9861 8396

House of MG

A 20th century family mansion converted to a boutique heritage hotel.
$$$ / https://houseofmg.com/ / +91 79 2550 6946

WHAT TO DO

Sabarmati Ashram

Also known as Gandhi Ashram, Sabarmati is located on the banks of Sabarmati River. Mahatma Gandhi stayed at the ashram for many years and facilitated all major activities related to India's independence and the upliftment of society. The museum houses personal memorabilia of Mahatma Gandhi, including various books, manuscripts, personal writings and letters, his writing desk, and the spinning wheel.

Mahatma Gandhi

Entry: Free
Hours: 8:30 am - 6:30 pm daily
https://gandhiashramsabarmati.org/en/

Sarkhej Roza

Sarkhej was once a prominent center of Sufi Culture in the country, as well as the residence of the revered Sufi saint Shaikh Ahmed Ganj Baksh. Located 8 km southwest of Ahmedabad in the village of Makarba, the complex includes a mosque and tombs that make up the beautiful Sarkhej Roza. Like many monuments built during this time, the design of Sarkhej Roza has both Indian and foreign elements making it an architectural marvel.

Entry: Free
Hours: Open daily from 9 am - 6 pm
https://www.sarkhejroza.org/

Kankaria Lake

Spread over 76 acres, the 500-year-old lake is one of the largest in Ahmedabad. After the recent reconstruction and renovation, the lake has become a hub of activities for people of all ages. Attractions include the Zoo, Zoological Gardens, a small amusement park for kids, toy trains, boat rides, hot air balloon rides, and food stalls.

Entry: INR 25 per person for adults and INR 10 per person for kids above 3; The entry is free for children below 3 years of age, senior citizens, and morning walkers.
Hours: 4 am - 8 am and 9 am - 10 pm daily. Closed on Mondays.

Sidi Saiyyed Mosque

Sidi Saiyyed (also spelled Sidi Saeed) was a royal slave of African descent in the service of Sultan Mahmoud III, the last ruler of Gujarat. Upon the Sultan's death, he joined the company of another general. By the time Saiyyed retired, he had amassed enough wealth to build himself a mosque. The architecture and the intricate detailing of the mosque represents the extraordinary legacy of the African diaspora in India. The beautiful latticework on the windows and the intricately carved jalis depicting the 'tree of life' showcases the contribution of art and architecture by the African community in India.

Entry: Free
Hours: 24/7

Bhadra Fort

Built in 1411, the Bhadra Fort gets its name from the famous

Bhadrakali temple located in the complex. Spread across 43 acres, the fort was captured by the British in 1817 and used as a prison until Independence.

Entry: Free
Hours: 9 am - 5 pm daily

The Calico Museum of Textiles

As one of the most famous museums in Ahmedabad, the Calico Museum houses collections of the finest Indian textiles. Displayed across several galleries, the museum contains handmade textiles spanning centuries, along with 19th century regional embroideries, religious and tie-n-dye textiles, royal garments, tribal costumes, and miniature paintings. The museum also displays various Jain sculptures, manuscripts, and ceremonial objects.

Entry: Free
Hours: A single guided tour starts at 10:30 am and ends at 1 pm. Entry is permitted only between 10:15 am and 10:30 am. The maximum number of visitors per tour is restricted to 20 and you need to pre-register online at least four weeks in advance. The museum is closed on Wednesdays and public holidays.
www.calicomuseum.org

Auto World Vintage Car Museum

With a collection of over 110 vintage cars, Auto World is a delight for all car enthusiasts. Displaying the history and the evolutionary journey of automobiles, the museum showcases vintage buggies, railway saloons, and spectacular convertibles and cars. Some of the brands represented are Rolls-Royce, Buick-Cadillac, Daimler, Bentley, Chryslers, Lincoln, Maybach, and Mercedes.

Entry: INR 50 per person
Hours: 8 am - 9 pm daily

Hutheesing Jain Temple

Jainism is an ancient religion with a strong influence in Ahmedabad. The numerous Derasars (Jain Temples) in the city are a testament to its belief. Completed in 1848, the Hutheesing temple is an architectural masterpiece. Named after the Jain Merchant who commissioned its building, the ornate white marble structure with stunning carvings pays reverence to Dharmanath, the fifteenth Jain Tirthankar (religious guru).

Entry: Free
Hours: 9 am - 5:30 pm daily

Akshardham Temple

Dedicated to Bhagwan Swaminarayan, the temple complex has a main Mandir (temple), several exhibitions, and lush gardens. Built completely in pink sandstone, the architecture is a masterpiece and a tribute to Hinduism. The 7-foot-tall gold-leafed statue of Bhagwan Swaminarayan is the focal point of the temple complex. The exhibitions and daily water show depict the life and journey of Bhagwan Swaminarayan, history of ancient India, and Hindu heritage, culture, and universal values.

Entry: Free to the main temple. The exhibitions and water show in the evening are ticketed at a cost of INR 60 per person for adults (11+ years) and INR 40 per person for children from 3-11 years of age. Children under 3 years of age can visit for free.
Hours: 11 am - 5:30 pm daily

https://akshardham.com/gujarat/

WHERE TO SHOP

Law Garden

Law Garden is a popular public garden in Ahmedabad. On one side of the garden is the market lined with shops and stalls with traditional clothes, ethnic jewelry, and handicrafts. Law Garden becomes crowded and lively during Navratri, selling traditional Chaniya Cholis and oxidized metal jewelry worn during the festival.

Hours: 5:30 am - 10:30 pm daily
Location: Netaji Road, Ellisbridge

Gujarat Jewelry

CG Road

A bit on the higher end, CG Road has malls, emporiums, and branded shops. The market is a local favorite for both trendy and traditional clothes as well as branded jewelry showrooms. Fuel up with *Sev Puri*, a cheap and delicious savory snack sold by vendors along the main road.

Hours: 11 am - 10 pm daily
Location: CG Road

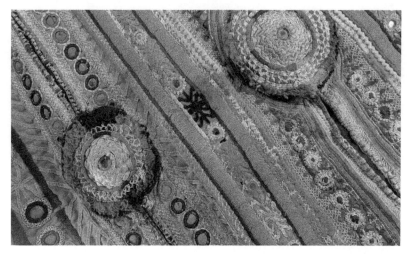

Gujarat Embroidery

Dhalgarwad Market

A popular market for traditional wear and cotton clothes, Dhalgarwad comes alive during the wedding season and Navratri. It's a great spot to buy traditional Bandhej/Bandhani Sarees along with Chaniya Cholis (traditional outfit worn by girls during Navratri). Not just for readymade clothes, the market also sells handicrafts and ethnic jewelry along with all the raw materials required to embellish the traditional clothes.

Hours: 10 am - 9:30 pm daily
Location: Dhalgarwad, Khadia

Sindhi Market

Close to the old city center, the Sindhi market is a hot spot to buy traditional Indian clothes. The wholesale market has more than 200 shops selling footwear, sarees, bedsheets, dress materials, and handicrafts all at wholesale prices. Bargaining is encouraged for stellar deals!

Hours: 11 am - 10 pm daily
Location: Sindhi Market, Revdi Bazar, Kalupur, Ahmedabad

WHAT TO SHOP FOR IN AHMEDABAD

Cotton Textile Work
Ahmedabad is famous for cotton textiles. Arvind Mills is the biggest textile manufacturer and produces denim for jeans worldwide. It was launched in response to Mahatma Gandhi's call for Swadeshi (Made in India) during the struggle for Indian Independence. Apart from Arvind Mills, the city has almost 62 cotton mills, making it the second largest producer of cotton in India and a renowned destination for unique textiles.

Ahmedabad Diamond
Jean Baptiste Tavernier, a French traveler and gem merchant, made several visits to Ahmedabad in the 1600's. Impressed with the quality, he famously named the diamond after the city.

WHERE TO EAT

Agashiye
The word *Agashiye* in Gujarati means 'on the terrace' and the rooftop seating of the restaurant stands true to its name. The converted heritage property is a favorite for an authentic Gujarati thali experience.
House of MG, Opposite Siddi Sayyed Mosque, Lal Darwaza

Swati Snacks
Starting as a small Mumbai restaurant in 1963, Swati Snacks served only a small selection of homemade chaats and ice cream. Through the years they expanded their locations and menu. Try the traditional Gujarati *dhokla* (steamed rice/chickpea flour snack), *patra* (steamed and fried taro leaf dumplings), *handvo* (savory vegetable cake), and *chaas* (buttermilk).
Panchavati Road Law Garden
ONE42, Off Ambli Road

Vishalla

Dining at Vishalla is truly an authentic Gujarati cultural experience. Guests are encouraged to sit on the floor as a traditional thali is served following the system of Ayurveda. The meals are accompanied by various shows and dance performances.

Opposite APMC Market, Vishalla Circle / http://www.vishalla.com/index.html

Narmada - The Ummed

Live music, ghazals, and authentic Awadhi/Mughlai cuisine makes Narmada a popular eatery for galawati and kakori kebabs.

The Ummed Ahmedabad Hotel, International Airport Road, Hansol

Wind and Water

A casual multi-cuisine restaurant with lush green surroundings and a waterfall. Try the Chinese starters and Tom Kha Chicken and Lamb broth.

Fortune Landmark Hotel, Ashram Road

Yanki Sizzlers

Popular among the locals, Yanki Sizzlers offers a variety of veg and non-veg sizzlers. There are several branches in Ahmedabad, all equally good.

4 Binori Ambit, Next to Renault Showroom, Thaltej Circle

WHERE TO DRINK

Because Gujarat is a dry state, alcohol is not easily available in restaurants. However, foreigners can obtain a special permit for the purchase and consumption of alcohol.

Since alcohol is not publicly available, be sure to try *aam panna*, *chaas* (buttermilk), Kokum juice, and flavored iced teas.

Zen Cafe
Try the watermelon juice and basil juice at this relaxed cafe near the iconic Amdavad ni Gufa.
Kasturbhai Lalbhai Campus, University Road, University Area, Navrangpur

The Project Cafe
A unique cafe curated by artists and designers where everything is on sale, including the furniture and crockery! You can also customize your dessert at the live bakery.
Yellow House No 7, Polytechnic Road, Ambavadi

Makeba - The Lounge Cafe
Popular with young professionals, Makeba is a terrace restro cafe with a live mocktail bar.
IIM Road, University Area, Vastrapur

LOCAL TOURS AND EXPERIENCES

Best of Street Food Tour

Discover the popular street foods of Ahmedabad and sample the regional specialities that the locals love and enjoy.

http://www.a4ahmedabad.com/culinary-tours/23-best-of-street-food-tour.html

Heritage Walking Tour of Ahmedabad Old City

Learn about the history and cultural significance of a 600-year-old city that was built inside a fortress. Visit the markets, monuments, and sacred spaces as you walk through the community-based residential areas (pols) and old markets.

http://www.a4ahmedabad.com/heritage-walking-tours/20-heritage-walk-tour-ahmedabad-city.html

Photography Tour

Join a professional photographer as you capture unique angles and lighting of the old city market, flower market, ancient monuments, and residential communities.

http://www.a4ahmedabad.com/photography-tours/24-photography-tour.html

Learn to Cook a Gujarati Delicacy

Sample Gujarati foods at popular Ahmedabad eateries and learn to cook a Gujarati delicacy from a celebrity chef.

http://www.a4ahmedabad.com/culinary-tours/22-learn-to-cook-gujarati-delicacy-dhokla.html

Adalaj Stepwell

DAY TRIPS

Adalaj Stepwell

A walk around the Adalaj will transport you to an ancient civilization. The entire structure is covered with carvings, sculptures, and ornamentation, combining Indo-Islamic architectural elements and designs. Built in the 15th century, the site is brimming with legends and a tragic love story. Adalaj is the only stepwell with three sets of entrance stairs that meet on the first level at a large square platform. As the stairs descend down to the fifth story, the air grows noticeably cooler. The small town of Adalaj was on a trade route and provided refuge to passing travelers. Try to visit when the morning rays of sunlight cast a soft glow.

Entry: Free; Guides charge INR 200-300 depending on experience
Hours: 6 am - 6 pm daily
How to Reach: Rent a car or catch a bus from Ahmedabad for the 30-minute journey

Zanzari Waterfall
The only waterfall in close proximity to Ahmedabad, Zanzari is a scenic spot for picnics or a day trip during monsoon months (July - September). Not a perennial waterfall, the falls come alive during monsoon when the rainwater creates thunderous cascades on the rocky riverbed.

Entry: Free
Hours: 6 am - 7 pm daily
How to Reach: Hire a private car or catch a local bus for the 75 km journey from Ahmedabad

Lothal
Lothal was an important trade center and pottery village during the Harappan Civilization. Today it is one of the most excavated sites and a delight for historians. The vast ruins are a popular attraction and tell a story about the Indus Valley Civilization. The museum also displays objects that were excavated from the site.

Hours: 10 am - 5 pm, open all days of the week except Friday. Remains closed on Friday.
How to Reach: There are direct trains from the Ahmedabad Gandhigram station to Lothal, but the most convenient way is by road. Hire a private car for the 1.5 hour (78 km) journey.

Dandi Kutir

Located in Gandhinagar, Dandi Kutir is India's largest museum dedicated to the life and teachings of Mahatma Gandhi. Shaped as a mound of salt, this is the only interactive museum that uses the sophisticated 3d and 4d technology to depict the biography of the Father of the Nation.

Entry: INR 10
Hours: 10:30 am - 5 pm daily; Closed on Mondays
How to Reach: Direct buses are available from Ahmedabad to Gandhinagar. You can also hire a private car or taxi for the short 40-minute ride.
https://dandi-kutir.com/

GLORIOUS GUJARAT

Historically, Gujarat was known as the home of Mahatma Gandhi and the base of the Indian independence movement. Although the western state offers travelers many diverse attractions, including wildlife, handicrafts, tribal villages, and temples, it is less often visited by foreigners. With modern infrastructure and incredibly friendly locals, we highly recommend spending more time in one of the most industrialized states in India.

Although Ahmedabad is the only Gujarati city we are featuring in GGG (with the exception of Gir National Park, pg. 407), here are a few of our favorite regional experiences:

Palitana Jain Temples

Palitana is considered the most sacred pilgrimage site of the Jain community. Ādinātha, the first of the Jain tirthankaras, is said to have meditated on Shatrunjaya Hill. Over generations, 3k+ temples were carved from marble; Palitana is presently the world's largest temple complex. The steep walk on the mountainside stone staircase is arduous and no food can be carried or consumed. However, the views and craftsmanship are breathtaking. Fact: In 2014, Palitana became the first city in the world to be legally vegetarian. In adherence to Jain philosophy, the buying and selling of meat, fish, and eggs is forbidden.

Rann of Kutch

Rann of Kutch is a large area of salt marshes, divided into two zones: Great Rann of Kutch and Little Rann of Kutch. Designated a world heritage site in 2002, it is India's second largest wildlife sanctuary and one of the largest salt deserts in the world. During the summer monsoon, the desert of salty clay and mudflats fills with standing water. From the city of Bhuj, various wildlife conservation areas of Kutch can be visited such as the Indian Wild Ass Sanctuary, Kutch Desert Wildlife Sanctuary, Narayan Sarovar Sanctuary, Kutch Bustard Sanctuary, Banni Grasslands Reserve, and Chari-Dhand Wetland Conservation Reserve.

Tribal Villages

It is estimated that more than five million people in Gujarat are tribal. Many are experts in weaving techniques, textiles, and handicrafts, the skilled embroidery often passed down from woman to child. We suggest visiting the Rabari Tribe of Kutch, a gypsy community of cattle herders with vibrant clothing and turbans. Also explore the 180+ weekly rural village Haats (markets), established to incentivize the rural population and ensure a platform to showcase and sell not only agricultural and allied goods but also handicrafts and textiles.

VARANASI

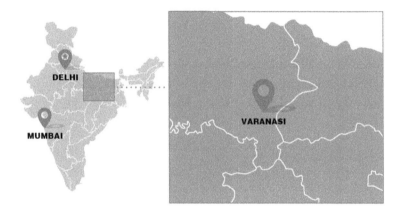

The City of Death and Rebirth

Varanasi is a sacred city of legends and liberation; a destination where intimate rituals are performed publicly. Also known as *Banaras* or *Kashi*, it is one of the oldest inhabited cities in the world. According to ancient texts, Varanasi was founded by the Hindu deity Shiva, making it one of the most important pilgrimage sites in India. The morning rays prompt locals to gather at the ghats for prayers and baths in the Ganges River. From the Aarti ceremony to the blazing funeral pyres, visitors are often in awe of the intensity, mysticism, and spiritual resonance.

TRANSPORTATION HUBS

Varanasi is located in the northern Indian state of Uttar Pradesh.

Lal Bahadur Shastri Airport (VNS)
Shahganj District, Babatpur, Uttar Pradesh

Varanasi is well connected to major Indian cities and the airport services both domestic and international flights. From the airport, you can take a local bus or hire a taxi/private car/rideshare to reach the city.

Varanasi Cantt Railway Station (BSB)
Azad Nagar Colony, Phulwari Village, Varanasi Cantonment, Varanasi

Manduadih Railway Station (MUV)
Manduwadih Rd, Manduwadih, Varanasi

Deen Dayal Upadhyaya Railway Station (DDU)
32101 Pandit Dindayal Upadhyaya Marg Pandit Dindayal Upadhyay Nagar Uttaresh

There are several railway stations in Varanasi, but the three main locations are BSB, MUV, and DDU. Varanasi is well connected with major rail lines across the country.

Chaudhary Charan Singh Bus Stand
Opposite to Varanasi Cantt Railway Station, Vijay Nagar Colony, Chetganj, Varanasi

Varanasi is very well connected by road. However, the driving distance to other destinations can be long, so it is recommended to book a flight or train.

AREAS TO AVOID

In the past decade, Varanasi has seen an increase in local crime, particularly theft and harassment. It's best to stay in well-lit, lively places after dark and avoid walking through the narrow lanes by the *ghats*. Beware of unlicensed guides who may overcharge or follow you until you strike a deal. Also, Varanasi has become a refuge for exiled Sadhus or Aghoris who are often intoxicated or under the influence of hard drugs. Try not to make direct eye contact or offer money for "religious" services.

LOCAL FESTIVALS

Ganga Mahotsav

The Mahotsav is organized on Dev Deepavali, or the full moon day in the Hindu month of Kartik (November), to thank the river goddess Ganga for providing nourishment and livelihood to Varanasi. The city is illuminated with thousands of diyas and cultural programs are organized near the riverbank. The festival celebrates the religious significance and cultural identity of Varanasi.

Buddha Mahotsav

The Buddha Mahotsav celebrates the day when Gautam Buddha was born in 563 BC. Because Buddha attained enlightenment on the same day he was born, the festival also marks Mahaparinirvana. The annual celebration is held in Sarnath on a full moon day in the month of Vaisakh (April or May).

Maha Shivaratri

Maha Shivaratri is an annual Hindu festival that celebrates Shiva. Devotees chant prayers, fast, meditate, visit temples, and even make a pilgrimage. Unlike most festivals that are celebrated during the day, Maha Shivaratri is observed at night. Ardent devotees will remain awake all night to overcome darkness and ignorance. It is celebrated on the 14th day of the dark fortnight of Phalguna (February/March).

Dev Deepavali

Dev Deepavali, or the *Diwali of the Gods*, celebrates the gods descending to earth and bathing in the Ganges River. The festival is observed 15 days after Diwali, the Festival of Lights, on the full moon of the Hindu month of Kartika (November - December). More than one million *diyas* light the Varanasi ghats and Ganges River to welcome and honor the deities. Thousands of devotees gather to observe the Aarti ceremony, chant, and pay reverence.

Makar Sankranti

Celebrated annually when the sun enters Capricorn season, Makar Sankranti is one of the only Hindu festivals observed according to solar cycles and not lunar cycles. Also known locally as Khichdi, the festival is dedicated to Lord Surya. Devotees bathe in the River Ganga and offer prayers to the sun god.

WHERE TO STAY

International Travellers Hostel (ITH)

An award-winning hostel with dormitories, tents, and family cottages in close proximity to the Varanasi Junction Railway Station.

$ / www.itravellershostel.com /+91 54 2222 0058

Moustache Hostel

A centrally located hostel near Assi Ghat that offers a glimpse of Ganga Aarti from the balcony.

$ / https://moustachescapes.com/ +91 89 2910 0705

Wander Station

A lively backpacking property in a convenient, walkable neighborhood.

$ / +91 94 1579 8378

Hotel Ganges View

A 19th century home at Assi Ghat converted to boutique accommodations.

$$ /www.hotelgangesview.co.in / +91 54 2231 3218

NamaSTAY Varanasi

A rural boutique hotel in the Varanasi countryside with an organic cafe and swimming pool.

$$ / https://www.namastayvaranasi.com/ +91 79 0900 7364

Amritara Suryauday Haveli

A restored haveli originally built by the Royal Family of Nepal as a retreat for the elderly.

$$$ / www.amritara.co.in/amritara-suryauday-haveli-varanasi-uttar-pradesh.html / +91 78 0049 0390

Brijrama Palace

A luxury riverside property with regal architecture and panoramic sunset views.

$$$$ / https://brijhotels.com/ +91 91 2941 4141

WHAT TO DO

New Vishwanath Temple (Birla Temple)

Dedicated to Lord Shiva, the Birla Temple is located inside Benaras Hindu University. The mandir actually features nine interior temples and is open to all castes and religions. The entire text of the sacred Bhagavad Gita is inscribed on the temple walls. Try and plan your visit during the Aarti ceremony that is performed several times daily.

Entry: Free

Hours: 4 am - 12 pm and 1 pm - 9 pm daily; Aarti timings are 4 am, 4:45 am, 10:30 am, 11:45 am, 12 pm, 1 pm, 6:45 pm, 7:30 pm, 8 pm and 8:45 pm.

Shri Kashi Vishwanath Temple

One of India's oldest temples, Kashi Vishwanath is commonly identified as the Golden Temple of Lord Shiva. It is one of the twelve *jyotirlingas*, or holiest of Shiva Temples. The name, Kashi, refers to the ancient title of Varanasi. The temple was demolished several times by Muslim rulers and the current structure was constructed in 1780.

Entry: Free
Hours: 3 am - 11 pm daily; Aarti timings are 3 am (Mangala Aarti), 11:15 am (Bhoga Aarti), 7 pm (Sandhya Aarti), 9 pm (Shringara Aarti), and 10:30 pm (Shayana Aarti)

Dashashwamedha Ghat

Dashashwamedha is one of the oldest ghats in Varanasi; it is also the sacred space of the nightly Ganga Aarti. The presiding priests stand on a Chauki (wooden stand) near the water. To the chant of Sanskrit mantras and the clash of cymbals and drums, the river is worshipped with flowers, incense, sandalwood, milk, and vermilion. The blazing camphor lamp and flaming Aarti lamps are raised high and then arched back to the water, the dark river reflecting the golden flames as the Ganges accepts the worship.

Entry: Free
Hours: 24/7

Manikarnika Ghat

Manikarnika Ghat is one of the holiest cremation grounds in the country.
According to Hindu philosophy, a death is a transition to the next life
based on karma. A cremation at this sacred ghat will break the cycle of
rebirth as the soul attains enlightenment.

Please remember that this is a highly emotional space of grief and
bereavement. Be respectful and refrain from laughing, eating, or drinking;
keep any discussions to a minimum and maintain a state of reverent
observation.

Entry: Free
Hours: 24/7

Man Singh Observatory

Also known as the Jantar Mantar of Varanasi, the astronomical
observatory was constructed in the 16th century by Raja Man Singh.
Located on the rooftop of a 300-year-old palace, the observatory
features ancient geometric instruments for preparing the lunar calendar,
measuring time, and computing celestial events. There is also an
interactive display that showcases the historical and cultural significance
of Varanasi. Although located near the popular Dashashwamedh Ghat, the
observatory is lesser known and considered a "hidden jewel" of the city.

The rooftop views are epic!

Entry: INR 250
Hours: 9 am - 5 pm daily

WHERE TO SHOP

Vishwanath Gali

As one of the oldest and busiest streets in Varanasi, Vishwanath Gali has rows of shops and stalls selling local artifacts, silk sarees, and jewelry. The market runs from Dashaswamedh Ghat to Gyanvapi Chowk and the narrow lanes leave very little room for personal space!

Hours: 9 am - 10 pm
Location: Dashaswamedh Ghat to Gyanvapi Chowk, Varanasi

Banaras Art Gallery

Operating since 1988, Banaras Art Gallery (BAG) promotes Varanasi's artistic and cultural development. View and shop the contemporary collections while learning about the development of Indian art.

Hours: 9 am - 9 pm
Location: B 1/256, Asi Main Road, Varanasi

Godowlia Market

The popular bazaar stretches for 3 km around the vicinity of Kashi Vishwanath Temple. As one of the busiest markets in the city, you can find household essentials, clothes, artifacts, silk embroidery, and even groceries at reasonable prices.

Hours: 10 am - 9 pm
Location: Dashashwamedh Road, Ramapura Luxa, Varanasi

Rajan Silk Store

Established 40 years ago, the Rajan Silk Store has become a Varanasi institution. Locals flock here for the finest collections of banarasi sarees, embroidered materials, stoles, and dresses.

Hours: 11 am - 8 pm daily; Closed on Sunday
Location: Ground Bulanala Maidagin Road Besides Bank Of India New Market Ash Bhairo, Govindpura, Varanasi

Harmony The Book Shop

If you're a bibliophile, make time to visit this unique shop near Assi Ghat. From spirituality to sociology, the owner has curated a collection of rare finds with books for every interest. Check out the section on Hindu poetry!

Hours: 10 am - 8 pm daily
Location: B1/158 Assi Ghat Road Below Sahi River View Guest House, Assi Ghat, Varanasi

WHAT TO SHOP FOR IN VARANASI

Banarasi Silk Sarees

Silk sarees of Banaras are famous worldwide for fabric quality and embroidery work. Every market has a collection of these sarees, including the Rajan silk store.

Crystal and Stone Shivalinga

The city of Varanasi is the abode of Lord Shiva. Devotees buy the Shiva Linga from markets like Vishwanath Gali to take home for worship. The lingam is the primary devotional icon that represents the eternal process of creation and regeneration.

Gulabi Meenakari

Adopted from Persia in the early 17th century, Meenakari is an art form that fuses metals in different colors. It is one of the rarest crafts of India found near Gai Ghat.

Glass Beads
Varanasi is the hub of multicolored glass beads, also known as *kaanch ke moti*. The practice of bead making and bead production dates back thousands of years with the city now employing over 2,000 artisans.

Rudraksha Mala
The Mudela Village near Varanasi is world-famous for making jewelry from rudraksha that includes garlands, crowns, bracelets, armlets, jackets, and caps. The malas are a symbol of devotion to Lord Shiva.

Wooden Toys
Wooden toy making and lacquerware are traditional Varanasi crafts. Artisans initially specialized in ivory carving, but after it was banned, they shifted to woodcarving.

Indic Literature
As one of the oldest cities in the world, Varanasi houses many bookstores with material related to Hinduism and religious ideology.

WHERE TO EAT

Shree Shivay Restaurant
Shree Shivay specializes in vegetarian thali, a selection of dishes served on a single platter. A traditional thali should include six flavors: sweet, salty, bitter, sour, spicy, and astringent. Did we mention it's unlimited? Come hungry!
S-1/118-6-M-1P Ground Floor, Shivpur, Varanasi / +91 99 3531 1449

Aum Cafe
A cozy cafe serving Ayurvedic and vegan dishes near Assi Ghat. (Ayurveda + Yum = Aum!) Save room for a slice of vegan cake with vegan whipped cream.
B1/201, Assi Rd, opp. Shri Ram Janki Math, Assi ghat, Shivala, Varanasi / +91 93 3536 1122

The Great Kabab Factory

Yes, it's a chain restaurant. Yes, it's in a hotel. But the veg and non-veg kebabs at The Great Kabab Factory are savory sticks of heaven.
Radisson Hotel, The Mall Cantonment, The Mall Road, Varanasi Cantt, Varanasi

Kaashi Chat Bhandar

The crowds say it all. Kasshi Chat Bhandar serves the best street food in the city, including our favorite aloo tikki with chickpea curry and topped with chutney.
D.37/49 Godowlia Road, Girja Ghar Chauraha, Badadev, Godowlia, Varanasi / +91 94 1561 8081

Canton Royale Restaurant

When you're not quite sure what sounds good, head to CRR. The extensive menu serves Indian, Mediterranean, Chinese, Mexican, and Continental cuisine. Good food and affordable prices.
S.20 / 51, Hotel Surya A-5, The Mall Rd, Cantt, Varanasi / +91 54 2250 8465

Dosa Cafe

Come for the South Indian food but stay for the chai. The peanut chutney is a favorite, as well as the chocolate banana dosa.
Maan Mandir D 15/49 Dashaswamedh, Varanasi / +91 79 8502 2907

WHERE TO DRINK

Because Varanasi is a pilgrimage destination, there are fewer spots to get your drink on. The bars and nightclubs will usually be inside or adjacent to a hotel.

Blue Lassi Shop

There are 80+ creamy flavors at this 75-year-old lassi shop with a

bright blue exterior. Be
prepared for a wait, both
due to crowds and the loving
preparation of the lassi.
*Near Vishwanath Temple,
Varanasi / +91 54 2240 1124*

Princep Bar

Established in honor of the
famous artist James Prinsep,
the colonial bar inside Taj
Ganges has an old-school vibe
and classic interior.
*Ground, Taj Ganges Nadesar
Palace, Varanasi /
+91 54 2666 0001*

Mangi Ferra Cafe

Order a beer and take a seat
under the mango tree at this
colorful pub in the Hotel
Surya Kaiser Palace.
*S-20/51A Hotel Surya Kaiser
Palace, The Mall Road, Varanasi / +91 88 5300 2353*

Varanasi Sadhu

LOCAL TOURS AND EXPERIENCES

Varanasi Heritage Walking Tour

Start early at 5 am for a walk through India's oldest city. The tour
starts from Assi Ghat and includes a sunrise boat ride on the Ganges.
https://cityonpedals.com/tours/varanasi-heritage-walking-tour

Varanasi Street Food Walking Tour

On this walk to impressive eateries in Varanasi, enjoy a special
Varanasi breakfast and try 8+ different local culinary treasures.
https://cityonpedals.com/tours/varanasi-street-food-walking-tour

Photography Walk

Learn about framing, composition, and lighting with a professional photographer who also teaches at the prestigious Banaras Hindu University.

https://www.roobaroowalks.com/walk/lucknow/

Death and Rebirth

One of our favorite walks that begins at a fertility temple and ends at the cremation grounds. Reserve the evening walk to observe the Aarti.

https://www.varanasiwalks.com/walks-boats

DAY TRIPS

Sarnath

Sarnath, where Buddha preached his first sermon after attaining enlightenment, is one of the four most important pilgrimage sites in the world. There is an archaeological museum, stupa complex, landscaped park, and remains of Buddhist monasteries. There are also contemporary Buddhist temples scattered around the town.

How to Reach: Hire a taxi, ride-share, or private vehicle for the 40-minute drive from Varanasi. Once at Sarnath, bicycle rentals are available to cruise around the park. Note: The museum is closed on Friday.

Ramnagar Fort

Built in the 18th century by Maharaja Balwant Singh, the red sandstone Mughal fort is located on the eastern bank of the Ganges River. The museum inside the fort showcases royal antique scripture, furniture, cars, and weapons. There is also a temple dedicated to Ved Vyasa, the author of *Mahabharata*.

How to Reach: Hop on a 30-minute boat ride from Assi Ghat.

Chandraprabha Wildlife Sanctuary

Named after the Chandraprabha River, the wildlife sanctuary is famous for blackbucks, chital, sambar, leopard, python, and 150+ species of birds. Developed in the 18th century as a hunting preserve for Varanasi's elite, the rare and rich vegetation in the dense forests have been a source of Ayurvedic medicine for centuries. Check out the majestic waterfalls and prehistoric cave paintings.

How to Reach: Hire a private car for the 2-hour journey from Varanasi.

Chunar Fort

Also known as Chandrakanta Chunargarh and Charandri, the fort is a famous Bollywood filming location. Dating back to 56 BC, its elevation above the Ganges River affords commanding panoramic views.

How to Reach: From Varanasi, you can take a local bus or hire a private car/taxi for the 32 km ride.

Bodh Gaya

At a driving distance of six hours from Varanasi, Bodh Gaya is obviously not a day trip. However, many travelers use Varanasi as a stopover en-route to the sacred town.

Bodh Gaya is where Siddhartha Gautama attained enlightenment, making it one of the most important Buddhist pilgrimage sites. During his travels to understand life, Siddhartha arrived in the Gaya district of Bihar. Here he sat under a large fig tree and, upon meditation, achieved enlightenment. This is also where he discovered the Noble eight-fold path, known as the Middle Path or Middle Way, which demonstrates a balanced life. Travelers and pilgrims visit the monastic rural town for meditation, studies, and the Mahabodhi Temple.

How to Reach: Hire a private car for the six-hour drive from Varanasi. There are also nonstop flights available from Delhi - Gaya.

GIVING BACK

KIRAN

As a ray of hope into lives, KIRAN aims to support and empower
differently abled youth from marginalized communities. Founded in
1990, the organization offers rehabilitation, education, and vocational
training so children can become fully integrated in Indian society.
https://kiranvillage.org

Ramaiya Charitable Foundation

Ramaiya works for the betterment of stray animals by providing
food, medical aid, and adoption services. They also educate the public
about animal cruelty cases and humane animal care.

LUCKNOW

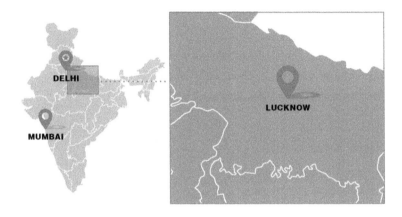

The City of Nawabs

With grand Islamic architecture and incredible cuisine, Lucknow is known for its *adab* and *tehzeeb* (manners and hospitality). The culture of Uttar Pradesh's capital is influenced by the refined and extravagant lifestyles of the Nawabs who ruled in the 18th and the 19th centuries. With a prominent art scene and bustling bazaars, Lucknow is a sleeper destination often overlooked by travelers - until now.

TRANSPORTATION HUBS

Lucknow is the capital of the northern Indian state of Uttar Pradesh.

Chaudhary Charan Singh International Airport (LKO)
Amausi, Lucknow

Domestic flights connect Lucknow to Delhi, Mumbai, Ahmedabad, Hyderabad, Bangalore, and Chennai.

Lucknow Charbagh NR Railway Station (LKO)
Railway Colony, Charbagh, Lucknow

Lucknow Junction Railway Station (LJN)
Preeti Nagar, Railway Colony, Charbagh
Daily trains connect Lucknow with most major Indian cities, including Delhi, Mumbai, Kolkata, Patna, and Chennai.

Alambagh Bus Terminal
Kanpur Road, Lucknow

AREAS TO AVOID

Overall, Lucknow is a safe destination for women travelers. However, avoid using public transportation after dark.

LOCAL FESTIVALS

Ramadan
With the history of Lucknow's ruling Nawabs, Ramadan/Ramazan is a significant festival. Ramadan is the 9th month of the Islamic calendar and a time of fasting, prayer, and reflection. During the daily fast from dawn until dusk, Muslims refrain from eating, drinking, smoking, or engaging in any sexual activity. It is also a time of spiritual discipline by practicing self restraint, performing community service, and studying the Quran.

The streets of the old city come alive in the evening when people break their fast. If you are in Lucknow during Ramadan, make time to attend prayers at Bara Imambara.

WHERE TO STAY

Backpackers Den
A clean and comfortable hostel with a garden and full American breakfast.
$ / 69, Avas Vikas Colony, The Mall Avenue, Lucknow /
+91 96 9527 2101

Lebua Lucknow
A sprawling traditional bungalow that reflects the Art Deco architecture from the early 1900's.
$$$ / https://lebua.com / +91 52 2223 8333

Taj Mahal Lucknow
A splash of luxury that captures the true essence of Lucknow through its architecture, decor, and hospitality.
$$$$ / www.tajhotels.com / +91 52 2671 1000

WHAT TO DO

Bara (Asfi) Imambara
Built in 1784, the Bara Imambara is an architectural marvel. An imambara is a place for religious gatherings during the month of Muharram. Inside is the largest vaulted hall in the world without any external support of wood, iron, or stone beams. With more than 1000 passages and hundreds of identical doorways, it takes a guide to navigate the maze without getting lost. The other side of the complex houses the Asfi mosque and a five-story baoli (stepwell).

Entry: INR 632
Hours: 6 am - 5 pm daily

Sadat Ali and Begum Tombs

Built on an emerald grassland are a pair of maqbarasi (tombs) of the 5th Nawab of Awadh, Sadat Ali Khan, and his wife, Khurshid Zadi. Both the tombs are fine examples of Indo-Islamic styles of architecture prominent in the early 19th century. It is easy to overlook the memorial among other heritage buildings in Lucknow, but the tombs exemplify the architecture of Khan's reign.

Entry: Free; Hiring a guide will cost approximately INR 40
Hours: 5 am - 8 pm daily

Rumi Darwaza

An imposing structure between the Bara Imambara and the Chota Imambara, Rumi Darwaza was built in 1784 and served as the entrance to the old Lucknow city. With an impressive height of 60 feet, the Rumi Darwaza is a visual delight during the day time and completely transforms during the night with lights illuminating the architectural marvel.

Entry: Free
Hours: 24/7

Hussainabad (Chota) Imambara

Hussainabad Imambara, also known as the Chota Imambara, stands to the west of Bara Imambara. The beautiful structure is known for its five arching doorways with verses from the holy Quran written in calligraphic Arabic script. Built on an elevated platform with a gilded dome surrounded by turrets and ornate minarets on each side, the entire complex is a striking sight. The stunning marble work, grand interiors, and sprawling gardens all add to the majestic charm of the Hussainabad Imambara.

Entry: INR 260
Hours: 6 am - 5 pm daily

Lucknow Residency (British Residency)

Resting on high ground to the south of the Gomti River are the ruins of the Lucknow Residency (British Residency). Spread over 33 acres, the residency was a city within a city. Originally built to house the British and the Europeans, the residency provided shelter and safety from invaders. During the siege of 1857, the residency was attacked continuously for five months. Some buildings were razed down to the ground while others suffered heavy damages. The residency and its ruins are a reflection of the past and each building in the complex has a story to tell.

Entry: INR 385
Hours: 10 am - 5 pm daily

La Martiniere

Designed and built by Claude Martin, La Martiniere (also known as Constantia) is 200 years old. A Frenchman who later joined the English and settled in Lucknow, Claude Martin, amassed immense wealth and built several buildings in Lucknow, the grandest of them all being Constantia. After his death, Martin's fortune was used to maintain three schools with the same name of La Martiniere in Lucknow, Calcutta, and Lyon (his birthplace).

Claude Martin may have been ignored by the history books but will remain alive in the hearts of the students who sing his praises. The buildings are a testament to his sincere intent and contribution to education in India and beyond.

Entry: Free
Hours: Since it is an operational school, it is advised to visit either in the morning or after school hours

Dilkusha

Built in the 18th century by the Nawab Saadat Ali Khan, Dilkusha Palace was the summer resort of the Nawabs. Much of it is in ruins, but one look at the structure will show the historical and the cultural significance of its time. The design bears a resemblance to a country house in England including perfectly manicured gardens.

Entry: INR 385
Hours: 8 am - 6 pm daily

WHERE TO SHOP

Hazratganj Market
Modeled after the Queen Street of London by the British, Hazratganj is a popular market for various handicrafts and other handmade products. Most of the shops sell high-quality products at fixed prices, so bargaining here is almost non-existent.

Hours: 1 oam - 9 pm/ Closed on Sundays
Location: Parivartan Chowk, Lalbagh

Chowk
Located in the old city, Chowk is one of the oldest markets in Lucknow. It is known for jewelry encrusted with semi-precious stones, precious stones, and antique products. The narrow bylanes with the fragrance of Attar and the Lucknowi cuisine is a treat for your senses. Various shops adorn the streets selling Chikankari clothes, traditional Indian clothes with Zardozi embroidery, handmade 'Nagra' footwear for men and women, and various handicrafts made from metal and silver. Chowk is a must visit to experience the old charm of Lucknow city and the famous Lucknowi kebabs.

Hours: 11 am - 10:30 pm / Closed on Thursdays
Location: Near Bara Imambara

Aminabad Market

Aminabad is also one of the oldest markets in Lucknow. Known as the street shopping hub, the market will spoil you with choices. You will find Chikankari clothes, elegant embroidered sarees, and stoles/wraps/dupattas with dazzling thread, beads, and zari work.

Hours: 11:30 am - 10:30 pm / Closed on Thursdays
Location: Mumtaz Market, Aminabad

Janpath Bazaar

Janpath comprises a number of small street shops and is quite popular among the city's youth. A great place to test your bargaining skills, Janpath offers a great variety of leather goods, chikankari clothes, and amazing deals on readymade garments at throwaway prices.

Hours: 9:00 am - 6:00 pm / Closed on Sundays
Location: Janpath Road, Lalbagh

WHAT TO SHOP FOR IN LUCKNOW

Chikankari

Chikan is one of the oldest traditional textile embroidery styles in Lucknow. The technique of creating delicate hand embroidery and thread work is called *Chikankari*. Traditionally, white cotton thread was used to hand embroider various fabrics like cotton, silk, muslin, organza, georgette, crepe and chiffon. Today, chikankari has evolved to many artistic forms, but the machine-made embroidery is no match to the manual stitching.

Zardozi

Another famous textile embroidery from Lucknow is Zardozi. Zardozi comes from two persian words: *Zar* meaning 'gold' and *dozi* meaning 'sewing'. In literal terms, it is hand embroidery using gold threads. Zardozi designs are often created with gold and silver threads on heavy fabrics such as velvet, silks, and satin.

Ittar/Attar

Ittar (Attar) are essential oils derived from botanical sources like flowers, leaves, aromatic herbs, sandalwood, musk, and other spices. The oil-based perfumes are locally made in Lucknow and can be mixed to make a custom fragrance. The fine perfumes are packaged in beautiful bottles of cut glass work.

WHERE TO EAT

Tunday Kababi

A local favorite, Tunday Kababi is best known for its Tunde Ke Kabab (Buffalo meat Kebabs) prepared with 160 spices! With a rich blend of flavors and melt in your mouth kebabs, this iconic joint is a must visit in Lucknow for a traditional gastronomic affair.

168/6, Old Nazirabad Rd, Mohan Market, Khayali Ganj, Aminabad

Rahim's

The 125-year-old restaurant in the old city is known for its Nalla Nihari. Nihari is a slow cooked meat in thick flavorful gravy served with Kulcha, a soft leavened flatbread. Rahim's is a Lucknow institution and bustling with people even early in the morning.

29 Phool Wali Gali, Akbari Gate, Chowk

Royal Cafe

Chaat (street food) has its origins in Uttar Pradesh. The deep fried potato cutlets/patties doused with generous amounts of spices and chutney are a must try in Lucknow. There are many eateries in the bylanes of the city, but the chef at Royal Cafe has become a social media sensation with his unique snack baskets.

9/7 opposite Sahara Ganj Mall, Shahnajaf Road, Hazratganj

Lucknow Food

Chanakya
A kulfi heaven! Kulfi is a traditional Indian ice cream that is denser and creamier than most western variations. Order the original flavor with a rich blend of milk, cream, dry fruits, and saffron.
Behind KD Singh Babu Stadium, Subhash Chandra Bose Crossing

WHERE TO DRINK

Underdogs Sports Bar and Grill
With live music and an international food menu, Underdogs is a preferred spot for young millennials.
4 City Mall, Vipul Khand 4, Gomti Nagar

Münick Bistro & bar

With the decor inspired from the city of Munich, the bar has an exhaustive Indian and continental menu.

27 & 31, Rohtas Presidential Arcade, Vibhuti Khand, Gomti Nagar

The Pebbles Bistro and Bar

A European inspired bistro with casual outdoor garden seating located in the heart of the city.

1/208A In front of Jaipuria School, Vineet Khand, Gomti Nagar

Molecule Air Bar

A local favorite, Molecule features a rooftop bar with live music and an eccentric food menu.

RiverSide Mall, Vipin Khand, Gomti Nagar

UP'S Bar

A stylish lounge serving premium beverages and creative cocktails, UP'S was the first bar to introduce international brands of draft beers in Lucknow.

Bar First Floor, Hyatt Regency

Ayodhya

LOCAL TOURS AND EXPERIENCES

Lucknow Colors
Walk through the bustling bazaars and witness the contrasts between the old and new neighborhoods of Lucknow.

https://www.indiacitywalks.com/package/lucknow-colors/

DAY TRIPS

Ayodhya
As the birthplace of Lord Rama, Ayodhya is regarded as one of the seven sacred cities in India. It is not just the center of Hindu pilgrimage but also features several Jain temples, ghats, and palaces. Don't miss the A Ram Janmabhoomi Temple.

Entry: Free
Hours: Summer hours are 7:30 am - 11:30 am and 4:30 pm - 9 pm; winter hours are 7 am - 11 am and 4 pm - 9 pm

How to Reach: Direct trains are available from Lucknow or you can hire a private car for the 2-hour journey

Dewa Sharif Sufi Sojourn
Dewa Sharif, the mausoleum of the saint Waris Ali Shah, represents and promotes an architectural harmony of Hindu and Iranian styles. You can pay your respects by offering Chadar-Posh, a grave covering cloth with flowers, and enjoy the soulful sufi music by devotional singers known as Qawals.

Entry: Free
Hours: 5:30 am - 9 pm daily

How to Reach: Hire a taxi or private car for the one-hour journey from Lucknow

GIVING BACK

SEWA (Self Employed Women's Association)

SEWA was founded by Ms. Runa Banerjee, a highly decorated Indian social worker. Her involvement with the craftswomen of Lucknow won her several accolades, including the highest civilian honor of 'Padam Shri'. A study conducted by UNICEF and Literacy House revealed that the women and children in the Chikankari industry were exploited and inadequately paid for their art. SEWA removes the middlemen and establishes a sustainable and viable production system with direct exposure to the market.

The chikankari store run by SEWA Lucknow is located in Halwasiya Market, near Habibullah Estate. You can also visit their factory outlet in Brahm Nagar.

Location: 11 A.C. Market, Halwasiya, Hazratganj AND 474 /1KA / 4 Brahm Nagar, Sitapur Road

http://www.sewalucknow.org/home.php

Sheroes Hangout

Sheroes Hangout is run and managed by survivors of acid attacks, a gender-related violence in India. The entrepreneurial project started to help the survivors become financially independent through education, training, and employment. The women can then support their families and use their collective voice to advocate for societal change. Sheroes also features a boutique apparel and handicraft store with items made by acid attack survivors. There are currently two locations - Agra and Lucknow.

Location: Opposite Dr. B R Ambedkar Park, Vipin Khand, Gomti Nagar

https://www.facebook.com/SheRoesLKO/

AGRA

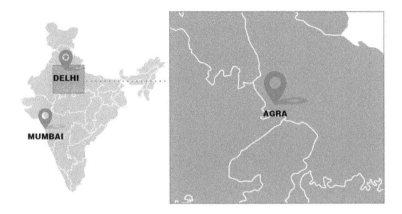

The City of Love

Welcome to Agra, the home of the majestic Taj Mahal. Once the capital of the Mughal Empire, Agra was a hub for education, commerce, and the arts. Beyond the Taj, there are spectacular tombs, wildlife sanctuaries, and vibrant markets. The city is also known for Muhglai cuisine and some of the best street eats in North India.

TRANSPORTATION HUBS

Agra is located in the state of Uttar Pradesh, 230 km southeast of Delhi.

Agra Airport (AGR)
59/10, VIP Road, Agra

The Agra airport is a military airbase and public airport. Domestic commercial flights are limited.

Agra Cantt Railway Station (AGC)
Siroli Rd, Agra Cantt, Idgah Colony, Dhanauli

Agra Fort Railway Station (AF)
Bijli Ghar, Near Agra Fort Crossing, Pipal Mandi, Mantola, Agra

Located near the Sadar Bazaar, Agra Cantonment (AGC) is the primary railway station.

The Gatimaan Express, a semi high-speed express train, departs from Delhi at 8:10 am and arrives in Agra at 9:50 am, shortening a four-hour drive to only 100 minutes by train. The return trip departs Agra at 17:50 and arrives in Delhi at 19:30. Gatimaan Express runs six days a week, except Friday, in both directions.

The Shatabdi Express departs New Delhi Railway Station (NDLS) at 6 am daily, arriving in Agra Cantt (AGC) at 7:50 am. The return train departs Agra at 21:20, arriving in Delhi at 23:50.

Skip the train if you are traveling in December/January as the heavy fog can often delay the rail operations.

Agra ISBT Bus Station
Near Gurudwara, Transport Colony, Transport Nagar, Agra

Agra is well connected by road to Delhi, Varanasi, Jaipur, Lucknow, and other cities in North India. It takes approximately four hours one-way from Delhi - Agra.

AREAS TO AVOID

Despite Agra being the most visited city in India, we don't recommend venturing out late at night. Many restaurants and bars are located inside hotels so you can stay close to your property in the evening hours.

Definitely avoid the tap water in Agra. It's not the cleanest city and has poor water filtration systems. When we do hear of clients or travelers becoming ill, it's often in Agra. Even at hotels, don't brush your teeth with tap water and be cautious in the shower.

LOCAL FESTIVALS

Taj Mahotsav

As the most popular festival in Agra, Taj Mahotsav promotes the arts and crafts of Uttar Pradesh. Organized annually in February, the 10-day event is held at Shilpgram, an open-air crafts village near the Taj Mahal. The Mahotsav kicks off with a grand procession of elephants, camels, folk artists, and traditional drummers. On display are regional goods and handicrafts, including Chikankari from Lucknow, handmade carpets from Badohi, wood carvings from Saharanpur, silk from Varanasi, and blue pottery from Khurja.

Bateshwar Fair

Located 70 km from Agra, the town of Bateshwar is named after the presiding deity, Bateshwar Mahadev. With 108 temples dedicated to several Hindu gods and goddesses, Bateshwar has a strong spiritual resonance. The annual fair, dedicated to Lord Shiva, is organized annually in October/November. Thousands of devotees attend the cattle fair, trade livestock, and take a dip in the holy waters of River Yamuna.

Ram Barat

Organized before Dussehra, Ram Barat is the special marriage procession of Lord Ram. It is a part of Ramleela, which ends on the day of Dussehra when Ravana is killed. The idol of Lord Ram is displayed on a special chariot adorned with silver leaves. The procession commences at a temple, traversing through the city lanes before arriving at a lavishly decorated venue. (Interestingly, the roles of female characters are played by local teenage boys.) Ram Barat is one of North India's largest Janakpuri and thousands of people attend the royal wedding.

Agra Itimad

WHERE TO STAY

Joey's Hostel
A backpackers delight with free breakfast, dormitories, and private rooms near the Taj Mahal.
$ / www.joeyshostel.com/agra.html / +91 98 1864 2824

Coral Court
A boutique homestay with a large terrace for sunrise yoga or sundowners.
$$ / https://coralcourthomestay.com/ +91 75 0534 0604

Ekaa Villa
A modern property with 13 beautifully curated rooms and farm-to-table cuisine.
$$ / www.ekaahotels.com / +91 74 5500 44 77

ITC Mughal
An upmarket hotel with landscaped gardens and several eateries.
$$$ / www.itchotels.com/in/en/itcmughal-agra / +91 56 2402 1700

Oberoi Amarvilas
A luxury hotel offering unobstructed Taj Mahal views from every room.
$$$$ / www.oberoihotels.com / +91 56 2223 1515

WHAT TO DO

Taj Mahal

As a Wonder of the World, the Taj Mahal is often considered the iconic image of India. The ivory-white marble mausoleum was built in the 17th century by the Mughal Emperor Shah Jahan for his beloved wife, Mumtaz Mahal. Located on the banks of the Yamuna River, the Taj took over 22 years and 20,000 men to build. The 42-acre garden complex also houses a mosque and a small guest house. The Taj is often regarded as the best example of Mughal architecture and a symbol of India's rich history. Note: The Taj Mahal is closed every Friday.

Entry: INR 1300 / The main mausoleum costs an additional INR 200
Hours: On normal operating days, the complex opens 30 minutes before sunrise and closes 30 minutes after sunset

Agra Fort

With a rich, historical background, the Agra Fort marks its place as the most-visited site after the Taj. It may be popular, but it is magnificent. Built as a military fort by Emperor Akbar between 1565 and 1573, it was repurposed as a palace by his grandson Shah Jahan, who spent his last years detained as a political prisoner by his own son who took over the throne. Although several of the buildings inside the fort have been destroyed, some mosques, public and private audience halls, palaces, towers, and courtyards still remain as testimony of the flourished past.

Entry: INR 600
Hours: Sunrise to sunset

The Tomb's

Before the Taj Mahal was built, Agra boasted of two beautiful tombs – the imposing red tomb of Emperor Akbar (which he himself commissioned and laid out) and the dainty white tomb of Itmad-ud-daulah (commissioned by his daughter, Empress Noor Jehan).

Akbar's Tomb was built in the early 17th century by Akbar's son, Jahangir. The mausoleum is famous for its white marble walls that are encrusted with semi-precious stones and adorned with fine inlays of geometric patterns and flowers. The Tomb also houses the mortal remains of Emperor Akbar.

Itmad-ud-daula was the first to be made of white marble (instead of the red sandstone typical of Mughal architecture) and is often referred to as "Baby Taj." It features some of the most beautiful inlay work in all of Agra and is the first example of the outstanding pietra dura. It was this new style that was later manifested in the Taj Mahal.

Entry: INR 310 for both Itmad-ud-daulah and Akbar's Tomb
Hours: Sunrise to Sunset

Mehtab Bagh
Did you know that the best place to view the Taj Mahal is not actually inside the complex? According to Shah Jahan, the Taj was best viewed from across the Yamuna River in the flood plains. Mehtab Bagh or the "Moonlit Garden" was created for the emperor to view his creation at night with an octagonal pool and the river reflecting the grandeur of Taj. The garden is relatively less crowded, so it offers you the best chance to take your photos/ portraits without people photo bombing. For the best light, visit at sunset.

Entry: INR 300
Hours: 6 am - 6 pm daily

Colonial Agra
Walk through the private bungalows in the cantonment area built in the early 19th century, still well maintained and featuring churches and cathedrals. Visit the post office, an art deco building constructed in 1905 with grand details reflecting the importance of this method

of communication to the community. John Hessing's tomb, known locally as the Red Taj Mahal, was commissioned by Ann Hessing in the memory of her beloved husband. You can also explore the telegraph office, St. George Cathedral, St. John's college and St. Mary's church.

GGG TIPS FOR VISITING THE TAJ MAHAL

Smog and Fog

The best time to explore North India is from October to March when the days are pleasant and the nights are cool. December and January can be foggy, so sunrise and morning viewings of the Taj Mahal may be obstructed. Additionally, the smog that envelopes Delhi, Agra, and surrounding areas in November (due to stubble burning) may also affect viewings at any time of day. It is difficult to predict, but be aware of these seasonal interferences. Generally speaking, most foreign tourists pack the Taj Mahal from December - March, but the popular monument remains busy all year.

Beware of the Local "Guides"

There are local touts who will approach foreigners - especially women - to avail of their guiding services. Use caution, as they are not licensed by the government, have limited English comprehension, and offer incorrect information. Many will not quote the guiding fees up front, leading to haggling and disappointment after the tour. Instead, hire a guide in advance through a reputable company.

When to Visit

Timing is everything when it comes to a Taj Mahal visit, and this is one spot where the early bird definitely gets the worm. Sunrise is usually the best time to arrive, with less crowds and soft light for photos (provided there isn't any smog, which the midday sun sometimes burns off). Sunset is another good option for the same reasons, although it is still busier compared to sunrise. Avoid morning visits in the months of December and January due to dense fog.

Remember, the Taj Mahal is closed every Friday! The monument is popular with both Indians and foreigners, so try not to become overwhelmed by the crowds, especially on weekends.

What to Wear

There is no enforced dress code by law, but rules of modesty do apply. It's recommended that women who visit the Taj Mahal cover their knees. If you're worried about the heat, maxi skirts, loose fitting dresses, or floaty linen trousers are a great option. Men may find it comfortable to dress to the weather but shirts or t-shirts with sleeves (rather than tank tops) and trousers or long shorts are a smarter choice. Some visitors stage formal photo shoots inside the complex, complete with traditional clothing and accessories.

At the entrance, all visitors receive a pair of shoe covers. You'll need to wear them if you plan on heading up to the Taj, to protect the ivory marble.

Leave it Behind

There is a security check before entering the monument with separate lines for men and women. Large bags and day packs are not permitted. Lines can become long during the security check, so the smaller the bag, the better. Prohibited items include tobacco products, lighters, knives or weapons, idols (including stuffed animals), camera tripods, food/snacks, and electrical items (including phone chargers, batteries, and headphones).

Eating, smoking, or group activities (including yoga or meditation) are not allowed inside the monument.

Entrance Fee Inclusions

The entrance fee for a foreigner

is currently INR 1300 and free for children below 15 years. The main mausoleum costs an additional INR 200. The foreigner entry fee includes shoe covers, a water bottle, a tourist map, and battery bus and golf cart services. You may also purchase the tickets directly from the ASI Website. It is much more time efficient and convenient than buying the ticket at the monument. (Note: You will still need to carry your passport to the point of entry).

Foreigners can also enter the complex ahead of Indian ticket holders. Shoe racks are available just below the main mausoleum free of cost. Remember, the entry ticket is only valid for three hours. If the time is exceeded, you are required to repay the fees equivalent to INR 600.

Choose the Gate

To help combat pollution, vehicles are not allowed within 500 meters of the Taj Mahal. You can enter the complex from the East and West gates only. The South gate is for exit only.

We suggest the East gate as the West gate is very congested. Once you park near the East gate, hop on a battery bus or golf cart to reach the entrance.

Moonlight Viewing

The Taj Mahal is open for night viewing every full moon and two days before and after the full moon. The experience can only be booked one day prior to the full moon date and the weather plays a significant role in the visibility of the monument. Visitors are not allowed on the grounds and can only view the Taj from a distance of 500 meters.

A total of 400 tourists are allowed inside the Taj complex at one time. These 400 are further categorized in eight batches with 50 members each. The night visit duration is 30 minutes between 8:30 pm and 12:30 am. Please note the moonlight viewing is not available on Friday or during the holy month of Ramadan.

WHERE TO SHOP

Sadar Bazaar

Being located near the Agra Cantt railway station makes Sadar Bazaar a busy yet convenient market. Although frequented by the locals for housewares and pethas (sweets), vendors also sell leather goods, handicrafts, and costume jewelry.

Hours: 11:30 am - 6 pm daily; Closed on Sundays
Location: Near Agra Cantt railway station, Agra

Kinari Bazaar

Located near the Taj Mahal, Kinari is Agra's largest wholesale market with fountains, sandstone architecture, and a central courtyard. The colorful (and crowded!) lanes wind around the 17th-century Jama Masjid mosque. The bazaar is a melting pot of spices, garments, handicrafts, and zardozi embroidery.

Hours: 11 am - 9 pm daily; Closed on Mondays
Location: Hing ki Mandi, Mantola, Agra

The Emporiums

Agra sells high quality and reasonably priced marble inlay, jewels, gold, and rugs. Although some emporiums are overpriced and target foreigners, there are also emporiums that not only sell upmarket goods but also ethically support the artisans. Also, unlike markets and bazaars, emporiums generally offer a product guarantee and there is recourse for returns and exchanges. Please refer to the Shopping section of GGG for more info on government vs. private emporiums. We recommend:

Marble Art Palace
18A/32, Fatehabad Road, Agra / www.marbleartpalace.in

U.P. Handicraft Palace / U.P. Crafts Palace
Fatehabad Road, Agra / www.uphandicraftpalace.com

WHAT TO SHOP FOR IN AGRA

Marble Inlay

Also called parchin kari or pietra dura, marble inlay is commonly found on Mughal monuments across North India. The skilled process involves cutting and engraving a design on a marble slab that is filled with precious and semi-precious stones. You will find marble inlay table tops, vases, coasters, statues, and plates. (I still have a small marble inlay elephant I purchased during my very first visit to Agra in 2005!)

Marble Inlay

Zardozi Embroidery

Originating in Persia, Zardozi is a heavy and elaborate metal embroidery. Once used exclusively to embellish the attire of Indian royalty, Zardozi has been prevalent in India since the Mugal Empire.

Jewelry

Agra is a popular destination for gold, jewels, and precious/semi-precious stones. You will find good deals on high quality diamonds, rubies, and sapphires, as well as antique and silver jewelry.

Carpets

Like Zardozi, Agra carpets and rugs also originated in Persia and were once reserved for Mughal emperors. They are now considered among the highest quality international home decor.

Leather Goods

Agra is considered "The Leather Market" of India. You will find high-quality shoes, jackets, belts, and bags that rival Italian durability.

WHERE TO EAT

The Salt Cafe
Reserve a table on the Santorini-themed rooftop terrace with grand views of the Taj Mahal.
1C, 3rd Floor, Fatehabad Rd, near Taj Mahal, Tajganj / +91 99 1097 8774 / www.thesaltcafe.com/agra

Café TC Agra
Good food and good vibes welcome you to Cafe TC (Turquoise Cottage). The cozy spot also features live music and DJ sets.
2nd floor, 76, Fatehabad Rd, Near Amar Hotel, Vibhav Nagar, Tajganj, Agra / +91 80 0680 7333

Sugar N Thyme
A relaxed bakery with starters, sandwiches, and 15+ shakes and smoothies.
1374-1375, Agra-Fatehabad Road, Near ITC Moghal Hotel Tajganj, Dinesh Nagar

Bamboo Café
Bamboo Cafe is one of those spots you are happy to support. Family owned, super friendly service, and delicious food. Try the Indian breakfast!
Shilpgram Rd, Taj Nagari Phase 1, Telipara, Agra / +91 81 7199 1693

Chainess
Pop by this local favorite for a masala chai, samosa bun, or paneer sandwich.
Shop G-11, 12 & 13, Block 34/2, Opposite LIC Building, Civil Lines, Agra / +91 56 2430 2727

WHERE TO DRINK

Molecule Air Bar
Head to the modern rooftop terrace for a curated cocktail and innovative menu.
E-4, Fatehabad Rd, Taj Nagri Phase 2, Tajganj, Agra / +91 90 6847 7477

The Palm Burj
A chill rooftop spot to get your drink on.
6, The Mall Rd, Agra Cantt, Rakabganj, Agra / +91 75 3588 8888

Beep Uncensored
A gastropub with indoor/outdoor seating and a fully stocked bar.
Fatehabad Road U.P.Handicrafts Complex, Agra / +91 74 6691 8000

Lord of the Drinks
A themed restaurant and bar with gold, glitz, and extensive drink menu.
5th Floor, E-4, Sector - E, Taj Nagri Phase 2, Agra / +91 95 2088 9311

LOCAL TOURS AND EXPERIENCES

Agra Heritage Walking Tour
A leisurely, curated walking tour that includes five religious sites, the old city, and breakfast!
https://cityonpedals.com/tours/agra-heritage-walking-tour

Agra Street Food Walking Tour
Experience the local flavors of Agra with chaats, curry, and world-famous Petha (sweets).
https://cityonpedals.com/tours/agra-street-food-tour

Agra Beat

Explore the unexplored with several specialized tours, including artistry, photography, cycling, and street eats.

https://agrabeat.com/ / +91 98 9705 5383 / info@agrabeat.com

DAY TRIPS

Vrindavan and Mathura

En-route from Delhi to Agra are the religious sister towns of Vrindavan and Mathura. Rediscovered in the 16th century, Vrindavan is considered the center of Krishna worship. It is also known as the "City of Widows" for the number of women who settled here after losing their husbands. (Historically, if a woman was widowed, she was exiled from the family and left on her own.) Several homes and organizations were established to offer resources, housing, and professional training.

Mathura is believed to be the birthplace of Krishna and therefore one of the seven cities considered holy by Hindus (Sapta Puri). It was also an important center of commerce and trade. Located on the Yamuna River, there are 25 ghats or bathing steps and several prominent temple complexes dedicated to Krishna.

How to Reach: Hire a private car or taxi from Agra for the two-hour journey on the Agra-Delhi National Highway

National Chambal Sanctuary

Located just 80 km from Agra is Chambal, a small town on the banks
of Chambal River. Chambal Valley features the National Bird and
Wildlife Sanctuary, a habitat to unusual and endangered species
including 340 species of birds which migrate from different parts
of the world during winter. Also check out the small villages and
Bateshwar temples that dot the riverbank.

How to Reach: Hire a private car or taxi for the 90 minute trip from
Agra; reserve the vehicle for the entire day since transportation is
difficult to find in Chambal

Fatehpur Sikri

A perfectly preserved red sandstone city, Fatehpur Sikri is an ideal
spot to capture insta-worthy shots. It was founded in 1571 by Emperor
Akbar as the capital of the Mughal Empire, only to be deserted 40
years later. Fatehpur Sikri was once a popular attraction on every
itinerary to Agra, but recent changes have made it less appealing.

Private vehicles are no longer allowed at the entrance and all visitors must take a government bus from the parking lot. The bus only leaves when full, resulting in long wait times and standing room only. If you do visit, skip the guide and explore independently.

Hours: Sunrise to Sunset daily; The museum is open daily from 9 am - 5 pm and closed on Sundays
Entry: INR 610
How to Reach: Hire a taxi, private car, or rideshare from Agra for the 45-minute journey. You can also catch a local bus from the Idgah bus stand in Agra

Keoladeo Wildlife Sanctuary
Formerly known as Bharatpur Bird Sanctuary, Keoladeo is a renowned avian sanctuary that hosts resident and migratory birds. Once a royal game reserve, the World Heritage Site is considered one of the richest birding areas in the world.

How to Reach: Hire a taxi or private car from Agra for the one-hour drive

GIVING BACK

Wildlife SOS Agra Bear Rescue Center
As one of the largest bear rescue centers in the world, Wildlife SOS has been working towards ending the brutal practice of dancing bears. The organization has rescued over 600 bears, mainly from tribal communities who have been harming the cubs to entertain the public and make a living.

https://wildlifesos.org/get-involved/volunteer-with-us/

Sheroes Hangout
Step off the Agra tourist track and visit a humble café only a block away from Taj Mahal. Sheroes Hangout is run and managed

by survivors of acid attacks, a gender-related violence in India. The entrepreneurial project started to help the survivors become financially independent through education, training, and employment. The women can then support their families and use their collective voice to advocate for societal change. Sheroes also features a boutique apparel and handicraft store with items made by acid attack survivors.

Behind Go Stops Hostel, Taj Nagari Phase 1, R.K. Puram Phase-2, Tajganj, Agra / +91 99 5806 6951

Sheroes Hangout

JAIPUR

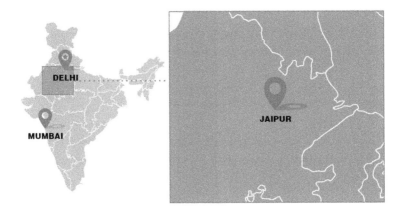

The Pink City of Rajasthan

Jaipur, Rajasthan's capital, is a fusion of history and mystery; a quintessential and dazzling representation of India in all her glory. Founded by the great astronomer and warrior Maharaja Jai Singh II, Jaipur was India's first planned city. It is fondly called the "Pink City" as the rose-hued buildings and avenues were once painted to welcome foreign guests. Historically a center of trade and commerce, Jaipur proudly maintains its reputation as one of the best shopping destinations in India.

TRANSPORTATION HUBS

Jaipur is located in the state of Rajasthan. The city joins Agra and Delhi on the popular "Golden Triangle" tourism circuit.

Jaipur International Airport (JAI)
Airport Rd, Sanganer, Jaipur, Rajasthan
www.jaipurairport.com

As the capital of Rajasthan, Jaipur services domestic and international flights from across India and beyond. JAI was also awarded the "World's Best Airport" for its passenger size. From the airport, hire a taxi or rideshare to reach your destination.

Jaipur Junction Railway Station (JP)
302006, Railway, Station Rd, Gopalbari, Jaipur

There are three train stations in Jaipur: Durgapura, Gandhinagar Jaipur, and Jaipur Junction, with Jaipur Junction being the primary location.

Daily trains connect Jaipur both regionally in Rajasthan and to most major Indian cities. As part of the Golden Triangle, Jaipur also has multiple connections daily to both Delhi and Agra. Check the rail schedules to see what classes are available on the respective lines.

Sindhi Camp Bus Stand
Kanti Nagar, Sindhi Camp, Jaipur

AREAS TO AVOID

Overall, Jaipur is a relatively safe destination for women. We do recommend caution when venturing out after dark - avoid narrow alleys and dim streets. Theft is common at crowded markets so keep a watch on personal belongings. There is a higher concentration of petty crime and harassment in Raja Park, Hasanpura, and Ramganj.

LOCAL FESTIVALS

Jaipur Literature Festival

Founded in 2006, the Jaipur Literature Festival is the world's largest free literary festival. The annual event brings together a diverse panel of the world's greatest writers, thinkers, humanitarians, politicians, business leaders, athletes, and entertainers to express and engage in thoughtful debate and dialogue. The festival is held in January at the Diggi Palace Hotel.
www.jaipurliteraturefestival.org

Elephant Festival

Celebrated on Holi, the Elephant Festival is a celebration of India's pachyderms. According to Rajasthani traditions, elephants are a symbol of royalty. The festival launches with a grand procession of decorated elephants, horses, camels, and folk dancers. There is also elephant racing, an elephant polo tournament, and games between elephants and their mahouts. Animal activists have been fighting for years to end the festival and its unethical treatment of the domesticated elephants.

Gangaur Festival

As one of the most prominent Rajasthani festivals, Gangaur celebrates spring, marriage, fidelity, and fertility. The 16-day festival commences the day after Holi and concludes with a procession of the deities. Unmarried women worship the Goddess Parvati for a husband, while married women pray for a long marriage and their partner's good health. Devotees fast, apply mehendi, dress auspiciously, and distribute *ghewar* (a sweet dish) to friends and family.

Teej

Dedicated to the Hindu goddesses Shiva and Parvati, Teej is celebrated at the beginning of monsoon season in July and August. Swings are hung from trees and decorated with flowers as married women pray for a long and happy union.

Kite Festival

The Jaipur Kite Festival is observed on January 14th, the day of Makar Sankranti or Uttarayan. It marks the auspicious transition from Sagittarius to Capricron in the sidereal zodiac. Locals take a pilgrimage to nearby Gatalji, share sugary delights, and fill the sky with colorful kites.

WHERE TO STAY

Jaipur Janta Hostel

A large bungalow converted to a delightful hostel with dorm rooms and a large garden.
$ / www.jaipurjantarhostel.com / +91 98 2904 0897

Zostel Jaipur

A classy backpacker hostel in a prime location.
$ / www.zostel.com / +91 22 4896 2267

Moustache Jaipur
A youth hostel with a rooftop terrace and plunge pool.
$ / www.moustacheescapes.com / +91 89 2910 0705

Jaipur Haveli B&B
A beautifully restored 200-year-old haveli with eight private rooms.
$$ / www.jaipurhaveli.com / +91 98 2901 8833

Shahpura House
An early 19th century palace located in a quiet residential neighborhood.
$$ / www.shapura.com / +91 14 1408 9100

Dera Mandawa
An all-suite boutique heritage hotel owned by descendants of a royal family.
$$$ / www.deramandawa.com / +91 14 1403 7377

Khas Bagh
A boutique farm retreat tucked away in the Aravalli Hills.
$$$ / www.khasbagh.com / +91 98 2906 2392

Tree of Life Resort and Spa
A wellness retreat with 13 luxury villas offering yoga, meditation, and therapies.
$$$ / www.treeofliferesorts.com / +91 90 1524 2000

Dera Amer Wilderness Camp
A glamping retreat with resident elephants, village walks, and bird watching.
$$ / www.deraamer.com / +91 90 0151 2512

Samode Haveli
A 225-year-old mansion that is still occupied by the royal descendants
$$$ / https://www.samode.com/samodehaveli / +91 14 1263 2407

Royal Heritage Haveli

A royal abode built in the 18th century by His Highness, Madho Singh Ji of Jaipur.

$$$ / www.royalheritagehaveli.com / +91 99 8331 7271

RAAS Rajmahal Palace

A fusion of contemporary and traditional at this exquisite heritage hotel.

$$$$ / www.raashotels.com /

WHAT TO DO

Amber Fort (Amer Fort)

With magnificent palaces and mirrored mosaics, Amber Fort is the principal tourist attraction of Jaipur. Perfectly picturesque, the 16th century hillside residence boasts grand pavilions and embossed silver doors that open to flourishing gardens and courtyards. Although Amber's main construction started in 1592 by Maharaja Man Singh, successive rulers added to the fortress during their respective reigns. Overlooking Maota Lake, the complex is connected by a subterranean passage to Jaigarh Fort.

Note: Visitors may ascend the fort by elephant or jeep. We do recommend reserving the jeep, as the elephants are often abused and overworked.

Entry: INR 550; elephant and jeep ride avail a supplement
Hours: 8 am - 7 pm daily

City Palace

The stunning City Palace was built in the late 1720's by Maharaja Sawai Jai Singh II. Located in the center of Old Jaipur, the palace is an amalgamation of three different styles - Rajput, Mughal, and

A woman at Amber Fort

European. The entire complex is structured in 'Grid Style' with four gates to enter and exit. The museum features antiques and belongings of the royal family and the royal residential area is accessible to the general public for an additional fee. Inside are smaller palaces, lush green gardens, courtyards, and open terraces.

Entry: INR 700
Hours: 9:30 am - 17:00 daily

Hawa Mahal (Palace of the Winds)
Constructed in red and pink sandstone, the 5-story Hawa Mahal is an iconic image of Jaipur. The original lattice design served two purposes: allow cool air to pass through the 953 windows, and allow female royalty to observe festivals and daily life without being seen by the public. The palace is an extension of a larger complex and also features an archaeological museum. It is a popular spot for photo-ops so be prepared to fight the crowds.

Entry: INR 200
Hours: 9 am - 5 pm daily

Elefantastic

Spend quality time with the elephants at a no-ride sanctuary that
provides a critical foundation for breaking the cycle of elephant
tourism. Guests can spend time feeding, bathing, and interacting
with the rescued and rehabilitated elephants. The founder, Rahul,
also supports the welfare and education of the caretakers and their
families through the human-elephant interaction program.
www.elefantastic.in

Nahargarh Fort

Perched on the edge of the Aravalli Hills, Nahargarh Fort was built as
a defense unit for Jaipur. Construction began in 1734 as a royal retreat
and the complex features stunning views of the city. Plan your visit
at sunset and then watch the sky twinkle with stars above the Jaipur
skyline.

Entry: INR 200
Hours: 10 am - 10 pm daily (The entry gate closes at 5 pm)

Jai Singh Observatory (Jantar Mantar)

The solar observatory built in the 18th century includes 20+ main fixed instruments. Designed for the observation of astronomical positions with the naked eye, they embody several architectural and instrumental innovations. Jantar Mantar is the most significant, most comprehensive, and the best preserved of India's historic observatories. It is an expression of the astronomical skills and cosmological concepts of the court of a scholarly prince at the end of the Mughal period.

Entry: INR 200
Hours: 9 am - 4:30 pm daily

Albert Hall Museum

Completed in 1887, Albert Hall is the oldest museum in Rajasthan. Historically a center of spreading knowledge to artisans, the museum now houses exhibits from all over the world. The collections include coins from the Gupta and Mughal periods, paintings, carpets, and metal sculptures. Visitors also flock to view the main attraction, an Egyptian mummy.

Entry: INR 300
Hours: 9 am - 6 pm daily

Panna Meena ka Kund

Tucked away behind Amber Fort is Panna Meena ka Kund. From one side you can view the massive Jaigarh Fort; from the other, a forest reserve. The site is well preserved with symmetrical stairs on all four sides and a small room that was once used for religious ceremonies before festivals, weddings, and other important occasions. Although the stepwell is free, it's not uncommon for security guards to approach visitors asking for an entrance fee. If you are not with a guide, politely decline and just walk away. The Panna Meena ka Kund beautifully depicts the architectural legacy of Rajasthan. Bonus: the zig-zag stairs make for spectacular photos.

Entry: Free
Hours: Sunrise - Sunset

WHERE TO SHOP

Johri Bazaar (Johari Bazaar)

Located near Hawa Mahal, Johri is the best market for buying jewelry and gemstones. You will find precious and semi-precious stones, as well as traditional Thews and Kundan Rajasthani jewelry. With orange and pink exteriors, the shops also feature artisans creating original pieces at their workstations.

Hours: 11 am - 10 pm daily
Location: Johri Bazaar, Jaipur

Nehru Bazaar

You can find clothes and accessories at many markets in the city, but head to Nehru Bazaar for traditional *jutis*. The colorful shoes line the streets, though women with a larger shoe size may find it challenging to score a pair that fits.

Hours: 11 am - 8 pm; Closed on Sunday
Location: Film Colony, Jaipur

Bapu Bazaar

Be prepared to bargain at this popular market in the Old City. The one-stop shopping destination sells handicrafts, bags, ready-to-wear garments, and other local goods.

Hours: 11 am - 8 pm; Closed on Sundays
Location: Old City, between Sanganer Gate and the New Gate of the Pink City

Chandpole Bazaar

Almost three-centuries old, Chandpole is the place to buy handlooms, marble sculptures, and wooden handicrafts. The pink symmetrical buildings also add a splash of color to the creative collective.

Hours: 11 am - 8 pm daily
Location: Walled City, from Choti Chaupar to Chandpole Gate

Sireh Deori Bazaar

You can easily spend a day buying and bargaining your way through Sireh Deori. Shop for puppets, razai (lightweight Jaipuri quilts), leather shoes, wall art, and other novelties at this popular market opposite Hawa Mahal.

Hours: 11 am - 8 pm daily
Location: Tulsi Marg, Gangori Bazaar, J.D.A. Market, Pink City, Jaipur

WHAT TO SHOP FOR IN JAIPUR

Blue Pottery

Although Turko-Persian in origin, Blue Pottery is widely recognized as a traditional craft of Jaipur. The name comes from the eye-catching cobalt blue dye used to color the clay. You will find beautifully decorated plates, flower vases, soap dishes, *surahis* (pitchers), trays, coasters, fruit bowls, doorknobs, and glazed tiles for your home decor.

Wool and Silk Carpets

Jaipur is a haven for hand-tufted wool and silk carpets. Cozy and colorful, the distinctive rugs are exported all over the world. Choose from a wide variety of colors, patterns, and sizes that reflect the traditional art of rug weaving.

Miniature Paintings

The art of miniature paintings is a fusion of Mughal and indigenous Indian styles. The paintings usually depict folk tales, religious stories, or literature and are designed on silk, ivory, cotton, and paper.

Lac Bangles

Lac bangles are the quintessential Indian female accessory. From weddings and festivals to everyday wear, the multicolored bangles can be customized and resized. Often adorned with colored glass or semi-precious stones, they add a pop of sparkle to both Indian and western attire.

Jewelry and Gemstones

As the *City of Gems*, Jaipur is the hub for buying and trading precious and semi-precious stones. In addition to gold, platinum, and silver, you will find a unique collection of rubies, garnets, diamonds, and sapphires. The creative craftsmanship produces original pieces directly from the artisans.

Puppets

Puppet dances are a popular folk entertainment in Jaipur. With faces shaped out of wood, the puppets are made from gotta cloth and cotton fillings. Many of the males also represent the snake charmers of Jaipur.

Jutti shoes

Jutti

Colorful and with well-cushioned soles, *juttis* (shoes) were once worn by Mughal royalty and adorned with fine gems and precious stones. The popular footwear can be hand-painted, embroidered, sequined, or threaded with beads and other accessories.

Custom Clothing

Whether shopping for formal sarees or casual t-shirts and hoodies, Jaipur is an excellent option for custom clothing. Depending on the attire, you can even request same-day service. Check out Kishanpole Bazar (walled city, from Ajmeri Gate to Choti Chopad) for custom tailors.

Razai

Razai is a traditional lightweight Jaipuri quilt. Similar to a duvet or comforter, it is filled with cotton and often adorned with a floral print. Characterized by their softness and warmth, the handmade quilts can also feature block printing.

Block Printing

The Pink City has become synonymous with block printing on

Block Printing

cotton fabrics, including sarees, dupattas, salwar-kameez, bed covers, curtains, and scarves. Sanganer and Bagru are neighboring towns outside Jaipur known worldwide for innovative block and screen printing techniques.

Sweets

Jaipur offers mouth-watering sweets like *pheeni* (sugar-soaked fried vermicelli), *churma* (ground flour-dumplings), *til patti* (jaggery and sesame crisp), *makkhan bada* (layered dish with dried fruits), and *ghewar* (sweet cake). Often served and shared during holidays and festivals, the sweets have become an iconic ingredient in Jaipur's culinary heritage.

WHERE TO EAT

1135 AD

Reservations are recommended for this distinguished dining in the

Maharaja's dining room at Amber Fort.
Amer Palace, Jaleb Chowk, Amer, Jaipur / +91 98 2974 4416

Anokhi Cafe

Anokhi is a small cafe that uses seasonal organic produce from their local farm. The non-Indian menu includes soups, salads, sandwiches, snacks, and sweets.
KK Square, C 11, Prithviraj Rd, Panch Batti, C Scheme, Ashok Nagar, Jaipur / +91 14 1400 7245

Thali and More

A thali is a platter with several small dishes, repeatedly filled to your heart's (and stomach's) content.
1st floor Plot No. C 46, Sarojini Marg, Panch Batti, C Scheme, Ashok Nagar, Jaipur / +91 76 6560 4777

Laxmi Misthan Bhandar

Established in 1954, LMB's sweets are the pride and joy of Jaipur.
No. 98, 99, Johari Bazar Rd, Bapu Bazar, Biseswarji, Jaipur / +91 90 2460 9609

Rawat Misthan Bhandar

RMB is a friendly local eatery renowned for kachoris (spicy deep-fried snacks).
Station Road, in front of Polo Victory Hotel, Sindhi Camp, Jaipur / +91 14 1236 8288

Kesar Sweets

Visit this mithai boutique for classic and innovative Rajasthani sweets.
Tonk Road, K-44, SL Marg, Lal Bahadur Nagar, Income Tax Colony, Milap Nagar, Jaipur / +91 98 2805 9033

Chaisa Cafe

Chaisa is a casual space to enjoy traditional breakfast staples like poha, idli, and aloo paratha. The cafe also pours classic chai and international teas.
Close to Vidhan Sabha, 8A-Satya Vihar, Pankaj Singhvi Marg, Vidhayak Nagar, Lalkothi, Jaipur / +91 96 6011 1145

WHERE TO DRINK

Lassiwala
Established in 1944, the original Lassiwala is a Jaipur icon serving the popular yogurt-based drink. Plan your visit early, as they close (or sell out) by 4 pm daily.
312, MI Rd, Jayanti Market, New Colony, Jaipur

Steam
All aboard! Order a cocktail (or dinner!) inside a restored steam train with an adjoining Victorian-style station.
Rambagh Palace, Bhawani Singh Rd, Jaipur / +91 14 1238 5700

Bar Palladio
Located in the Narain Niwas Palace Hotel, Bar Palladio has an insta-worthy blue interior inspired by Mughal and Italian designs. Did we mention the wandering peacocks and mango trees?
Kanota Bagh, Narayan Singh Rd, Jaipur / +91 14 1256 5556 / www.bar-pallidio.com

Blackout
Grab a drink and hit the dance floor at this all-weather rooftop lounge and terrace.
Hotel Golden Oak, 8th & 9th Floor, Landmark Building, Ashok Marg, D38A, Ahinsa Cir, C Scheme, Jaipur / +91 99 2811 6900

LOCAL TOURS AND EXPERIENCES

Pink City Rickshaw Company
Pink rickshaws in the Pink City! GGG loves this Jaipur initiative of ACCESS Development Services that provides employment to over 200 women from low-income households. Reserve a tour in the

custom rickshaws knowing your dollars are directly benefiting the economic independence of Pink City Hostesses.

We recommend: The Pink City Heritage Tour, Wake Up with Jaipur
www.pinkcityrickshawcompany.com / +91- 80 9455 6333 /
vishal@accessdev.org

Virasat Experiences

A community-based tourism initiative that promotes activities in alliance with grassroot development agencies. Virasat encourages the awareness of living heritage through sustainable directives.
We recommend: Amber Hiking, Amber Heritage Trail, Temples and Haveli's Walking Tour.
https://virasatexperiences.com

Regal Ride of Jaipur

Experience the hidden gems of Jaipur as you cruise around the city on a savvy electric bike. Choose fun over fuel!
www.blive.co.in

DAY TRIPS

Galtaji Temple

Built in the Aravalli Hills outside Jaipur is the ancient pilgrimage site of Galtaji. A series of temples surround a natural spring that flows downward and fills sacred bathing tanks. Climb to the highest temple for hilltop views of Jaipur's fortifications. Galtaji is also called "The Monkey Temple" for the large number of monkeys who call the complex home. Be cautious - they often steal and become hostile!

How to Reach: From Jaipur, hire a taxi, private car, or rideshare for the 10 km ride.

Sanganer and Bagru

Sanganer and Bagru are neighboring towns outside Jaipur known worldwide for innovative block and screen printing techniques.

During the 16th and 17th centuries, the East India Company exported the prints to Europe in bulk and several of the traditional designs were produced under the patronage of the royal family. Sanganer prints are facilitated on a white or off-white background; Bagru prints are printed on an Indigo or a dyed background.

It is believed that in the 16th century, the ruler of Amber, Raja Man Singh, brought *Kagzis* (paper makers) to Sanganer where abundant water was available from the Saraswati River. The town emerged as one of the biggest paper making centers in northern India.

How to Reach; There is no direct bus from Jaipur to Sanganer and Bagru; hire a taxi or private car for the 30 km (45-minute) journey

Chand Baori

Dating back to the 9th century is Chand Baori, an architectural gem in Abhaneri Village. With over 3,500 steps descending 13 stories, it is one of the deepest stepwells in India. Until just a few years ago, locals - especially children - would cool off by jumping into the pond. Chand Baori is said to be named after a local ruler called Raja Chanda, but there is little evidence about its construction or the adjoining Harshat Mata Temple. This particular stepwell is also a popular filming location for Bollywood films.

How to Reach: Hire a private car for the two-hour (80 km) journey from Jaipur

Jhalana Safari Park

The apex predator at Jhalana is the leopard - 35 to be exact (at the time of publication). Approximately seven have territories in the park's tourism zones. The usually shy cat does not have many predators, availing for more visibility and better sightings. There are currently two safari routes operational in the non-profit park dedicated to education and conservation.

There are two jeep safaris daily: 6 am - 9 am and 3:30 pm - 6:30 pm. The cost is INR 6000 + 5% GST per jeep (maximum six guests per jeep).

How to Reach: Hire a taxi, private car, or ride share for the short 10 km drive.
www.jhalanaleopardsafari.com / +91 99 2940 0009

GIVING BACK

Ladli

Ladli is a vocational training program for orphaned, abused, and impoverished children. The youth at risk for prostitution or child labor are taught to make jewelry and handicrafts. They attend school, take dance and art classes, and receive meals and medical care. Guests can donate, volunteer, and/or buy handmade products.
www.ladli.org

PUSHKAR

Bordering the Thar Desert, Pushkar is a Hindu pilgrimage destination nestled on the sacred Pushkar Lake. There are 500+ temples in the town, including the 14th-century Jagatpita Brahma Mandir dedicated to the god of creation. The lake is also surrounded by 52 bathing ghats where pilgrims perform a cleansing ritual.

Pushkar is most widely known for the annual Pushkar Camel Fair in October/November. Traditionally, the fair served a religious and economic purpose; livestock would be traded and Hindu devotees would perform rituals during auspicious dates. Today, the multi-day cultural event has become very commercialized and caters to curious foreigners. Over 50,000 camels are dressed in the finest attire and then paraded, raced, and traded. Most of the activities take place on the fairground, including a carnival with acrobats, dancers, musicians, and carousels.

Prices skyrocket during the annual festival as over 200,000 visitors converge on Pushkar. Luxury tented camps are temporarily constructed in the desert near the fairground, or you can try and reserve a hotel or guest house in the vicinity. The influx of tourists also means more beggars and gypsies, so be prepared to be hassled for money.

How to Reach
The closest train station is 15 km away in Ajmer; the Ajmer-Pushkar link connects Ajmer and Pushkar every morning except Tuesdays and Fridays. It is an unreserved train, so you cannot book tickets in advance for the one-hour journey. You can also hire a taxi for the 30-minute drive to Pushkar from the Ajmer station.

If traveling between Jodhpur and Jaipur, Pushkar is a popular and convenient stopover destination. The town is three hours (150 km) from Jaipur and four hours (190 km) from Jodhpur.

Where to Stay

Rawai Luxury Tents
Swiss cottage-style tents at a boutique glamping site.
$$ / http://rawailuxurytents.co.in/ / +91 83 0685 0811

The Westin Pushkar Resort & Spa
An exclusive haven of wellness and renewal near the spiritual sites of the city.
$$$ / www.marriott.com / +91 14 5277 4400

JODHPUR

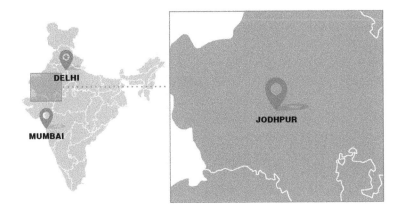

DELHI

MUMBAI

JODHPUR

The Blue City of Rajasthan

Jodhpur's fortifications inspire legendary tales of victory. Named "The Blue City" for the azure alleys and buildings, Jodhpur was historically the capital of the Kingdom of Mewar. It was founded in 1459 A.D. by Rao Jodha, chief of the Rathore clan of Rajputs. The majestic Mehrangarh Fort rises over the city as a testament to the royal past, while a maze of fragrant streets lead to temples and bustling bazaars.

TRANSPORTATION HUBS

Jodhpur is located in the state of Rajasthan, 245 km to Udaipur and 350 km to Jaipur.

Jodhpur Airport (JDH)
Civil Airport Road, Air Force Area, Ratanada, Jodhpur

Jodhpur services domestic flights to Delhi, Mumbai, Bangalore, and Chennai.

Jodhpur Junction (JU)
Maharaja Umaid Singh Statue Circle, Station Rd, Ratanada, Jodhpur

As the second largest city in Rajasthan, Jodhpur is well connected by rail to major Indian cities. Some of the popular trains are Rajasthan Sampark Kranti, Howrah Jodhpur SF Express, Chennai Jodhpur Express, Suryanagari Express, Jaisalmer Delhi Express, and Yesvantpur Bangalore Jodhpur Express.

Jodhpur Bus Stand
Raika Bagh Station Rd, Bhadwasiya, Paota, Jodhpur

AREAS TO AVOID

Overall, Jodhpur is a safe destination for female travelers. We do advise using caution at night by walking in busy and well-lit areas.

LOCAL FESTIVALS

Rajasthan International Folk Festival (RIFF)
The Jodhpur RIFF is an annual music and arts festival that promotes the traditional folk artistry of Rajasthan. Held at the Mehrangarh Fort, the cultural event is endorsed by UNESCO as a People's Platform for Creativity and Sustainable Development. RIFF is scheduled during the brightest full moon of the year (Sharad Purnima) in September/October.

www.jodhpurriff.org

Marwar Festival

As the capital of the Marwar state, Jodhpur enthusiastically celebrates Rajasthan's royalty. The Marwar Festival is an annual cultural fair featuring folk music and dances. Performers dress in colorful traditional attire to honor the Rajput heroes of Jodhpur's princely past. The festival is held in September/October at Mehrangarh Fort, Umaid Bhawan Palace, and Mandore.

International Desert Kite Festival (Makar Sankranti)

The Jodhpur International Desert Kite Festival attracts the best kite flyers from India and abroad. The 3-day event is held at the polo grounds on January 14th (Makar Sankranti). During the inaugural ceremony, children release colorful bunches of balloons as Air Force helicopters also release hundreds of kites. With kite competitions and displays, the Jodhpur skyline transforms to a multicolored rainbow.

Nagaur Fair

Popularly known as the Cattle Fair of Nagaur, the festival is a gathering of livestock traders. Over 70,000 bullocks, horses, and camels converge on the historic town of Nagaur, located between Jodhpur and Bikaner. The animals and their owners dress in their finest for games, bargaining, and trading. The fair also includes the Mirchi Bazaar, the largest red-chili market in India.

WHERE TO STAY

Zostel Jodhpur

A bright blue backpacker hostel overlooking the majestic Mehrangarh Fort.
$ / www.zostel.com / +91 22 4896 2266

Juna Mahal

A boutique homestay in old town decorated with ancient sandstone carvings.

$$ / www.junamahal.com / +91 29 1244 5511

Devi Bhawan

A family-owned heritage hotel with Indian and colonial British architecture.

$$ / www.devibhawan.com / +91 29 1251 1067

Pal Haveli

A classic 18th century noble home in a central location.

$$$ / www.palhaveli.com / +91 29 1261 2519

The Rohet House

A family home that has been lovingly restored to exclusive boutique accommodations.

$$$$ / www.houseofrohet.com / +91 12 4465 4330

RAAS Jodhpur

A grand hotel that fuses modern and ancient styles with epic fort views.

$$$$ / www.raashotels.com / +91 29 1263 6455

Umaid Bhawan Palace

A luxurious palace hotel and the world's 6th-largest private residence.

$$$$ / www.tajhotels.com / +91 29 1251 0101

WHAT TO DO

Mehrangarh Fort

With seven gates, the Mehrangarh Fort is one of the largest in India. The massive complex includes several palaces known for intricate

carvings and expansive courtyards. Mehrangarh's museum houses a collection of palanquins, howdahs, royal cradles, miniatures, musical instruments, costumes, and furniture. Craving a side of adrenaline with your history lesson? Head to Flying Fox Jodhpur for a zipline course with epic fort views.

Entry: INR 650 (including elevator access)
Hours: 9 am - 5 pm daily

Jaswant Thada

The "Taj Mahal of Marwar" is the marble cenotaph of Maharaja Jaswant Singh II. Because ancestry worship is common in Rajput clans, the main hall was built as a temple where pujas (rituals) are performed. The intricately carved marble stone is reflective of the iconic Taj Mahal. Now serving as the cremation ground for the Royal Rajput family of Marwar, the complex also features tiered gardens and a small lake.

Entry: INR 50
Hours: 9:30 am - 5 pm daily

Mandore Gardens

Mandore Gardens was the former capital of the Maharajas.

Abandoned in 1459 CE for the security of Mehrangarh Fort, it remains one of the best preserved sites in Rajasthan. The gardens house temples and the cenotaphs of Jodhpur's former rulers. Be sure to visit the Hindu temple and Hall of Heroes to view paintings and sculptures of the bygone era.

Entry: Entry is free to the gardens, but the museum costs INR 50
Hours: 9 am - 10 pm daily

Chamunda Mataji Temple
Located at the southern end of Mehrangarh Fort is a temple housing the deity Devi Chamunda Mataji. Previously based in Mandore, the idol was installed in the fort temple in 1460 by Rao Jodha. In present times, the royal family still considers Devi Chamunda Mataji as the adopted family goddess. She is one of the many forms of Durga, or the goddess of destruction.

Entry: Free
Hours: Sunrise to Sunset

Toorji Ka Jhalra Stepwell
Built in the 1740s, Toorji Ka Jhalra was submerged for decades until a recent restoration uncovered 200+ feet of intricate sandstone carvings. Located close to the Clock Tower, the stepwell remains off the popular touring circuit, allowing for moments of reflection. An urban regeneration has modernized the surrounding neighborhoods with restaurants, cafes, and shops.

Entry: Free
Hours: Sunrise to Sunset

WHERE TO SHOP

Sadar Bazaar

Located near the Clock Tower, Sadar Bazaar (or Sadar Market) is one of the oldest markets in Jodhpur. A fusion of vibrancy and chaos, the colorful lanes spiral into narrow alleys filled with leather shoes, embroidered carpets, and rare antiques.

Hours: 9 am - 8 pm
Location: Sardar Market Clock Tower, Paan Gali, Jodhpur

Mochi Bazaar

Do you love shoes and accessories? Mochi Bazaar is your one-stop destination for Jodhpuri Jutis, known locally as mojaris, and lac bangles.

Hours: 9 am - 8 pm
Location: Korna House Rd, Bhistiyon Ka Bas, Jodhpur

Stepwell Square

Toorji Ka Jhalra, a stepwell built in the 1740's, was submerged for decades until a recent restoration.. An urban regeneration has modernized the surrounding neighborhoods with restaurants, cafes, and shops. Located near the Clock Tower, it's an urban jewel where tradition meets modernity.

Hours: 9 am - 10 pm
Location: Sutharo Ka Bass Rd, Gulab Sagar, Jodhpur

Umaid Bhawan Palace Market

Visit the palace road between Ajit Bhawan and Umaid Bhawan for exclusive antiques, metal works, and designer furniture. The market does not entertain bargaining, but the treasures are worth the price.

Hours: 9 am - 8 pm
Location: Circuit House Rd, Cantt Area, Jodhpur

Tripolia Bazar

Tripolia, meaning three gates, is tucked between Manak Chowk and Chhoti Chaupar. The popular market sells almost everything - handicrafts, clothes, shoes, marble statues, apparels, brassware, textiles, and silver jewelry.

Hours: 9 am - 9 pm
Location: Between Manak Chowk and Chhoti Chaupar

WHERE TO EAT

Stepwell Cafe
Perched above an 18th century stepwell, the 3-story cafe with a view serves starters, calzones, and sandwiches. Choose to dine on the A/C first floor, al fresco upper level, or the rooftop lounge.
Tunwarji Ka Jhalra Makrana Mohalla, Jodhpur / +91 29 1263 6455 / www.stepwellcafe.com

Indique
Reserve a table at this rooftop restaurant in Pal Haveli. Savor classic Rajasthani dishes while gazing at the majestic Mehrangarh Fort and the azure exteriors of the city.
Pal Haveli, near Clock Tower, Pal Haveli, Ghantaghar, Gulab Sagar, Jodhpur / +91 29 1263 8344

Janta Sweet Home
Established in Jodhpur, JSH is a traditional sweet and savory brand that is "by the people, for the people."
3, Nai Sarak, opposite Priya Hotel, Chauraha, Jodhpur / +91 29 1263 6666 / https://jantasweethome.com/

Gypsy
A popular local eatery specializing in thalis (a platter with small plates) and Rajasthani favorites.
689, 9th C Rd, Sardarpura, Jodhpur

Chokelao Mahal
Chokelao Mahal is an exclusive garden and terrace restaurant near the Mehrangarh Fort. Wear your finest attire and make a reservation for the royal experience.
Mehrangarh Fort, Sodagaran Mohalla, Jodhpur / +91 95 7157 1000

WHERE TO DRINK

Shri Mishrilal Hotel
Founded in 1927, the iconic sweet shop wears the crown for the best lassi in the city. Try the Makhaniya Lassi, a Jodhpur specialty prepared with cardamom, sugar, milk, and compressed curd.
Clock Tower Rd, Sardar Market, Jodhpur / www.shrimishrilal.com / +91 98 2905 8782

The Laughing B
A gastropub in a garden setting that attracts the younger crowd with an innovative bar menu.
Hotel Residency Palace, near Senapati Bhawan, Ratanada, Jodhpur

Geoffrey's
An Irish pub in the Park Plaza Hotel with a pool table and dance floor.
House, Jhalamand, Airport Rd, Air Force Area, Jodhpur

LOCAL TOURS AND EXPERIENCES

Virasat Experiences
A community-based tourism initiative that promotes activities in alliance with grassroot development agencies. Virasat encourages the awareness of living heritage through sustainable directives.

We recommend: Majestic Marwar, Brahmins & the Blue City Walking Tour, Stepwells & Temples of Jodhpur
https://virasatexperiences.com

Flying Fox Jodhpur

Soar on six ziplines over the lakes and fortifications of Mehrangarh. Join two instructors as you glide over two desert lakes, trek through the Rao Jodha eco-park, and enjoy the best views of Mehrangarh and the Blue City. Catch the view other travelers miss!
https://www.flyingfox.asia/jodhpur/

DAY TRIPS

Bishnoi Village

Created by the Rajas and Maharajas of Jodhpur, Bishnoi Village offers a glimpse of rural tribal life. Although a planned community, the villagers call Bishnoi home and work as potters, shepherds, weavers, and block printers. They also worship nature in all forms, especially the sanctity of plant and animal life.

How to Reach: Hire a taxi or private car for the 22 km drive from Jodhpur

Indian woman with chilis

GIVING BACK

Sambhali Trust

Sambhali Trust works with women and children experiencing daily discrimination and violence due to economic, gender, and caste status. Many lack any autonomy in their domestic lives and face severe verbal, physical, and sexual abuse within their communities. Sambhali equips underprivileged women with the tools to become financially independent, provide for their children, and establish self-sustaining communities of support.

www.sambhali-trust.org

Mandore Project

The Mandore Project was established to share skills, creativity, and learning with the aim of building a fairer world through the active involvement and collaboration between volunteers and the host community. The projects are primarily aimed at improving the quality of education in rural areas surrounding Jodhpur. There are several departments seeking active volunteers, including health, sanitation, and outdoor sports.

https://mandoreproject.org/

UDAIPUR

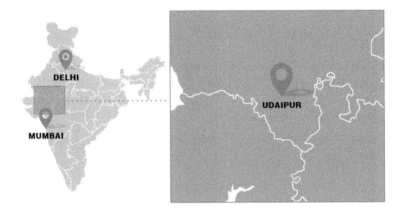

The White City of Rajasthan

With a wealth of enchanting lakes, Udaipur is a true oasis in Rajasthan. The City of Dawn is dotted with marble palaces, hibiscus gardens, and fountain pavilions. Udaipur's inherent romance, beauty, and heroic past appeals to the imagination of poets, painters, and writers.

TRANSPORTATION HUBS

Udaipur is located in the state of Rajasthan, 250 km from Jodhpur and 400 km from Jaipur.

Maharana Pratap Dabok Airport (UDR)
NH 76, Dabok, Rajasthan
www.udaipurairport.com

Domestic flights connect Udaipur to Mumbai, Delhi, Hyderabad, and Kolkata.

Udaipur City Train Station (UDZ)
8, Station Rd , Jawahar Nagar, Udaipur

Daily trains connect Udaipur with most major Indian cities, including Delhi, Mumbai, Jaipur, Agra, and Ahmedabad.

Udaipur City Bus Depot
Roadways Bus Stand Udaipole, Ganesh Ghati, Udaipur

AREAS TO AVOID

Overall, Udaipur is a safe destination. After dark, be cautious in the narrow lanes of the Old City and at the bus/train stations.

LOCAL FESTIVALS

Mewar Festival of Gangaur

The Mewar Festival is perhaps the most important celebration in Udaipur. After locals dress up in various images of Isar and Gangaur, there is a large procession that moves throughout the city and eventually aboard boats on Lake Pichola. Celebrated in April, the festival also includes religious ceremonies, cultural activities, Rajasthani folk dances, and music performances.

Teej

Dedicated to the Hindu goddesses Shiva and Parvati, Teej is celebrated at the beginning of monsoon season in July and August. Swings are hung from trees and decorated with flowers as married women pray for a long and happy marriage.

Shilpgram Utsav

Located just 8 km from Udaipur, Shilpgram is known for handicrafts from Rajasthan, Goa, and Gujarat. The village hosts a 10-day festival in late December with craft demonstrations, multiple bazaars, and live music and dancing in the amphitheater.

WHERE TO STAY

Zostel Udaipur

A centrally located hostel with lovely lake views from the rooftop cafe.
$ / www.zostel.com/zostel/udaipur/ / +91 22 4896 2266

Gypsy Child Lake Hostel

A budget property on Lake Pichola offering private rooms and female dorms.
$ / www.gypsychildhostels.com / +91 98 1160 4848

Shalom Backpackers Udaipur

A hip hostel with a dedicated library and evening bonfires.
$ / shalombackpackers.com/udaipur / +91 89 7992 8988

Jagat Niwas Palace

A family-operated 17th century haveli in the Old City.
$$ / www.jagatcollection.com/jagatniwas / +91 70 7300 0378

Bloom Boutique

A highly awarded mid-market hotel with colorful interiors.
$$ / staybloom.com/hotels/udaipur/bloom-boutique-lake-pichola / +91 11 4122 5666

Premkunj

A luxury boutique homestay surrounded by the hills.
$$$ / www.premkunj.in / +91 98 2951 3883

Fateh Garh

A luxury heritage hotel with the best pools in Udaipur.
$$$ / www.fatehgarh.in / +91 86 9694 5109

Taj Lake Palace

An ultra romantic, top-10 global hotel located in the middle of Lake Pichola.
$$$$ / www.tajhotels.com / +91 29 4242 8800

WHAT TO DO

City Palace

Built by Maharana Uday Singh in 1559, the magnificent City Palace graces the banks of Lake Pichola. It features courtyards, corridors, mahals, pavilions, terraces, and hanging gardens. There is also a renowned museum that features the finest Rajput elements of art and culture including brilliant sculptures and colourful paintings.

Entry: INR 300
Hours: 9:30 am - 5:30 pm daily

Ahar Cenotaphs

Ahar Cenotaphs are the royal cremation grounds of the Mewar Kingdom. The village and architectural ground is a time machine. There are over 250 structures, finely carved pieces of pottery, and a museum to view excavated artefacts that date back over 1,000 years. Make time to visit nearby Dhulkot, a village that is over 4000 years old according to archaeological records. To visit Ahar, you will need to take a taxi or train from Udaipur.

Entry: Free
Hours: 10 am - 5 pm daily

Jagdish Temple

The four-hundred-year-old Jagdish Temple is dedicated to Lord Vishnu. Fun fact: The space follows Vastu Shastra, a traditional Indian design pattern that integrates architecture and nature to create a positive flow of energy. The temple has been in continuous worship since 1651.

Entry: Free
Hours: 4:15 am - 1 pm and 5:15 pm - 8 pm daily

Jag Mandir Island

Jag Mandir is an island palace in Lake Pichola. James Bond fans will instantly recognize this spot, as it was famously featured in *Octopussy*. This is one of our favorite spots to grab a cocktail and watch the glorious Udaipur sunset.

Entry: There is no fee to enter the island but the boat ride costs INR 700. Boats depart from Bansi Ghat Jetty.

Sahelion Ki Bari

Built in memory of Maharana Sangram Singh's 48 maidens, Sahelion

Ki Bari features a lush park, rain fountains, lotus pond, and a museum displaying items from the royal household. Known locally as the *Pleasure Gardens*, it is a whimsical space to frolic in nature and take insta-worthy photos.

Entry: INR 50
Hours: 9 am - 7 pm daily

WHERE TO SHOP

Hathipole
Hathipole (or Hathi Pole), one of the largest markets in the city, is known for reasonably priced handicrafts and folk art. Shop for Rajasthani miniature paintings, Pichwai and Phad; authentic souvenirs; wooden handicrafts; and colorful 'Nagra' slippers made from camel skin with beautiful embroidery.

Hours: 9.30 am to 5.30 pm / Closed on Sundays.
Location: Adjacent to the City Palace

Bada Bazaar
Bada Bazaar is THE market for accessories, bags, clothes, and jewelry. You will find small shops, big showrooms, outlets, and exhibitions that display a variety of unique Rajasthani items.

Hours: 9.30 am to 6 pm / Closed on Sundays.
Location: 1 km from City Palace

Sadhna

Established in 1988, Sadhna is a handicraft enterprise that provides alternative incomes for women in rural, tribal, and slum communities. Registered under the Mutual Benefit Trust Act, the organization offers training and teaches patchwork/embroidery skills. Sadhna started with 15 women and now employs over 700 female artisans.

Hours: 10 am - 7 pm daily
Location: Seva Mandir, Sevamandir Rd, Old Fatehpura
Phone: +91 294 245 4655
www.sadhna.org

Indian fabrics

WHAT TO SHOP FOR IN UDAIPUR

Bandhani

Dating back to 4000 BCE, Bandhani is a type of tie-dye textile that is formed by plucking the cloth into a figurative design. The highly skilled process creates stunning and original patterns for sarees, salwars, scarves, and other wearables.

Leather Diaries and Journals

Udaipur is a hot spot for leather diaries, journals, and handmade paper. You will find vintage journals and embossed book covers with contemporary and traditional designs.

Pottery

Like Jaipur, Udaipur is a popular shopping destination for Blue Pottery. The name comes from the eye-catching cobalt blue dye used to color the clay. You will find beautifully decorated plates, flower vases, soap dishes, *surahis* (pitchers), trays, coasters, fruit bowls, doorknobs, and glazed tiles for your home decor.

Embroidered Bags

Visit any local market and you will find rows of embroidered gypsy banjara bags on display. Available in several sizes, the bags are lightweight and easy to pack, making them a popular ethnic gift to bring home.

Miniature Paintings

The Mughal artistry of miniature paintings is alive and flourishing in Udaipur. Irrespective of size, the intricate Rajasthani paintings are colorful, opulent, and tell a story.

WHERE TO EAT

Udai Art Café

Nestled next to the Jagdish Temple is this popular bohemian hotspot serving delicious coffees, crepes, and sandwiches. Owned by a photographer from Greece, Udai Art Cafe is cozy, simple, and offers the best breakfasts in Udaipur - including Turkish and Greek coffee with almond and soy milk options.

Jagdish Temple Rd, Near Jagdish Temple

Savage Garden

Even Italians love the homemade pasta at this unassuming spot above Cafe Edelweiss. However, the real star of the show is the Chicken Wajid Ali, boneless chicken breast stuffed with cashews and paneer. It is the restaurant's signature dish that hails from the royal kitchens of Awadh.

71 Gangour Ghat, above Cafe Edelweiss

Krishna Dal Baati Restro

A feast for only INR 250! This local favorite specializes in Rajasthan's famous dish, *Dal Baati Churma*. There is only item on the menu - a *thali* (platter) with *daal* (lentils), *baati* (balls of wheat flour), *churma* (sweetened and fried baati), *gatte ki saag* (chickpea flour dumplings in yogurt-based curry), chutneys, papad, salad, rice, and the quintessential buttermilk. Skip the utensils and eat with your hands!

17, 1st Floor, Jal Darshan Market Hotel Green View Street, Gulab Bagh Rd / http://krishnadalbatirestro.in

Upre

Perfectly positioned on the rooftop terrace of Lake Pichola Hotel, Upre is a dynamic spot to enjoy the open-air bar and cabanas with lakeside views. For fine dining, reserve a table at their sister restaurant, 1559 AD.

Lake Pichola Hotel, Lake Pichola Road Outside ChandPole / www.1559ad.com

Charcoal by Carlsson

As the name suggests, Charcoal by Carlsson specializes in food cooked over coal. Opened by Swedish chef Henric Carlsson, menu items include meats and veggies grilled on a barbeque, tandoor, or in traditional pots over an open flame. Bonus: The restaurant makes the BEST authentic Mexican tacos in Udaipur.

12, Lal Ghat Road, Behind Jagdish Temple, Old City, Silawatwari / www.charcoalpb.com

Millets of Mewar

Millets of Mewar has branded itself as Udaipur's first dedicated health-food restaurant. The menu includes vegan and gluten-free items with ingredients that are organic, sustainable, and locally sourced.

Sajjangarh Monsoon Palace, 25, Sajjan Vihar, near Biological Park / www.milletsofmewar.org

WHERE TO DRINK

Panera Bar
Whether drinking it up poolside or on a plush sofa under a grand chandelier, the palatial setting at Panera Bar offers a royal experience.
Shiv Niwas Palace Hotel, Lake Pichola, The City Palace Complex

Brewz Rock Café
The beertails - cocktails made of beer - are wildly popular at this bar and cafe featuring live music and Bollywood nights.
Celebration Mall G-20 Bhuwana Bypass Road, Opposite Devendra Dham, Pulla Bhuwana

Hook & Irons Café & Bar
A chill spot with live music, ample seating, and savory starters.
Hotel Paras Mahal, Railway Colony

Frangipani by the Lake
A lakefront setting with an incredible selection of international liquors.
Hotel Lakend, Fatehsagar Lake

Sangria
This lively lounge comes alive during sports games with a community table, bonfires, billiard tables, and abundant TV screens.
No 6 Ambavgarh, Opposite Lake Swaroop Sagar

LOCAL TOURS AND EXPERIENCES

Pink City Rickshaw Tours
Experience the legacy, culture, and history of Udaipur on eco-friendly rickshaws driven by female guides from low income communities.

We recommend: Old City Rickshaw Tour and Udaipur at a Glance

http://pinkcityrickshawcompany.com/udaipur

Virasat Experiences
A community-based tourism initiative that promotes activities in alliance with grassroot development agencies. Virasat encourages the awareness of living heritage through sustainable directives.

We recommend: Udaipur Village Tour, Udaipur Heritage Walk, and Udaipur by Cycle

https://virasatexperiences.com

Enteyoga
Reserve a yoga class or private session beside a 350-year-old temple

on Lake Pichola. The instructor, Seethu, belongs to the revered yoga lineage of Shri T. Krishnamacharya, an influential guru of the 20th century. www.enteyoga.com

Shashi's Cooking Classes

Shashi teaches 14 delicious dishes during her small-group classes, including her famous magic sauce. She also openly shares her remarkable story of overcoming stringent gender and caste boundaries. Tourists actually helped Shashi develop her business model, including the website and cookbook. Classes start at 10:30 am and 5:30 pm. Contact: Shashicooking@gmail.com / +91 99 2930 3511

DAY TRIPS

Ranakpur

Surrounded by tangled forests with monkeys abounding in the courtyard, Ranakpur is one of the five important pilgrim centers for the Jain community. The temple, including the extraordinary array of 1144 pillars, is distinct in design with carved ceilings and arches decorated with friezes depicting scenes from the lives of the Jain saints. The architecture of this space is magnificent - don't miss it! Note: Shoulders and knees must be covered and no leather (purses, belts, etc) are allowed.

Hours: Open daily from 12 pm - 5 pm (The morning is strictly reserved for prayers and no tourists are allowed)
Entry: INR 200 for the audio guide and INR 100 for a camera.
How to Reach: A local bus from Udaipur stops just outside the temple or you can hire a taxi/private car for the two-hour drive from Udaipur

Deogarh

A delightful and charming town just two hours from Udaipur. Off the popular tourist circuit, it's a lovely area to shop at local markets, taste regional specialities, and engage in lively conversations. If possible, book an overnight at either Deogarh Mahal or Dev Shree.

How to Reach: A local bus goes directly to Deogarh or you can hire a taxi from Udaipur for the 2-hour ride

Kumbhalgarh Fort
Nestled in the Aravalli Hills is Kumbhalgarh, a fort that has made its mark in history as the second largest wall after the Great Wall of China. Built by Rana Kumbha in the 15th century, the fort was declared a UNESCO World Heritage Site under the group Hill Forts of Rajasthan. It is also spectacularly lit for a few minutes every evening.

Hours: Open daily from 9 am - 6 pm
Entry: INR 200
How to Reach: Local buses are not advised for this route so hire a taxi for the 2-hour drive from Udaipur

GIVING BACK

Manjari Foundation
Established in 2015, Manjari's vision is to empower women from marginalized communities both socially and economically so they become catalysts of change.
https://www.manjarifoundation.in

Animal Aid Unlimited
AAU rescues and rehabilitates ill, injured, and abused street animals in Udaipur. The organization also offers training programs, cruelty response, and education and outreach.
https://www.animalaidunlimited.org

JAISALMER

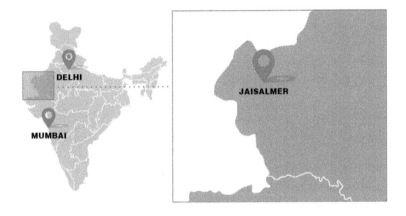

The Golden City of Rajasthan

The remote location of Jaisalmer kept it almost untouched by outside influences, even during the days of the Raj. Founded in 1156 AD by Rawal Jaisal, the city was the last to sign the Instrument of Agreement with the British. In Medieval times, Jaisalmer's prosperity was due to its location on the main trade route linking India to Egypt, Arabia, Persia, Africa, and the West. The imposing Jaisalmer Fort rises from the Thar Desert surrounded by golden sandstone havelis and Jain temples.

TRANSPORTATION HUBS

Jaisalmer Airport (JSA)
Air Force School Road, Shastri Nagar, Jaisalmer

Jaisalmer's airport operates as a civil enclave on an Indian Air Force base. There are limited commercial flights to Delhi and Mumbai.

Jaisalmer Railway Junction (JSM)
Coulony, Gandhi Colony, Jaisalmer

Jaisalmer is well connected by the rail network with daily trains linking to Mumbai, Delhi, Udaipur, Jodhpur, and other major cities.

Jaisalmer Bus Depot
Jai Narayan Vyas Colony, Jaisalmer

Because of Jaisalmer's remote location, there are frequent buses to Udaipur, Jodhpur, and other cities in Rajasthan.

AREAS TO AVOID

Overall, Jaisalmer is a safe destination for female travelers. We do recommend caution when venturing out after dark - stay in lively and well-lit areas.

LOCAL FESTIVALS

Jaisalmer Desert Festival
The Jaisalmer Desert Festival celebrates the sun, sand, and ancestral traditions. Held annually in February, the 3-day event includes cultural performances, camel races, and turban competitions. The

festival concludes in the Sam Sand Dunes with Rajasthani folk music under the starry sky. www.desertfestivaljaisalmer.com

WHERE TO STAY

Zostel Jaisalmer
A colorful and quirky backpackers haven located inside Jaisalmer Fort.
$ / www.zostel.com / +91 22 4896 2266

The Wanderlust Guest House
A lovely 6-room guest house with fort and sunset views from the rooftop.
$ / www.facebook.com/thewanderlustguesthouse / +91 94 6115 7753

1st Gate Home Fusion
Clean and spacious rooms with a popular rooftop restaurant.
$$ / Near Fort Parking, Dhibba Para, Amar Sagar Pol, Jaisalmer / +91 29 9225 4462

Nachna Haveli
A 280-year-old haveli converted to a boutique heritage hotel.
$$ / www.nachnahaveli.com /+91 29 9225 2110

Killa Bhawan
A simple and refined heritage hotel located inside the fort.
$$$ / www.hotelkillabhawan.com / +91 29 9225 1204

Suryagarh
A luxury desert oasis with yoga, archery, and cultural performances.
$$$$ / www.suryagarh.com / +91 78 2715 1151

WHAT TO DO

Jaisalmer Fort
The bronzed sandstone Jaisalmer Fort rises from the desert like a majestic sand castle. With one-quarter of the city's population still residing within its walls, it is one of the few "living forts" in the world. Once positioned at the intersection of important trade routes, the fortification served as a center of commerce and communication. For almost 800 years, the fort was the actual city of Jaisalmer; only in the 17th century were settlements established outside the gates to accommodate a growing population. Enter through one of four gates to view Jain temples, merchant haveli's, and the Raj Mahal Palace.

Entry: INR 550
Hours: 9 am - 5 pm daily

Patwon ki Haveli
Built in 1805, Patwon ki haveli is actually a cluster of five havelis (mansions). As the largest haveli in Jaisalmer, it took workers and

artisans almost 55 years to complete the first wing. Once owned by a wealthy and renowned trader, the haveli is now occupied by Rajasthan's government arts and crafts department and features creative mirror work, intricate carvings, and rare paintings.

Entry: INR 250
Hours: 9 am - 5 pm daily

Jain Temples

Built in the 15th and 16th centuries, there are seven Jain temples inside the Jaisalmer Fort. Legends state that King Jaisal had land but not much wealth; however, the thriving trade routes (where the city was located) were controlled by Jains. Seeking protection, the king made a deal to include seven Jain temples if the wealthy traders financed the fort. Little has changed from the original construction and the temples now store one of the largest collections of sacred Jain literature.

Entry: INR 220
Hours: 8 am - 1 pm

Gadi Sagar Lake

Gadi Sagar Lake was originally a man-made reservoir that provided water to the residents of Jaisalmer. The banks of the lake feature shrines, temples, ghats and Chattris and it's a popular spot for boating and sunset strolls.

Entry: Free
Hours: 9 am - 7 pm daily

WHERE TO SHOP

Manak Chowk

Located near the railway station, Manak Chowk is known for leather goods, silver jewelry, and antiques. It's a popular spot for artisans to showcase their talents.

Hours: 10 am - 10 pm
Location: Amar Sagar Pol, Jaisalmer

Pansari Bazaar (The Villager's Market)

As one of the city's oldest street markets, Pansari Bazaar features ethnic wears, traditional dresses, and Jaisalmeri jewelry.

Hours: 9 am - 10 pm
Location: Dhibba Para, Amar Sagar Pol, Jaisalmer

Seema Gram

This government-run shop is a fan favorite for reasonably-priced shawls, garments, and stitched fabrics.

Hours: 9 am - 10 pm
Location: Jaisalmer Fort

Sadar Bazar

Sadar Bazaar is a wholesale and retail market selling trendy and traditional goods. Shop for genuine camel leather bags, tapestries, puppets, oil lamps, and carved wooden boxes.

Hours: 9 am - 10 pm
Location: Jaisalmer Fort

WHERE TO EAT

Gaji's Restaurant
A unique fusion of Indian and Korean cuisine on the rooftop of Gaji Hotel. Order the kimchi to soothe any sensitive digestion!
Gaji Hotel, Kalakar Colony Near Sunset Point, Jaisalmer / +91 98 2903 0701

Cafe the Kaku
The lively rooftop eatery offers an international menu, hookah, and epic fort views.
Patwa Haveli Road Sun Set Point, Suli Dungar, Jaisalmer / +91 96 7270 3070

Restaurant Romany
Located near Sunset Point, Romany features classic Rajasthani dishes. The best butter chicken in Jaisalmer!
Hotel Chirag Haveli, Fort Rd, Dhibba Para, Jaisalmer / +91 88 9075 4646

KB Cafe and Restaurant
We love this rooftop breakfast spot with golden haveli and fort views. It's also a cool cafe to enjoy afternoon tea and coffee.
Patwa Haveli, near Amar Sagar Pol, Jaisalmer / +91 29 9225 3833

WHERE TO DRINK

Because Jaisalmer has no private bars, you can enjoy cocktails at hotel pubs or purchase liquor from government-approved shops.

Kanchan Shree Shop

Every Rajasthani city has an iconic lassi shop, and Kanchan Shree is the local favorite in Jaisalmer. A 10-minute walk from the main gate, the shop also sells ice cream and kulfi.

Gadisar Road, Jaisalmer / +91 29 9225 0990

LOCAL TOURS AND EXPERIENCES

Golden Fort Heritage Walk

Embark on a 3-hour walking tour through the Jaisalmer Fort and learn about the legends and legacies of Sonar Kila.

www.jaisalmermagic.com

Desert Camping and Camel Safari

Located in the desert, Jaisalmer is a prime destination for jeep rides, camel safaris, and dune camping. Both the Sam Sand Dunes and Khuri Sand Dunes offer budget-friendly and luxury overnight desert camps. Camels sway in the distance while the sun sets against a shimmering sea of desert dunes, all culminating with epic stargazing.

One of our favorites is the desert camping by Vedic Walks: www.vedicwalks.com

DAY TRIPS

Bada Bagh

Bada Bagh (also known as Bara Bagh or Big Garden) are the royal cenotaphs of Jaisalmer Maharajas, including Jai Singh II. Overlooking a mango grove, the golden chhatris are striking against the desert landscape. To avoid the crowds and avail cooler temperatures, plan your visit at sunrise. (Remember to remove your shoes when entering a cenotaph!)

Hours: 8 am - 6 pm daily
Entry: INR 100
How to Reach: Hire a taxi or private car for the short 6 km drive from Jaisalmer

Khaba Fort

The ruins of Khaba Fort date back to the 13th century. Located in a barren desert village in the Thar Desert, the fort was once home to 80 families and abandoned 200 years ago for unknown reasons. The archaeological site features a small museum and hundreds of wild peacocks roaming the grounds.

Hours: 8 am - 5 pm daily
Entry: INR 50
How to Reach: Hire a taxi or private car for the one-hour (35 km) ride from Jaisalmer

Longewala War Memorial

The Battle of Longewala (December 4 - 7, 1971) was one of the first major engagements in western India during the Indo-Pakistani War. With audio narration, the complex showcases the conflict with military displays, tanks, weapons, exhibits, and murals of soldiers who lost their lives. A historical and reflective site for Indians, Longewala is also recommended for military and history enthusiasts.

Hours: 8 am - 6 pm

Entry: INR 40
How to Reach: Hire a taxi or private car for the one-hour (75 km) journey from Jaisalmer

Tanot Mata Temple

Located near Longewala is Tanot Mata Temple, constructed in 828 AD. According to Charan literature, Tanot Mata is an incarnation of the divine goddess Hinglaj Mata. The temple was attacked by 3000 bombs by the Pakistan Army during the war in 1971; however, there was no damage to the sacred structure and unexploded bomb shells still remain on temple grounds.

Hours: 5 am - 8 pm; the evening Aarti is generally scheduled from 6 pm - 7 pm
Entry: Free
How to Reach: Hire a taxi or private car for the two-hour (77 km) journey from Jaisalmer

UNIQUE STAYS IN
RAJASTHAN

Rajasthan offers a portfolio of unique accommodations outside major cities, including historic forts, wildlife camps, and restored heritage properties. Here are six GGG faves.

Dev Shree Deogarh

Located two hours from Udaipur, Dev Shree is an intimate 8-bedroom property that is personally managed by the scion of the Deogarh Family. Constructed in a traditional haveli style, the exclusive homestay features oversized verandahs, spacious interiors, and courtyards that reflect Rajput architecture. Bhavna and Shatrunjai, the owners and hosts, offer an impeccable guest experience that includes guided village walks, sunset jeep rides, poolside yoga, and some of the best home-cooked food in Rajasthan. www.devshreedeogarh.com

Ramathra Fort

A private fort perched on a hill, Ramathra overlooks miles of serene country, farms, and a large perennial lake. Around Ramathra are some of the best walking trails in the region, besides wilderness drives into scrub country and birding. This is a place to connect with the locals and integrate with the traditional village communities. Dinner time is very special in Ramathra as fragrant, home cooked recipes are served under the starry sky. www.ramathrafort.com

RAAS Chhatrasagar

A luxury tented camp for wildlife and birding enthusiasts,

Chhatrasagar is nestled on a man-made resoirvier in Pali (1.5 hours from Jodhpur). Enjoy a sunrise stroll around the lake or an evening jeep drive through the grasslands, spying myriad bird species and herds of blue bull. Finish the day with a sundowner and animated chats around a blazing fire under a canopy of stars. The cuisine incorporates local, organic home produce as much as possible and the age old family recipes receive some of the highest praise in Rajasthan. www.raashotels.com

Mihir Garh

Mihir Garh is an exclusive, 9-bedroom boutique property with private terraces, courtyards, and plunge pools. The infinity pool offers spectacular views of the desert wilderness and the property boasts one of the finest equestrian programs in Rajasthan. Spend your days visiting neighboring villages, learn royal recipes from the legendary kitchen, or reserve a royal picnic in the wilderness. www.houseofrohet.com

Alila Fort Bishangarh

Located in Bishangarh Village between Delhi and Jaipur is the 230-year-old Alila Fort. As one of the only warrior forts to be converted into a heritage resort, this historic landmark is a unique example of Jaipur Gharana architecture, influenced by both the Mughals and the British. Meet local artisans, reserve a masterclass on Rajasthani cuisine, or sit poolside while admiring the panoramic rural landscapes. www.alilahotels.com

Lakshman Sagar

At the fringe of the Badlands outside Jodhpur, Lakshman Sagar was built in the late 19th century as a hunting lodge to host other noble families and British emissaries. Seeped in history, every corner of Lakshman Sagar depicts the nuances of hunting holidays during the days of the Raj. Each room opens into a private splash pool overlooking the lake, creating a visual bliss with a panoramic view of the landscape. www.sewara.com

MUMBAI
(FORMERLY BOMBAY)

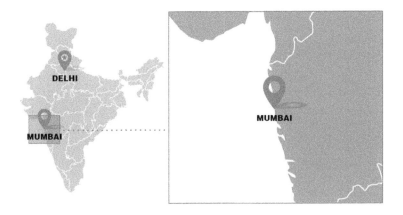

City of Dreams

Holding world records for the largest film industry and the largest slum, Mumbai is a city of contrasts. India's financial hub is gritty, contemporary, and incredibly resilient. Every year, millions of people come to Mumbai in search of a better future and the eclecticism leaves a permanent imprint on its culture.

GGG asked a good friend and local Mumbaiker, **Prachi Jatania**, to provide content for this destination. A Journalist and Digital Media Communications Specialist, Prachi has lived in India's financial hub for much of her childhood and professional years. She currently resides in Mumbai with her husband and 8-year-old daughter.

TRANSPORTATION HUBS

Mumbai is located on the coast of the western state of Maharashtra.

Chhatrapati Shivaji Maharaj International Airport (BOM)
Santacruz East Mumbai

Mumbai is India's second largest airport and was awarded the best Asia-Pacific airport (based on size) in 2020. There are two terminals: Terminal 1 at Santacruz for domestic flights and Terminal 2 at Sahar for both international and domestic flights. There is a 20-minute drive between the terminals, though they share the same airside facilities. Make sure to allow enough time to connect between international and domestic flights, as they may be in different terminals.

Mumbai Central Station (MMCT)
Mumbai Central

Chhatrapati Shivaji Terminus (CST)
Dhobi Talao, Chhatrapati Shivaji Terminus Area, Fort

As a major metropolitan city, Mumbai has several rail stations. The main locations are MMCT and CST. There is frequent connectivity to regional and major cities across India.

MSRTC Mumbai Central
R.B.I Branch, Vahatuk Bhavan (MSRTC), Dr Anandrao Nair Marg

Intercity and Interstate buses are available daily at regular frequencies.

AREAS TO AVOID

The Mumbai Police has broadly indicated to avoid isolated areas after 6pm IST, including subways, railway stations, and old mill compounds (where nightclubs, cafes, and eateries are located but may not have adequately lit entry and exit points). Also avoid Aarey Colony in Goregaon. This is often an isolated route in the late evenings with thickets and bushy spots being adjacent to nature reserves, alleyways, construction sites, and beach spots that may not be adequately lit.

LOCAL FESTIVALS

Ganesh Chaturthi
This ten-day Hindu festival celebrates the birth of Lord Ganesha, the elephant-headed God of new beginnings. The idols are worshipped every day with an Aarti celebration in the evening. The largest Ganesha statues on display to the public are immersed in water on the final day, Anant Chaturdashi. (In Mumbai, more than 150,000 statues are immersed every year!) Exact dates differ annually based on the lunar calendar, but the celebration generally falls in August or September.

WHERE TO STAY

Zostel Mumbai
A large and lively backpacker hostel near the Mumbai airport.
$ / www.zostel.com / +91 22 4896 2270

Mumbai Staytion
A clean, cozy, and comfortable hostel catering to free-spirited backpackers.
$ / www.mumbaistaytion.com / +91 98 3372 5472

Le Sutra

An art hotel in the heart of Mumbai that was crafted for creativity and curiosity.

$$ / www.lesutra.in / +91 22 6642 0020

Abode

A luxury boutique hotel in the trendy Colaba neighborhood.

$$ / www.abodeboutiquehotels.com / +91 80 8023 4066

The Gordon House

An intimate hotel that blends Scandanavian, Mediterranean, and English Country designs.

$$$ / www.ghhotel.com / +91 22 6124 5800

Taj Mahal Palace

An iconic and exclusive hotel overlooking the Gateway of India.

$$$$ / www.tajhotels.com / +91 22 6665 3366

Oberoi Mumbai

A luxury hotel featuring women butlers for female guests.

$$$$ / www.oberoihotels.com / +91 22 6632 5757

Mumbai

WHAT TO DO

Gateway of India

The Gateway of India was built to commemorate the December 1911 visit of King Emperor George V and Queen Mary. Overlooking the Arabian Sea, the monument is an icon of the city. Fun fact: At the time of the royal visit, the gateway was not yet complete and the royals were greeted by a cardboard structure. After construction was completed in 1924, the monument was used as a symbolic ceremonial entrance to British India for VIP's; it is also where the last British troops left India in 1948, following independence.

Entry: Free
Hours: 24/7; For best lighting, visit at sunrise or sunset

Dhobi Ghat (Mahalaxmi Dhobi Ghat)

Viewed from a distance, the 140-year-old open air laundromat appears disorderly and overwhelming; however, a closer look reveals an organized chaos. It is estimated that the workers at Dhobi Ghat

Dhobit Ghat

wash, bleach, dry, and iron about one million pieces of clothing every day. Spread across 15 acres, the best time to view the action is early morning.

Entry: Free
Hours: 7 am - 8 pm daily

Mani Bhavan Gandhi Museum

Mani Bhavan served as Gandhiji's Mumbai headquarters for 17 years. It is also where Mahatma Gandhi initiated his famous Satyagraha movement and propagated the causes of Swadeshi (made in India and using locally made products) and Khadi (handloom textile). Mani Bhavan was dedicated as a memorial to Gandhiji in 1955 and houses a library and a gallery depicting his life.

Entry: INR 20
Hours: 9:30 am - 6 pm daily
http://www.gandhi-manibhavan.org/

Chhatrapati Shivaji Maharaj Vastu Sangrahalaya

Chhatrapati Shivaji Maharaj Vastu Sangrahalaya, formerly known as the Prince of Wales Museum, is a premier art and history museum in Mumbai. The gallery was built in 1905 in honor of the Prince of Wales's (King George V) first visit to India. An architectural marvel, the heritage building was awarded the UNESCO Asia – Pacific Heritage Award for Cultural Heritage Conservation.

Entry: INR 200
Hours: 10 am - 3 pm daily
https://www.csmvs.in/

Marine Drive

Marine Drive is a landmark in Mumbai and featured in several Bollywood movies. The 3.5 km c-shaped boulevard is also called the *Queen's Necklace* as its nighttime aerial view resembles the shape of a necklace with "jewels" (glittering lights).

Entry: Free
Hours: As a public boulevard, the road is open 24/7

Chhatrapati Shivaji Maharaj Terminus

A historical train station and UNESCO World Heritage site, Chhatrapati is one of the largest and busiest train stations in the world. The architecture is a fusion of British and Indian elements that forged a unique and symbolic style in Mumbai.

Entry: Free
Hours: 24/7; Visit in the morning to experience rush hour

Sassoon Docks

Built in 1875, the Sassoon Docks define the mercurial character of Mumbai. It was named after David Sassoon, a Jewish man from Baghdad whose company built the docks for the trade of silk and cotton goods. Located in Colaba (South Mumbai), the docks offer a glimpse into the fishing community, including the largest wholesale fish market. The best time to walk the docks is between 5 – 8 am.

Entry: Free
Hours: 5 am - 8 pm daily

Sassoon Docks

WHERE TO SHOP

Crawford Market

A large wholesale market, Crawford is famous not only for fresh produce and poultry but also for its Victorian Gothic architecture. Look out for great deals on imported foods! In 1882, the building was the first in India to be lit up by electricity.

Hours: 11 am - 8 pm daily; Closed on Tuesdays
Location: 367 Abdul Rehman Street, Lohar Chawl, Kalbadevi

Fashion Street, Churchgate

Very popular among students and teenagers, the cluster of shops are spread across numerous streets and together referred to as Fashion Street. You will find trendy, export surplus and chic clothing at bargain prices. The vibrant flea market is a haven for fashionable attire, traditional wear, jewelry, and accessories.

Hours: 11 am - 8 pm daily
Location: Opposite Azad Maidan, Karamveer Bhaurao Patil Marg, M.G. Road, South Mumbai

Malad Market / Natraj Market

During festivals, Malad Market is packed with shoppers purchasing traditional attire, cosmetics, gold, silver, and artificial jewelry. It is one of the oldest neighborhood markets in Malad.

Hours: 10 am - 8 pm daily; Closed on Sundays
Location: Parekh Road, Malad

Bandra Hill Road and Linking Road

A posh suburb in Mumbai, Bandra is popular for shopping. Both Hill Road and Linking Road are famous for street shops selling clothes, jewelry, shoes, handbags, cosmetics, and other fashion trinkets. A wardrobe makeover at bargain prices!

Hours: 10 am - 9 pm daily
Location: Bandra Hill Road and Linking Road

Colaba Causeway
With street shops and fashionable boutiques, Colaba welcomes shoppers with clothes, jewelry, souvenirs, pashmina shawls, and replicated artifacts. The area is also filled with popular restaurants and bars.

Hours: 9 am - 10 pm daily
Location: Colaba Causeway

Dadar Flower Market
The vibrant colors and floral fragrances will awaken your senses. Also known as the Dadar Phool Gali, this is the biggest (and only) wholesale flower market in Mumbai. Flowers are sold by length, weight, and numbers and you can find varieties from the locally grown roses and marigolds to exotic tulips.

Hours: 6 am - 8 pm daily
Location: 302, Senapati Bapat Marg, Dadar West

WHERE TO EAT

Bombay Canteen

Bombay Canteen was launched by Floyd Cardoz, a four-time James Beard Award nominee, winner of Top Chef Masters, and the "godfather of modern Indian cuisine." The cafe and bar offers a creative Indian menu and colonial-inspired cocktails.

Unit-1, Process House, S.B. Road, Kamala Mills, Near Radio Mirchi Office Lower, Parel

Sardar Pav Bhaji

Pav Bhaji is one of the most popular street foods in Mumbai, and no one makes it better than Sardar Pav Bhaji. The no-frills joint has been dishing out vegetable curry on buttered buns since 1966.

Junction, 166-A, Tardeo Rd, Janata Nagar, Tardeo

Colaba Causeway

Just as shopping is great in Colaba, so is the food! Popular eateries include Cafe Mondegar, Theobroma Patisserie, Colaba Social, Bademiyan, and Kailash Parbat.

Colaba Causeway, South Mumbai

India Bistro

India Bistro serves regional specialities from North India and Punjab. Try the hearty chicken curry, dal makhani, and kebabs.

301, Safal Pride, Sion Trombay Road Deonar

Theobroma Patisserie

A boutique patisserie that first opened in Colaba, Theobroma has since branched out across Mumbai. The breads and pastries are a hit!
24, Cusrow Baug, Electric House, Colaba

Copper Chimney

With several locations across Mumbai, this restaurant serving authentic North Indian cuisine has been a local favorite since 1972. Although each location is delicious, the flagship store in Worli continues to be a favorite among its patrons.
Ground Floor, Door No.12-A, Lotus Court, Dr. A.B. Road, Worli

Woodside Inn

Popular for its burgers, pizza, and artisanal beers, Woodside Inn is famous with the younger crowd. With live music and attentive service, it's a hidden gem in Colaba.
Indian Mercantile Chamber Building Ground Floor Woodhouse Road, Opposite Regal Cinema

Pali Village Café

With simple, rustic interiors and a focus on food, Pali Village Cafe serves European cuisine and good wine. It's slightly pricey but worth it.
10, Pali Mala Road, Adarsh Nagar, Bandra West

Kulfi Centre

As the name suggests, Kulfi Centre is a small shop selling some of the best Kulfi (Indian milk desserts) in Mumbai. Try the traditional flavors like Kesar Pista and Malai and the seasonal favorites like Mango and Chiku.
Marina Mansion, 556, Sardar Vallabhbhai Patel Road, Sea Face, Sukh Sagar

WHERE TO DRINK

Leopold Café
Dating back to 1871, this Irani cafe bar is one of the most popular spots in Colaba. Leopold shot to international fame with Gregory Roberts's book *Shantaram* and sees lines of people every weekend.
Shaheed Bhagat Singh Road, Colaba Causeway

The Social
This urban cafe and bar has outlets in almost all metropolitan cities of India. With 11 locations just in Mumbai, this is the only cafe where work and play can happen simultaneously - with cocktails.
Unit.3, The Capital, G Block Rd, G Block BKC, Bandra Kurla Complex, Bandra East

Gateway Taproom
Gateway is an upscale yet casual pub serving award-winning brews and European cuisine. Enjoy a pint of their draft beer with Shrimp Tortellini and Malt Glazed Salmon.
Godrej BKC, Unit 3, Plot C - 68, G Block, Bandra Kurla Complex

LOCAL TOURS AND EXPERIENCES

Street Food Walk - Khau Gully
'Khau Gully' translates to 'Food Lane'. Learn about the history and evolution of Mumbai street food and taste the local favorites.
https://www.nfpexplore.com/product/street-food-walk-khau-gully/

Street Food Walk – Kebab and Curry
Residing in India since the 16th century, Bohra Muslims are a small business community whose food has become an important part of the country's culinary narrative. Sample some of their quintessential

delicacies, including 12 pot curry, Seekh Kebab, and hand churned ice creams.
https://www.nfpexplore.com/product/street-food-walk-kebab-and-curry-walk/

Mumbai by Dawn
"A city that never sleeps" is an apt expression for Mumbai. Grab a chai and experience the city early in the morning with a visit to a fish market, flower market, and herb mandi (market selling green leafy vegetables).
https://www.nfpexplore.com/product/mumbai-by-dawn-a-city-awakens/

Heritage Walk (Colonial Walk - Historical Sauntering)
This experiential tour will take you through the tourist precinct of Mumbai and showcase the heritage buildings and landmarks.
https://www.nfpexplore.com/product/colonial-walk-historical-sauntering/

Dharavi Tour
A visit to one of Asia's largest slums and experiencing life in the most bustling and economically proficient part of Mumbai.
https://www.nfpexplore.com/product/dharavi-tour/

Of Bold Spices and Thieves Market
Visit the Lalbagh spice market and the infamous Chor Bazaar (Thieves Market) where you will find everything from electronics to perfume. They say if you lose something in Mumbai, you can buy it back from the Chor Bazaar.
https://www.nfpexplore.com/product/of-bold-spices-and-thieves-market/

Bollywood Dance Workshop
Learn Bollywood dancing from the pros! With spirited music and dramatic facial expressions, Bollywood dancing is a fun way of learning about the culture of India.
https://www.nfpexplore.com/mumbai/workshops/bollywood-dance-workshop/

A Day with Dabbawalas
Dressed in white outfits and traditional Gandhi caps, an army of 5,000 dabbawalas fulfill the hunger of almost 200,000 Mumbaikars with home-

cooked food. The Dabbawallas, called the Lifeline of Mumbai, deliver meals from a customer's home to the offices and then return the Dabbas (metal lunch boxes) back on the same day. Started in 1890, the "meals-on-wheels" organization is the oldest food delivery service in the world. https://www.nfpexplore.com/product/a-day-with-dabbawallas/

Five Senses Tour

Engage your five senses through five different immersive experiences:

Sight - Walk through the historical precinct and cover the popular monuments and landmarks
Sound - Listen and groove to Bollywood music
Taste - Sample the local cuisine
Smell - Visit the Mumbai spice market
Touch - Volunteer and engage with the community
https://www.nfpexplore.com/product/the-five-senses-tour/

DAY TRIPS

Alibaug

Alibaug is known for its beaches like Kashid, Kihim, and Varsoli. Just offshore, the 17th-century Kolaba (Alibaug) Fort has carvings of tigers, elephants, and temples dedicated to Hindu gods. To the south, Portuguese-built Korlai Fort dates from 1521 and includes a lighthouse. Check out the island fort of Janjira with its high walls, turrets, and cannons.

Besides enjoying time at the beaches, you can also explore the Jewish legacy of the D Samson Soda Shop located between Alibaug and Poynad. It is a monument to the Bene Israeli community who settled in the area. Daniel Samson Digodkar established this iconic soda joint in 1938 after the local mills shut down. Today it's run by his son, Daniel Sydney, and a popular spot for the residents of Alibaug to catch up or chat about world affairs. If you enjoy conversations with strangers, plan to spend time here. If not, you can always just ask for a fizzy soda drink (pick from the large variety or dive into the rich ice cream soda) and enjoy the old-world charm.

How to reach: The beach town of Alibaug is a short ferry ride from the Gateway of India. You can use a Ro-Ro water taxi, recently introduced between South Mumbai and Alibaug beach town. From Mandwa Jetty take a local rickshaw or 45-minute bus ride. The most convenient way is via ferry or catamaran from the Gateway of India. Mumbai to Alibaug ferries are available throughout the year except during the monsoon season. By road, it takes up to three hours depending on traffic.

Elephanta Caves

A short boat ride from Gateway of India, Elephanta Caves are a UNESCO World Heritage Site and a collection of cave temples predominantly dedicated to the Hindu god Shiva. The island consists of five Hindu caves and a few Buddhist stupa mounds that date back to the 2nd century BCE, as well as a small group of two Buddhist caves with water tanks. The Elephanta Caves contain rock cut stone sculptures that show syncretism of Hindu and Buddhist ideas and iconography.

How to Reach: Boats operate to Elephanta Island (Gharapuri) every 30 minutes between 9 am and 2 pm. Boats operate *from* Elephanta every 30 minutes between noon and 5:30 pm. The ride takes approximately one hour. Elephanta Caves and the ferry service are closed on Mondays.

Karjat

Residents of Mumbai often visit Karjat to escape the monotony of city life or participate in various adventure sports. The city is full of rich vegetation, several waterfalls, and rocky terrain that make it the perfect abode for a weekend getaway. Visit Peth Fort, located in a small village in the vicinity of Karjat. The fort offers a panoramic view of the surroundings and forms the backdrop of the quaint village of Matheran. The entire Konkan countryside can be viewed from the fort, constructed by Maratha rulers to protect their kingdom against foreign invasion. Although Peth Fort is now almost in ruins, the water cisterns around the fort remain undamaged.

How to Reach: Karjat is a local railway station and there are trains running from Mumbai to CST every 30 minutes. The first train for Karjat starts at 4:15 am from CST and the last train at 12:43. With local trains, it takes 2-3 hours to reach Karjat from CST. There are also around 16 direct trains from Mumbai and it takes 20 mins to reach Karjat.

Lonavla

The area around Lonavala was an important Buddhist center in the 2nd century BC. Several rock-cut cave temples remain, including Karla and Bhaja. Located in the inhospitable terrain of the Sahyadri mountain range, Lonavla was not an important site in terms of history. Popular for trekking and hiking, the lush hill station is also known for its production of *chikki* (hard candy). The lush hill station offers trekking, hiking,

How to Reach: Reserve a private car for the 1+ hour drive from Mumbai. Alternatively, you can take an outstation train to Pune and get off at Lonavala railway station.

GIVING BACK

SNEHA Mumbai

SNEHA is a non-profit organisation that works with women, children, and public health and safety systems. Launched in 1999, the innovative work in urban informal settlements aims to reduce maternal and neonatal mortality and morbidity, child malnutrition, and gender-based violence. www.snehamumbai.com

Srujna

Srujna has created business opportunities for underprivileged women since 2011. The organization promotes economic and social empowerment through its Make and Market programs. Donations are welcome to continue the support of female entrepreneurship. https://www.srujna.org/

INTERVIEW WITH A LOCAL:
PRACHI JATANIA

What do you love and loathe about Mumbai?

I love the frenetic pace and the multicultural and cosmopolitan fabric of the city. People from various regions and cities come to live in Mumbai to fulfill their aspirations, ambitions of a modern, busy life. I also love how accepting Mumbai is to people from all strata, all walks of life. Locals don't care or bother about which brand of clothing you are wearing, what car you drive, or how much money you make. You are accepted regardless of your societal standing.

And it is this hectic, frenzy life that I also loathe. It takes an emotional toll sometimes because one has to consciously ensure there is time for self-care, family, and to pursue interests other than simply chasing work deadlines. Also, the local administration can do much more by providing better infrastructure in the forms of better-quality roads, a less congested organized metro-rail/local tube travel network, and cleaner public spaces.

There is so much to experience! What do you recommend?

1. Bicycle ride tours on evenings and weekends
2. Heritage walks in South Mumbai and other suburbs

3. Day treks in Yeoor Hills, Thane, or Sanjay Gandhi National Park (Please choose a local tour group for a safer, more immersive experience!)

4. Sunrise walks to Bhau-cha Dhakka or Ferry Wharf. This is Mumbai's largest and oldest fish market, on the eastern seafront. Catch a local train to Dockyard Road station on Mumbai's local railway network (Harbour Line) and walk to Ferry Wharf.

5. Watch the sunset at the Queen's Necklace/Marine Drive

6. Attend a cricket match organized via the official BCCI (Board of Cricket Control of India), possibly a T-20 game. This will require buying tickets to the game in advance. You can also catch a local cricket match at the Oval Maidan in Churchgate (free).

What advice would you give visitors to Mumbai?

Mumbai can be explored easily in 4 days/3 nights. This is enough time for you to see all the major architectural landmarks, the famous beaches, and take a Bollywood tour. Along with that, you can explore restaurants and cafes across the city to try a distinct variety of food. You can also do some shopping, as the city has markets ranging from the huge flea markets, to the famous Chor Bazaar and high street malls. The beautiful coastline, roadside street food, high-end restaurants and cafes, Bollywood (Indian film industry) tours, and many more elements make this a sensational place to visit.

Mumbai is known for its street food. Where can we find the best late-night snacks?

Mumbai sleeps late, so satisfying a midnight craving is easy. If you are adventurous with your palate, you can enjoy local snacks like vada-pav, Bombay sandwich, mango milkshakes, royal falooda, egg bhurji/masala scrambled eggs, meat rolls, seafood, and pav bhaji.

Ayub's, Kalaghoda
Badey Miyan, Apollo Bunder

Jaffer's Delhi Darbar, Grant Road
Trishna restaurant, Colaba
Amar Juice centre and fast food, Vile Parle
Go Biryani, Andheri
Bhagwati, Kandivli
Naturals Ice Cream, several outlets

Anything else you wish to share with our readers?

Mumbai is often called a microcosm of the old and new, contemporary and with glimpses of the past. The contrasts are stark and glaring. Here slums jostle for space with tall multi-storeys, the rich and wealthy stand out from the poor. For many tourists, seeing beggars at traffic lights at the same time as watching a luxury car drive by the same street could be an overwhelming experience. Come prepared with an open mind, without judgement, with a sense of adventure but also a sensitivity towards cultural and social differences. Mumbai is a bustling metropolis that offers an immersive experience if you allow it.

I've often had mixed emotions about living in Mumbai. I spent most of my childhood years here as well pursuing my undergrad and postgrad studies. Since my husband served in the Indian Armed Forces, we had an opportunity to travel and live in many other cities across India. But Mumbai holds a special place in our hearts. I met my husband here during a work assignment and we've built many memories together in this city. I love the local cuisine that is an amalgamation of many different culinary influences – Goan, Parsee, Maharashtrian, and Gujarati among many. My favorites include vada pav, missal, Bombay sandwich, sugarcane juice, and bhel-puri.

Mumbai shaped my career as a journalist, exposing me to the rugged, the raw, the fast-paced life that I found both intoxicating and challenging. But living here and accepting it with all its flaws has taught me to be more accepting, grateful, forgiving, and resilient.

NASHIK

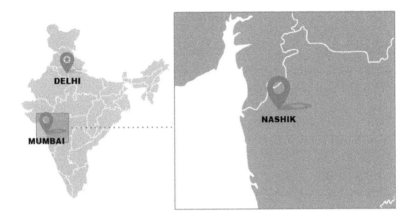

The Wine Capital of India

A favorable climate and ideal temperatures have attracted almost half of India's wineries and vineyards to Nashik. In addition to producing internationally recognized and award winning wines, many vineyards now feature modern tasting rooms and luxury accommodations. The city also has immense religious significance. Every twelve years, Nashik hosts the Kumbh Mela, considered one of the world's most massive religious gatherings.

TRANSPORTATION HUBS

Nashik is located in the state of Maharashtra, 160 km from Mumbai.

Chhatrapati Maharaj International Airport Mumbai
Santacruz East Mumbai / +91 22 6685 1010

The closest airport to Nashik is located in Mumbai. To reach Nashik, hire a private vehicle for the 3.5 hour (170 km) journey.

Nashik Road Railway Station (NK)
Slali Gaon, P&T Colony, Rajwada Nagar, Deolali Gaon

Nashik is well connected to major Indian cities by train, including Delhi, Allahabad, Punjab, Varanasi, and Kanpur. Day and night trains from Mumbai operate daily with high frequency.

Nashik Madhyawarti Bus Sthanak (Nashik Central Bus Station)
Near Nashik Court, CBS Rd, Police Staff Colony

Mahamarg MSRTC Bus Station
Mumbai Naka, Gaikwad Nagar

There are frequent intercity and interstate buses connecting Nashik to Mumbai and beyond.

AREAS TO AVOID

Overall, Nashik is a safe destination for female travelers. However, it is recommended not to travel alone in crowded areas or markets (such as Phule Market) after dark.

LOCAL FESTIVALS

Rathyatra

Janmotsava, the festival of the birth of Lord Rama, is celebrated at Sansthan Shri Kalaram Mandir, Panchavati, Nashik every year in March or April. The festival spans 15 days from the first day of Chaitra until the Chaitra Purnima (full moon). Janmotsava is witnessed by thousands of pilgrims every year and starts exactly at 12 pm. The auspicious Rathyatra, or procession, occurs on the second day when Lord Ram Rath and Garuda Rath move through Nashik.

WHERE TO STAY

The Source at Sula
A heritage vineyard resort surrounded by grape farms.
$$$ / https://sulavineyards.com/ +91 78 7555 5735

Grape County
A luxury eco-resort set on 150 acres with sky rooms and forest tents.
$$$ / www.grapecounty.in / +91 70 3091 5009

Beyond by Sula
The exclusive and intimate sister property to The Source by Sula.
$$$$ / https://sulavineyards.com/ +91 78 7555 5725

Viveda Wellness Retreat
An integrated wellness village infused with ancient knowledge of health and hospitality.
$$$$ / https://vivedawellness.com / +91 78 8780 5800

WHAT TO DO

Vineyard Tours
As the wine capital of India, vineyards are a major tourist attraction in

Nashik. Two of our favorites are Sula and York Winery.

Entry: Approximately INR 400
Hours: Please visit the individual websites for timings

https://sulavineyards.com/
http://www.yorkwinery.com/

Nasik Caves (PandavLeni Caves)
The Nasik Caves are a group of 23 Buddhist caves built on the outskirts of Nashik on Trirashmi Hill. The intricate carvings, craftsmanship, and outstanding sculptures reflect the transformation of Buddhist devotional practices.

Entry: INR 500
Hours: 8 am - 6 pm daily

Panchavati Temples
Panchavati got its name from the original five banyan trees in the area. In Marathi, 'Panch' means five and 'Vati' means banyan tree. It is believed that Lord Rama, Sita, and Laxman stayed in Panchvati,

making the temples a popular pilgrimage destination for Hindus in Maharashtra.

Entry: INR 200 per person
Hours: 24/7

Trimbakeshwar Temple
An ancient Shiva temple in the town of Trimbak, Trimbakeshwar is one of the 12 jyotirlingas. Located at the source of the Godavari River, it is a holy space and pilgrimage site for all Hindus.

Entry: INR 200 per person
Hours: 5:30 am - 9 pm daily

WHERE TO SHOP

Saraf Bazaar
As one of the busiest markets in Nashik, Saraf Bazaar is popular for gold shops. There are more than 400 jewelry showrooms selling necklaces, earrings, anklets, and rings. The market is also known for beautifully carved gold utensils.

Location: Panchavati, Nashik

Vithal Market
Famous for clothes and footwear, the market is popular among the ladies.

Location: Main Road, Shinde Wada, Shalimar

WHERE TO EAT AND DRINK

Sadhana Village

For a local flavor, visit Sadhana Village. Try the traditional Maharashtrian misal pav, a spicy sprouted bean curry topped with crunchy Farsan, crisp red onions, and fresh cilantro served with lightly buttered Pav or dinner rolls.

Haji Farms, Opposite Sula Vineyard, Govardhan

Cellar Door Wine Lounge

A short drive from the city center takes you to York Winery and their restaurant, Cellar Door Wine Lounge. An Indian restaurant and bar with an extensive food menu, the eatery aims to break the myth that Indian food does not pair well with wine.

Gat no. 15/2, Gangavarhe Village, Gangapur-Savargaon Road

The Foundry – Industrial Bar and Sport

An industrial sports bar with live music, The Foundry is a favorite among the younger crowd for a relaxed evening out with friends. Delivery is also available!

BLVD, Level 2, P20, Satpur MIDC Rd.

LOCAL TOURS AND EXPERIENCES

Grape Stomping at Soma Vine Village

Visit Soma Vine Village to experience the traditional method of producing wines. Feel the grapes between your toes as you jump in an oak barrel and extract juices with your feet.

Entry: INR 350
Hours: 11:30 am - 6 pm daily

Cheese Tasting at Le Fromage

A close drive to York Winery is Le Fromage, Nashik's first artisanal cheese company. Sample natural organic cheeses to pair with your wine, including mozzarella, feta, gouda (with chilli and black pepper variations), and cheddar. You can also view the cheese-making process upon request.

Entry: INR 200 per person
Hours: 9 am - 6:30 pm daily

DAY TRIPS

Shirdi

The town of Shirdi is the former home of spiritual leader Sai Baba. Identified as a saint and a fakir, Sai Baba was revered by both Hindu and Muslim devotees during and after his lifetime. Shirdi is a popular pilgrimage destination for followers who visit the Sri Saibaba Samadhi temple to pay their respects.

Entry: Free
How to Reach: Direct buses are available from Nashik or hire a private car for the 2-hour journey

AURANGABAD

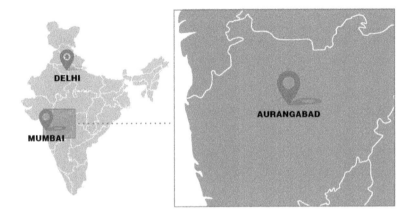

DELHI

MUMBAI

AURANGABAD

The City of Gates

Aurangabad is home to the renowned cave temples and UNESCO World Heritage Sites of Ajanta and Ellora. It is also a major center for Mughal relics, cotton textiles, and traditional silk fabrics. The historical significance and the medieval charm make Aurangabad a popular weekend retreat from Mumbai.

TRANSPORTATION HUBS

Aurangabad is located in the state of Maharashtra, 200 km to Nashik and 240 km to Pune.

Chhatrapati Sambhaji Maharaj Airport (IXU)
Jalna Road, Chikalthana, Aurangabad, Maharashtra 431006

Aurangabad is a smaller airport yet still well connected to Hyderabad, Delhi, Udaipur, Mumbai, Jaipur, Pune, Nagpur, and Indore.

Aurangabad Railway Station (AWB)
Silk Mill Colony, Aurangabad

Aurangabad has regular train service to Mumbai, Delhi, Hyderabad, Pune, Madurai, and other major Indian cities.

Aurangabad Central Bus Station
CBS Road, Mhada, Aurangabad, Maharashtra 431002

AREAS TO AVOID

Overall, Aurangabad is a safe destination for female travelers.

LOCAL FESTIVALS

Ajanta and Ellora Festival
Held annually in March, the Ajanta and Ellora Festival celebrates classical dance and music. Organized by the Maharashtra Government Tourism Department, prominent and talented personalities across the country showcase their genius in dance and music against the backdrop of the brilliant Ellora Caves.

Aurangabad Festival
The Aurangabad Festival celebrates the city's rich cultural and artistic heritage. Administered by the Aurangabad Festival Committee, the event features performances of classical dances, folk dances, popular songs, Mushaira, Ghazals, and Qawwali. Handlooms and handicrafts like Himroo, Mashru, Paithani, Bidri, and Paperwork are also exhibited by local artisans.

Khuldabad Urs
Khuldabad Urs is celebrated by Muslims in the month of Rabi-Ul-Awal (May). Devotees gather at the tomb of Khwaja for five days and pay respects to consecrated saints, namely Burhan-ud-din and Zain-ud-din.

Paithan Fair
The Paithan Fair is celebrated in March or April when pilgrims gather at Paithan and pay homage at the Eknath Maharaj Temple. Located on the banks of the Godavari River, the fair spans for ten days with incomparable enthusiasm and gusto.

WHERE TO STAY

Zostel Aurangabad
A lively and centrally-located backpackers hostel.
$ / www.zostel.com / +91 22 4896 2270

Lemon Tree
A local chain with modern amenities and a large swimming pool.
$$ / www.lemontreehotels.com / +91 24 0660 3030

Vivanta by Taj
An upmarket hotel in landscaped gardens featuring a traditional tea house.
$$$$ / www.vivantahotels.com / +91 24 0261 3737

WHAT TO DO

Bibi Ka Maqbara
Bibi Ka Maqbara was built by the last mughal emperor Aurangzeb in memory of his wife, Dilras Banu Begum. With intricate carvings and pristine marble, the tomb is also known as the Dakkhani Taj (Taj of the

Deccan) for its resemblance to the Taj Mahal.

Entry: Free
Hours: 8 am - 8 pm daily

Aurangabad Caves

The Aurangabad Caves are a total of 12 Buddhist caves carved out of soft basalt rock. Divided into three groups, the caves are maintained by the Archeological Survey of India. With a scenic hillside setting, each cave has a story to tell with scriptures, figurines, and sculptures.

Entry: INR 100
Hours: 9 am - 5 pm daily

Panchakki

Panchakki (the water mill) offers a glimpse into the scientific brilliance and technology during the medieval era. Nestled among beautiful surroundings with a view of the Kham River, the main purpose of the mill was to generate energy with water from a mountain spring. The mill would then grind grains to feed the pilgrims who visited the Baba Shah Musafir Dargah.

Entry: INR 100
Hours: 7 am - 9 pm daily

Ajanta Caves

A group of 30 caves, Ajanta is an acclaimed UNESCO World Heritage Site. The Buddhist Caves are an ancient architectural marvel and filled with ornate frescoes considered masterpieces of Buddhist art.
The caves were excavated in a horseshoe-shaped bend overlooking a valley. This serene and calm environment provided the Buddhist monks a secluded place to study, meditate, and further their religious pursuits. The murals of Ajanta are recognized as some of the greatest art produced by humankind. Even today, the colors glow with a brilliant intensity.

Entry: INR 600 per person
Hours: 9 am - 6 pm daily; Closed on Mondays

Ajanta

Ellora Caves

Ellora is a neighboring UNESCO cave complex with Hindu, Buddhist, and Jain temples. Of the 100+ caves, 34 are open to the public. Historically, Ellora was on the popular trade route and served as accommodation to the traveling Buddhist and Jain monks. The caves feature deities, carvings, and scriptures depicting the mythology of each religion and representing the harmony and solidarity among all faiths and beliefs.

Entry: INR 600
Hours: 9 am - 5:30 pm; Closed on Tuesdays

Salim Ali Lake and Bird Sanctuary

Calling all nature lovers! Located in the northern part of Aurangabad, the lake and sanctuary provides a safe haven for many local and migratory birds. Known as Khiziri Talab during the Mughal period, the lake was later renamed Salim Ali after the famous naturalist and ornithologist Dr. Salim "Birdman of India" Ali.

Entry: Free
Hours: 8 am - 5 pm daily

Jama Masjid

Known for its magnificent Islamic architecture, Jama Masjid is one of the oldest standing mosques in Aurangabad. The impeccably designed arches, towering minarets, and around 50 polygonal pillars showcases the architectural genius of the Mughals.

Entry: Free
Hours: 24/7

Daulatabad Fort

Daulatabad, meaning City of Prosperity or Fortune, is a 14th-century fort located 16 kilometers northwest of Aurangabad. Once known as Deogiri, the formidable structure of the fort rising amidst the surrounding greenery is often hailed as one of the 'Seven Wonders of Maharashtra'. To reach the top, there is a hike of almost 800 steps - but the views are well worth the climb!

Entry: INR 100
Hours: 9 am - 6 pm

WHERE TO SHOP

Gul Mandi Market

As the main market of Aurangabad, Gul Mandi is located in the heart of the city. The bazaar is a local favorite for clothes, handicrafts, food, costume jewelry, and Paithani sarees.

Hours: 10 am - 10 pm
Location: Shahgunj, Aurangabad

The Emporiums

There are several authorized emporiums in Aurangabad to buy high-quality Himroo fabric and apparel, bidriware handicrafts, and the famous Paithani Sarees. The prices at emporiums are higher compared to local markets (with less bargaining power), but the quality is well worth it.

WHAT TO SHOP FOR IN AURANGABAD

Himroo Fabric

A luxurious handwoven fabric made with cotton and silk, the word "Himroo" originates from the Persian word Hum-ruh meaning "similar.' Himroo is a unique interpretation of the Persian kinkhwab fabric. The designs are traditionally ornate in nature with paisleys, marigolds, vines, and fruits being popular motifs.

Paithani

A traditional Maharashtrian silk saree named after the Paithan town in Aurangabad, Paithani is also known as the Queen of Silks. Traditionally woven by hand with very fine silk, the saree is known for its kaleidoscope-colored designs and ornate motifs.

Bidri "Bidriware"

Bidriware is an indigenous handicraft that originated in Bidar, Karnataka. The ornate design impressions are made on an alloy of copper and zinc and then inlaid with gold and pure silver sheets. Bidriware is one of India's most important handicraft exports and prized as a symbol of wealth in homes across the world.

WHERE TO EAT

Kream and Krunch

Kream and Krunch is redefining gourmet food in Aurangabad. Try the

vietnamese paper rolls, chicken burger, and decadent Mac and Cheese.
Plot No 2, Jalna Road

Yalla Yalla
Despite being a fairly new restaurant, Yalla Yalla has already become popular for its richly spiced Biryani and North Indian dishes.
New Osmanpura Rd, Snehnagar, Konkanwadi

Tandoor
As the name suggests, Tandoor is loved for all things tandoori (made in a traditional Indian clay oven).
Shyam Chambers, Bhanudas Sabhahgrah Railway Station Rd, Bansilal Nagar

D'Curry House
Known for their daily buffets and mutton thali, D'Curry House is an intimate Indian restaurant located in Hotel Green Olive. Order the Dal Bukhara (slow-cooked black lentils), Roomali Papad (a fried crisp with savory toppings), and Aloo Pasanda (meat and potato gravy).
Hotel Green Olive, Next to Punjab National Bank, CBS Road, Bhagya Nagar

Icy Spicy
A casual restaurant known for street food and quick bites, Icy Spicy serves both Indian chaats and American sandwiches.
Mini Shop No. 65-66, Connaught Garden, CIDCO Cannought, Cidco

China Town
With reasonably priced Chinese dishes, China Town is popular with the locals. Try the Malaysian flat noodles!
Amarpreet Hotel, Amarpreet Chowk, Jalna Road

WHERE TO DRINK

Madhushala - Rama International ITC Hotel
Madgushala is one of the only bars in Aurangabad where you can reserve a Mixology class and make innovative cocktails.
Rama International Hotel, Chikalthana, Jalna Road

Slounge - Lemon Tree
A recreation bar with a playstation, pool table, and wonderful cocktails.
Lemon Tree hotel, Chilkalthana

Tease Bar - Vivanta by Taj
The exclusive Tease bar at Vivanta has a cool vibe and classic cocktails.
Vivanta by Taj, Rauza Bagh, Cidco

LOCAL TOURS AND EXPERIENCES

Explore the Cuisine
The cuisine of Aurangabad is a unique fusion of North Indian and Hyderabadi food. Sample popular dishes like the Biryani and Naan Qalia.

http://aurangabadwalks.com/explore-cuisines/

Life & Culture of Aurangabad
Be amazed by the majesty of Aurangabad! Explore the city's culture, glorious monuments, unique history, rich food, and famous textiles and artwork.

http://aurangabadwalks.com/life-culture/

Art & History of Aurangabad

With temples, monasteries, and Buddhist caves, the city of Aurangabad has an important religious significance. The tour will take you through the popular landmarks and let you absorb the glorious past.

DAY TRIPS

Gautala Autramghat Wildlife Sanctuary

A beautiful wildlife reserve known for its dense vegetation, the Gautala Autramghat Sanctuary is located approximately 70 kms from Aurangabad. The foliage and widespread grasslands provide an ideal environment for flora and wildlife to flourish. The resident wildlife includes panthers, Barking deer, chital, and peacock. The best time to visit is between January and March when the weather is ideal for long excursions.

Entry: INR 100 per car to enter the sanctuary
Hours: 9 am - 5 pm daily
How to Reach: Hire a private car for the 1.5 hour (70 km) ride from Aurangabad

Lonar Crater Lake

Lonar is a natural lake created by a meteorite in the Buldhana district of Maharashtra. The water of the lake is alkaline and supports numerous flora and fauna. For conservation purposes, Lonar was also declared a Wildlife Sanctuary.

Entry: Free
How to Reach: Hire a private car for the 3-hour (140 km) ride from Aurangabad

Pitalkhora Caves

Pitalkhora is a complex of 14 rock-cut Buddhist caves that date back to the 2nd century BCE. With magnificent architecture and beautiful sculptures, the basalt rock caves are among the oldest examples of rock-cut architecture. The caves are divided into two groups - *Chaityas* (prayer halls) and Viharas (residential halls).

Entry: Free
Hours: 8 am - 5 pm daily
How to Reach: Hire a private car for the 1.5 hour (80 km) ride from Aurangabad

Zainuddin Shirzai Maqbara

Zainuddin Shirzai was a sufi saint revered by many, including Aurangzeb, the mughal emperor. The tomb, considered an exceptional piece of art, is visited by many devotees every year.

Entry: Free
How to Reach: Hire a private car for the short (8 km) journey from Aurangabad

GOA

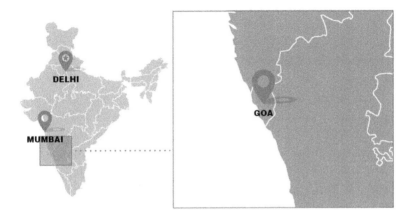

The Portuguese Oasis

There is more to Goa than golden beaches, full moon parties, and epic sunsets. Settled by the Portuguese in the 15th century, the popular sunkissed destination is a kaleidoscope of Indian and European traditions. With wildlife sanctuaries, spice plantations, seaside dining, adventure activities, and yoga retreats, Goa has many personalities.

TRANSPORTATION HUBS

Goa is a state in western India with coastlines on the Arabian Sea.

Goa International Airport (GOI)
Airport Road, Dabolim, Goa 403801

Goa is well connected with frequent (and cheap!) domestic flights from many Indian cities. The airport also services international and charter flights to Europe, Middle East, and South Asia.

Madgaon Junction (MAO)
Margao, Goa 403601

Vasco-da-Gama Station (VSG)
Karnataka-Goa, Swatantra Path, Vaddem, Vasco da Gama, Goa

There are several railway stations in Goa, but the primary locations are Madgaon Junction and Vasco-da-Gama. Both are located in the southern area of the state. There are frequent trains connecting Goa to Mumbai, Bangalore, Hyderabad, Kochi, and several other cities. Although Goa is very well connected by rail, most travelers prefer a flight for both cost and convenience.

Panaji Bus Terminus
Patto Centre, Panaji

AREAS TO AVOID

Overall, Goa is a safe destination for female travelers. If you are traveling solo and want to enjoy the nightlife, book a hotel near the popular clubs in North Goa near Baga Beach or Calangute.

BEACH GUIDE

Which Goa beach fits your mood?

Anjuna (North Goa): Backpackers and bohemians, lively / 20 km from Panjim

Baga and Calangute (North Goa): Crowded, commercialized, water sports / 18 km from Panjim

Vagator (North Goa): Split in two sections, Big Vagator (Indian tourists) and Little Vagator (Foreigners) / 23 km from Panjim

Arambol (North Goa): The newest hot spot, laid-back, a fusion of boutique and immersion / 50 km from Panjim

Candolim (North Goa): Beach shacks, sand dunes, a more mature vibe / 13 km from Panjim

Palolem (South Goa): The most animated beach in South Goa / 75 km from Panjim

Agonda (South Goa): Quiet, less crowded, foreigner friendly / 76 km from Panjim

Patnem (South Goa): A small, quiet beach with a laid-back vibe / 80 km from Panjim

Cola (South Goa): A secluded beach with its own lagoon / 68 km from Panjim

LOCAL FESTIVALS

Sunburn Festival

Launched in 2007, Sunburn is one of Asia's largest Electronic Dance Music (EDM) festivals. A fusion of music, entertainment, food, and shopping, the 3-day event features popular international and Indian artists on multiple stages.

Goa Carnival

Celebrated since the 18th Century, Goa Carnival is similar to the Carnival in Rio or Mardi Gras in the United States. During the four days before Lent, the streets transform into a flamboyant and joyous wonderland with colorful floats, competitions, fire dancers, acrobats, amazing food, and plenty of feni! The Goa Carnival is the largest in India and one of the few traditional Catholic festivals in Asia.

Sao Joao Festival

Not many people are familiar with the Sao Joao Festival, celebrated on June 23rd. Popular in North Goa, locals jump into wells, streams, and ponds to retrieve gifts thrown by villagers. The festival includes colorful boats, parades, free flowing feni, and good food all around.

St. Francis Xavier Festival

Celebrated annually on December 3rd, the festival marks the anniversary of St. Francis Xavier's death. Thousands of people joyously gather in the Basilica of Bom Jesus to commemorate his memory and service. The festival is also a public holiday in Goa.

Gudi Padwa

A springtime festival, Gudi Padwa is also celebrated as the New Year for Marathi and Konkani Hindus. It is said that Lord Brahma created the universe on this day when Lord Rama was re-crowned after his return from exile. People wear new clothes, decorate and clean their houses, and indulge in delicacies. Gudi Padwa occurs on the first day of the chaitra month of the Hindu calendar.

WHERE TO STAY

The Hosteller Goa
A hip, crazy, party hostel near Anjuna Beach with karaoke nights and beer pong parties.
$ / www.thehosteller.com / +91 98 1018 7717

Zostel Varkala
A seaside backpacking hostel near Varkala Beach with ocean views from the rooms and rooftop lounge.
$ / www.zostel.com / +91 22 4896 6122

Footloose Hostel
A popular hostel with foreign backpackers near Anjuna Beach.
$ / House No-640/4, Little Vagator, near Hilltop, Anjuna /
+91 95 8207 0845

Craft Hostels
A beautifully designed boutique hostel in North Goa with female dorm rooms.
$ / https://craft-hostels.business.site/ / +91 98 1170 0712

Siolim House
A beautifully restored Indo-Portuguese rural country house from the 17th century.
$$ / https://www.siolimhouse.com/ / +91 98 2258 4560

Ahilya by the Sea
A serene escape tucked away in a quiet corner of Dolphin Bay.
$$$ / www.ahilyabythesea.com / +91 11 4155 1575

Aashyana Lakhanpal

A unique retreat near Candolim Beach with a yoga pavilion and seaside sitouts.

$$ / www.aashyanalakhanpal.com / +91 83 2248 9225

Nilaya Hermitage

A boutique hotel in the hills with views of the Arabian Sea and Arpora Village.

$$$ / https://nilaya.com/ / +91 74 4779 3337

Cabo Serai

An eco-conscious resort with a barefoot luxury philosophy near Cabo De Rama Beach.

$$$$ / https://caboserai.com/ / +91 78 8788 2414

W Goa

A contemporary, cosmopolitan resort near night clubs on Vagator Beach.

$$$$ / www.marriott.com / +91 83 2671 8888

The Cape Goa

A luxe hotel overlooking the sea and surrounded by palm trees and paddy fields.

$$$$ / www.thecapegoa.com / Cabo De Rama Beach, Canacona

WHAT TO DO

Calangute Beach, North Goa

Crowned the Queen of Beaches, Calangute is the largest beach in Goa with restaurants, clubs, and shacks. Known for water sports and nightlife, it is a popular spot for the active and spirited crowd.

Baga Beach, North Goa

Popular for its nightlife and food scene, Baga is lively both day and night. The crowds and late-night music can make it unappealing for those seeking a quieter Goan experience, but it's a fantastic beach to survey the scene.

Candolim Beach, North Goa

Just like Baga and Calangute, Candolim is lively and full of clubs, shacks, and restaurants. However, it is less crowded (comparatively speaking) and offers a milder version of the Goan experience.

Vagator Beach, North Goa

Considered as one of the most beautiful beaches in Goa, Vagator Beach is in the Bardez district next to Anjuna Beach. Although famous for its rave parties and the weekly German flea markets, the white sand beaches generally cater to a quieter crowd. Vagator is also known for spectacular sunset views from the surrounding red cliffs. The beach is actually split in two sections, each flanked by the cliffs: North Vagator (Big Vagator) and Ozran Beach (Little Vagator). Before sunset, taste the local catch at one of the many seaside eateries and then take a dip at one of two natural freshwater springs adjacent to the shore.

Fort Aguada

Located at the confluence of the Mandovi River and Arabian Sea, the 17th century fort was the most prized fortification of the Portuguese. It was named after the fresh water spring that provided a consistent supply of potable water to passing ships. The fort was so well planned, built, and fiercely protected that it never fell into enemy hands. The Aguada Fort Lighthouse, constructed in 1864, is the oldest of its kind in Asia.

Entry: Free
Hours: 9:30 am - 6 pm daily

Basilica of Bom Jesus

With brilliant Baroque architecture, the Basilica of Bom Jesus is the oldest Roman Catholic church in Goa and houses the remains of Saint Francis Xavier. Located in Old Goa, there is also a nearby modern art gallery that showcases paintings by renowned artists of that time.

Entry: Free
Hours: Monday to Saturday, 9 am - 6:30 pm and Sunday, 10:30 am - 6:30 pm. A mass is held in English every Sunday at 8 am, 9:15 am, and 10:15 am

Our Lady of the Immaculate Conception Church

Overlooking the city of Panaji, the classic white structure with snaking staircases was used by sailors to thank god for their safe arrivals. Originally built in 1541, the chapel has since been rebuilt several times but still retains its original Portuguese and Baroque architecture. The church conducts mass daily in English, Portuguese, and Konkani.

Entry: Free
Hours: 9 am - 12:30 pm and 3 pm - 5:30 pm daily; Mass is held at 8 am daily

Casino Cruise

Gambling is legal and regulated on casino cruises in Goa. There are several luxury liners where you can roll the dice and spin the wheel. Enjoy a cocktail on the deck, view the coastlines, and play to win!

WHERE TO SHOP

Mapusa Market

Although operational every day of the week, Mapusa Market is particularly active on Fridays. Practice your bargaining skills for textiles, antiques, clothing, spices, handicrafts, pottery, carpets, jewelry, fruits, vegetables, and regional delicacies. (Luckily, most stalls

are grouped by category.) During peak season, merchants from other Indian states also descend on Mapusa to sell handmade bags and shawls.

Hours: 9 am - 8:30 pm; Closed on Sundays
Location: Municipal Market, Mapusa

Anjuna Flea Market

With origins as a hippie market to exchange goods and commodities, the Anjuna Market has become a bustling flea market. Held every Wednesday near the beachfront, many stalls are still run by foreigners who sell products from their countries.

Hours: Wednesdays from 9 am - 6 pm; Closed from June - September
Location: 10 St. Michael's Vaddo South, Anjuna

Panjim Market

As one of the largest markets in Goa, Panjim is a popular spot to experience the real Goan culture. Join the locals and peruse upmarket attire, footwear, trinkets, cashews, feni, and local handicrafts at a reasonable price.

Hours: 7 am - 9 pm daily; Closed on Sundays
Location: New Municipal Market, Panaji

Calangute Market

Calangute Market is a beachside flea market where you can buy clothing, souvenirs, accessories, metal goods, and various Goan artifacts. Visit the stalls and shacks lining the market to buy take away trinkets.

Hours: Saturdays from 6:30 am - 12 pm
Location: Saligao, Calangute

Makie's Night Bazaar

Popular with foreigners, Makie's Night Bazaar is held between November and April at River Baga. In addition to food and souvenir stalls, the market also has live performances, concerts, and a dance floor for a more interactive atmosphere.

Hours: Saturdays from 6 pm - 1 am
Location: Near 281, Baga River Bridge, Tamudki Vado, Marinha Dourada Road, Arpora

Colva Beach Market

Popular for trendy outfits and accessories, the Colva Beach Market in South Goa is known for luxury knockoffs. A good eye and strong bargaining skills will strike an exceptional deal!

Hours: 12 pm - 8 pm daily
Location: Colva Beachside

Tibetan Market on Baga Road

The Tibetan Market is lined with shops and stalls selling clothes, souvenirs, handmade products, food, shoes, and other everyday products. When the sun goes down, Baga Road comes alive with entertainment and live music.

Hours: 9 am - 9:30 pm daily
Location: Calangute - Baga Road, near Coffee Day, Umtav Vado, Khobra Waddo, Baga

Hollywood Fashion

A popular tailor shop in Candolim, Hollywood Fashion has highly trained tailors and designers with fast turnaround times. Successfully running for the last 20 years, their services are trusted and recommended.

Hours: 9 am - 10 pm daily
Location: Fort Aguada Road, near Souza Vaddo, Candolim

WHAT TO SHOP FOR IN GOA

Cashew Nuts and Feni

Goa is famous for good quality Cashew nuts. The nuts are also used to make a local fermented brew called feni. There are two popular types of feni - one distilled from Cashews and the other from toddy palm. Feni is very pungent and has a distinctive taste. Mostly used in cocktails, the spirit has a high alcohol content and is known to do its job well.

Goan Sausage (Chorizo)

A reflection of Indo-Portuguese cuisine, Goan sausage (Chorizo) is very popular. Made with pork, sea salt, and red chilis, it is spicy, tangy, and aromatic. Chorizo is available across India but best made and consumed in Goa.

Pottery and Terracotta

The districts of Bicholim and Calangute in North Goa are renowned for traditional red clay pottery. Artists make both utilitarian and decorative sculptures and artifacts which are then sold in the weekly markets in Panaji and Madgaon. Pottery and terracotta can also be purchased from handicraft emporiums across the state.

Kunbi Textiles

Considered the oldest weave of Goa, the red and white checkered Kunbi saris were mainly worn by farmers. The cotton sari was traditionally worn without the blouse, lightly draped across the waist, and fastened with a knot on one shoulder. The sari is now adorned with different types of blouses and the fabric is used to make other garments.

WHERE TO EAT

Gun Powder

With colorful, outdoor garden seating and a South Indian menu, Gun Powder is the first restaurant to make the Assagao area popular.
No. 6, Anjuna Mapusa Road, Saunto Vaddo, Assagao

Suzie's

A garden restaurant nestled in the by-lanes of Assagao, Suzie's is known for its fusion cuisine. The chef ensures that the menu changes every six weeks to accommodate the seasonal fresh Goan produce.
House no. 531, Suzie's Lane, Bouta Waddo, Near Chari Garage, Assagao

Pousada by the Beach

Hidden strategically at the end lane of Calangute Beach, the open-air eatery has epic beach views. Ocean waves complement the menu featuring crusty prawns and stuffed crab.
Holiday Street, Calangute

Martin's Corner

Ask any Goan for a restaurant recommendation and the response almost always includes Martin's Corner. The family-run restaurant has come a long way from its start as a corner shop, and many locals consider eating its sorpotel, lobster piri-piri, and chicken xacuti a rite of passage.

69, Binwaddo, Betalbatim, Goa / www.martinscornergoa.com

Fisherman's Wharf

Located by the banks of River Sal, the restaurant is popular for Goan cuisine paired with global flavors. Try the masala fried calamari, rava fried prawns, and fish curry with rice.

At the Riverside, Cavelossim

The Black Sheep Bistro

BSB is one of the few establishments in Panjim that can rightfully call itself farm-to-table: Most of its ingredients are sourced within a 100-mile radius.

1st Floor, Villa Braganca, Dr Braganza Pereira Rd, above Fab India Store, Panaji

Olive Bar & Kitchen

Perched on a cliff overlooking Vagator Beach, Olive Bar & Kitchen offers views of the Arabian Sea, an award-winning chef, and locally sourced ingredients.

Unit 1, Vagator Helipad, Big Vagator, Anjuna

Zeebop by the Sea, South Goa

Sunshine, surf, sea breezes, and an overflowing platter of curry prawns with rice await at the award-winning eatery specializing in Goan and South Indian cuisine.

Opposite Kenilworth Beach Resort, Utorda Beach, Salcete

Noronha's Corner

A food truck decorated with animated cartoon characters may not seem a likely spot to grab traditional Goan fare, but the three brothers

who manage Noronha's Corner know the art of food. The menu is separated into four sections: beef, chicken, pork, and fish. (This is not the place for vegetarians.)
MDR 10, Assagao, Goa

WHERE TO DRINK

Goan food is rightly accompanied by earthy local drinks. Try the banana lassi, kokum juice, and *Sol Kadi* - Made from Kokum juice and coconut milk with salt and coriander for flavoring, it aids in digestion after eating spicy Konkani cuisine.

To encourage tourism, the state has low taxes that mainly apply to alcohol; therefore, liquor is 1/3 the price compared to major cities like Delhi and Mumbai. Alcohol is served everywhere, from local restaurants and beach shacks to fine dining. The most popular local drink is Port wine - another Portuguese influence - with dry, semi-dry, and sweet varieties.

Tito's
One of the most recognized names in Goan nightlife, Tito's is a popular club in North Goa. The establishment is so famous that the entire stretch of road where Tito's sits is now called Tito's Lane.
Tito's Lane, Saunta Vaddo, Baga-Calangute

Thalassa
With sunset views and cold brews, the hillside Greek retro bar is a good way to end the day.
Plot No. 301, 1, Vaddy, Siolim

Curlies

A beach shack on Anjuna Beach, Curlies transforms from a beachside family restaurant during the day to a semi-club with music and UV lights at night.
St Michael, near Flea Market, Gumal Vaddo, Anjuna

Club Cabana

The 'Nightclub in the Sky' is located in Arpora Hills with breathtaking views and daily DJ sets. The neon-lit nightclub also also features a spacious outdoor area with a pool.
Aguada-Siolim Road, Arpora

Soro

An old Goan house transformed into a club, Soro The Village Pub is a retro space with creative cocktails.
Badem Junction, Siolim Road, North Goa, Assagao

Guru Bar

A typical beach shack with bamboo and cane accents, Guru Bar is a beachfront venue with live music.
St. Anthony Prais Waddo, North Anjuna, Anjuna, Bardez

LOCAL TOURS AND EXPERIENCES

Latin Quarter Walk

From the times of tobacco trade to the minting of coins and the final administrative center of the Portuguese, Goa has seen it all. With a special focus on the Fontainhas area, discover the making of Panaji.
https://www.soultravelling.in/tours/explore-panaji-64007

A Nature Trail at Chorao

Offering the best of both history and ecology, Chorao Island is one of the most popular areas in India to view migratory birds. Take a boat ride in the mangroves, explore the churches and temples, and view wildlife with a naturalist.
https://www.soultravelling.in/tours/the-island-of-chorao-74729

The Christian Art Trail

This trail is a favorite among art enthusiasts who want to learn and view the history of art in Goa's magnificent churches. Learn about the ancient art forms of Kaavi as you admire the colorful murals and stucco work.

https://www.soultravelling.in/tours/old-goa-christian-art-trail-61213

Rediscovering Candolim

There is so much more to Goa than just beaches. Discover the unexplored neighborhoods of Candolim and Sequirem as you visit a Goan home, enjoy a boat ride in the Mandovi River, explore Fort Aguada, and more! https://www.soultravelling. in/tours/rediscovering-candolim-82595

The Food Trail (North Goa)

Soak in the Indo-Portuguese architecture on a picturesque bicycle tour in the Latin Quarter.

https://www.blive.co.in/tours/goan-food-trail-90080

Stories by the Bay (North Goa)

Cycle by the sandy shores of Siridao Beach and experience the traditional side of Bambolim and the surrounding villages. Learn about sustainable fish farming and refuel at a scenic cafe. https://www.blive.co.in/tours/stories-by-the-bay-75853

Village Vistas of Cavelossim (South Goa)

Visit the more remote villages of Cavelossim, cycle along paddy fields and backwaters, and learn how to shuck oysters.

Goa Fish Vendor

https://www.blive.co.in/tours/village-vistas-of-cavelossim-70093

Boat Cruises

Located in Morjim, the outfitter leads guests by boat and then launches kayaks and SUP's for more immersive aquatic adventures. https://www.konkanexplorers.com/

DAY TRIPS

Mhadei Wildlife Sanctuary

Head north of Valpoi to reconnect with nature in the Mhadei Wildlife Sanctuary. The 80-square-mile preserve, nestled in the Western Ghats, is considered an area of high biodiversity, with wildlife ranging from black panthers and leopards to sloth bears and Bengal tigers. Look high! The sanctuary is also an important bird and biodiversity area (an official designation by BirdLife International and the Audubon Society), with 255 recorded species. Besides wildlife, the preserve is dotted with dozens of waterfalls, most notably the dual Vazra Sakla and Virdi Falls. There are no public tourist facilities; allow yourself three hours for a self-guided exploration of the sanctuary.

How to Reach: Hire a private car for the 1.5-hour (55 km) ride from Goa.

Nersa

A village located on the border of Karnataka and Goa, Nersa is considered one of the richest biodiversity spots in the world. Popular among nature enthusiasts, the hills and the lush green forests are ideal for trekking and bird watching.

How to Reach: Hire a private car for the two-hour (76 km) drive from Goa.

Chorla Ghat

Popular for its waterfalls during the monsoon season, Chorla Ghat lies at the intersection of three states: Maharashtra, Goa, and Karnataka. Home to rare wildlife and bird species, it is a utopia for ornithologists. The scenic route boasts views of water laden streams, waterfalls, and lush green forests.

Entry: Free
How to Reach: Travel like a local and rent a cycle or scooter for the 67 km drive from Goa. Start the trip early to allow for sufficient time. Pack food and water as there are not many hospitality stops. Carry a change

of clothes, an umbrella, or a raincoat if traveling during the monsoon season.

Divar Island

Board a ferry from Old Goa for the short crossing to Divar Island. With its single-lane roads that are virtually empty, the island is ideal for independent exploration. For years the government tried to persuade the residents of Divar to approve a bridge from the mainland. The locals resisted, however, and the island remains a quaint and traditional step back in time. Divar Island is not a typical tourist spot: there is one guest house, a few pubs, two bakeries, and a handful of restaurants that mostly cater to workers. The one exception to this tranquility comes in late summer, when Divar hosts Bonderam, a cultural festival that resembles Carnival. Otherwise, the island is an idyllic day trip overflowing with mangroves, grasslands, and old-world charm.

How to Reach: Ferries operate from 7 am - 8 pm. A boat from Viceroy's Arch (Old Goa) connects to the south side of the island; the east end of the island is connected by ferry to Naroa; the southwest of Divar is connected by ferry to Ribandar.

Dandeli

Calling all adventure enthusiasts! The Dandeli Wildlife Sanctuary is home to black panthers, monkeys, and elephants, as well as many bird species. The habitat offers game drives, white water rafting, canoeing, kayaking, mountain biking, rappelling, and trekking. With diverse flora and fauna, the forests are very popular for day trips and weekend getaways.

Entry: Free
How to Reach: It takes around 2.5 hours to cover the distance of 98 kms from Goa. You can take a train or a bus from Goa to reach here. Ideal and the most convenient mode of transport is the car. You can rent a car from Goa.

Dudhsagar Falls

The literal translation of Dudhsagar is 'Sea of milk' and the falls do justice to its name. The magnificent 4-tiered waterfall is among the tallest in India. At the base, a pool of water forms where people take a dip and enjoy the green forest cover. The waterfalls are at their best during the monsoon season.

Entry: Free
How to Reach: Grab a taxi or hire a rideshare/private car for the one-hour (29 km) drive from Goa

Karwar

If you want to escape from the touristy Goan beaches, the quaint town of Karwar will fill your cup. Known for its pristine beaches, you will find less crowds with golden sand and rows of palm trees.

Entry: Free
How to Reach: You can take a bus from Goa (INR 800) or hire a private car for the 2-hour ride.

NATIONAL PARKS:
CORBETT, RANTHAMBORE, GIR, KANHA, AND BANDHAVGARH

JIM CORBETT
NATIONAL PARK

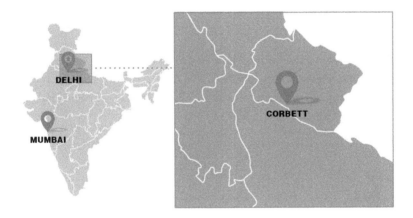

Established in 1936 to protect the endangered Bengal tiger, Jim Corbett
National Park is the oldest national park in India. Named after the
legendary naturalist and conservationist, it was also where Project
Tiger was launched in 1973. Corbett is one of the few Indian tiger
reserves that allows overnight stays, though entry permits and advance
reservations are required.

TRANSPORTATION HUBS

Corbett is located in the state of Uttarakhand and the closest town, Ramnagar, is 30 minutes away. Ramnagar is well-connected by road and rail network.

By Air

It is not convenient to reach Corbett by flight. The closest domestic airport is Pantnagar (50 km), but there are currently no regular commercial flights. The closest international airport is Delhi, six hours away by car.

By Road

Ramnagar and Corbett are well connected by road. From Delhi, the drive is approximately six hours (260 km). You can travel by bus or hire a private car. The Uttarakhand state government also links with interstate buses to Corbett directly from Dehradun and Nainital.

By Rail

Ramnagar Railway Station (RMR)
Station Rd, Shivlalpur Pandey, Uttarakhand

Overnight trains are available from Delhi - Ramnagar. Corbett is located 15 km from the station.

WHEN TO VISIT

The park is open from mid-November to mid-June, but the best chance to spot the elusive tiger is during the winter months from November - February.

There are five zones in the park: Jhirana, Sitabani, Dhikala, Durga Devi, and Bijrani. The coveted Dhikala zone is where you can usually find the highest number of tigers and cubs. The Jhirana and Sitabani zones are technically open all year, though there are frequent and unscheduled closures during the summer (monsoon) season.

WILDLIFE AND ATTRACTIONS

Jim Corbett is home to 110 species of trees, 488 species of plants, 50 species of mammals, 25 species of reptiles, and over 600 species of birds. Although Bengal tigers are abundant, the dense jungle keeps them camouflaged. The park is also home to leopards, elephants, jungle cats, Himalayan black bears, and the Indian python. Wildlife viewings are conducted by an open jeep or on the back of an elephant.

Adventure activities in the park include hiking, cycling, rappelling, river rafting, fishing, and mountain climbing.

Kath Ki Nav Village
35 km from Corbett is a small village of Kath Ki Nav. A 10-minute uphill walk leads to a viewpoint of the entire park with the Kosi River flowing on one side and the beautiful Ram Ganga Valley on the other. On a clear day, you can also view the snow-capped Nandi Devi range.

Kaladhungi (Choti Haldwani)
Retrace the steps of Jim Corbett on a heritage walk at Kaladhungi, also known as Choti Haldwani. The model village was established by the conservationist himself. There is also a museum housing Corbett's muzzle-loading gun.

PARK HOURS AND CLOSURES

PARK SAFARI TIMINGS	MORNING SAFARI TIME	EVENING SAFARI TIME
16 Oct - 30 Jun	6:00 am - 9:30 am	15:00 - 18:00

SAFARI COST

TYPE OF SAFARI	MORNING SAFARI	EVENING SAFARI
Exclusive Jeep Safari (1 to 6 pax)	INR 6500 Net	INR 6500 Net
Elephant Safari (1 to 4 pax)	INR 3500 Net	INR 3500 Net
Shared Safari by Canter (1 to 8 pax)	INR 1500 Per Person	INR 1500 Per Person

WHERE TO STAY

Jim's Jungle Retreat
A jungle retreat with 18 cottages and bungalow-style lodges.
$$ / www.jimsjungleretreat.com / +91 97 1178 9828

Dhikala Forest Lodge
A unique and earthy accommodation located inside the Dhikala zone
Note: This is one of five forest lodges managed by the Corbett Forest Department. Foreigners must reserve accommodations 91 days in advance.
$$ /www.dhikalaforestlodge.in / +91 97 6028 3617

Taj Corbett Resort & Spa
An exclusive hotel from Taj Group with cottage-style rooms on the Kosi River.
$$$ / www.tajhotels.com / +91 59 4726 6600

Lebua Corbett Resort

A luxurious jungle resort offering an ecologically sustainable haven.

$$$ / www.lebua.com / Phone: +91 72 5300 0908

Paatlidun Safari Lodge

A premium wildlife resort with in-house expert naturalists.

$$$ / www.patlidun.com / +91 99 9933 8886

Riverview Retreat, Corbett

A cozy retreat with private villas on the banks of the Kosi River.

$$$ / +91 59 4728 4135

Aahana

An award-winning luxury resort with ecological initiatives and an organic farm-to-table garden.

$$$$ / www.aahanaresort.com / +91 70 8860 0024

RANTHAMBORE
NATIONAL PARK

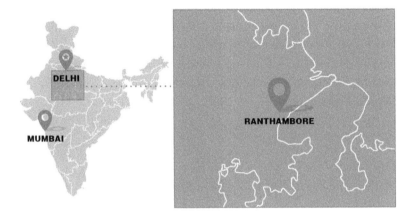

Welcome to Ranthambore National Park, one of the most filmed wildlife reserves in the world. Once the hunting ground of Rajput royalty, Ranthambore was declared a wildlife sanctuary in 1955 and became a part of Project Tiger in 1973. It's accessibility to both Agra and Jaipur makes the park a popular spot for travelers on the famed Golden Triangle path (Delhi, Agra, Jaipur). As Ranthambore is relatively small, you have a higher probability of spotting leopards, Bengal tigers, and jungle cats.

TRANSPORTATION HUBS

Ranthambore is located in the state of Rajasthan. The nearest city is Jaipur, a 4-hour drive (200 km).

By Road
Ranthambore is well connected to Delhi, Agra, Jaipur, and other cities in Rajasthan. The driving distance from Agra is approximately 302 km (six hours); from Jaipur, 200 km (four hours). There are also private and public buses available. Hire a private car from Jaipur for the fastest journey. Due to the distance, it is not advisable to drive from Delhi - Ranthambore in one day.

By Train

Sawai Madhopur (SWM)
Railway Station Road, Railway Colony, Sawai Madhopur

Ranthambore is 10 km away from the Sawai Madhopur station. There is daily connectivity to Delhi, Agra, and Jaipur. We highly recommend reserving the day train from either Delhi Nizamuddin (NZM) or Agra (AGC).

By Air

Jaipur International Airport (JAI)
Airport Road, Sanganer, Jaipur, Rajasthan

The nearest airport is Jaipur (200 km). You can hire a taxi or private car from the airport for the four-hour drive to Ranthambore.

WHEN TO VISIT

Although Ranthambore is open year round, the core zones (gates 1-5) remain closed from July - September. The buffer zones (gates 6-10) are open during the monsoon season.

October - March has the most favorable weather. Mornings and evenings can be chilly from December - February, so pack accordingly.

If you can bear the heat, the summer season (April - June) avails the best opportunity to spot tigers and their cubs at the watering holes.

WILDLIFE AND ATTRACTIONS

As part of Project Tiger, Ranthambore's prized resident is the Bengal tiger. The densely forested area dotted with lakes and watering holes is ideal for big cats. Other residents include leopards, sloth bears, chital (spotted deer), marsh crocodile, palm civet, jackal, desert fox, serpent eagle, and waterfowl. The park is home to 40 species of mammals, 35 species of reptiles, and 320 species of birds. Ranthambore also features India's largest banyan trees.

Ranthambore Fort
The Ranthambore Fort is tucked in the heart of the Ranthambore National Park. Perched on a 700-foot hill, it was declared a UNESCO World Heritage Site under Hill Forts of Rajasthan. The fort contains three temples of Lord Ganesh, Ramlalaji, and Shiva, constructed with red Karauli stone.

Chambal Crocodile Sanctuary
40 km from Ranthambore is the National Chambal Sanctuary, a 5,400 km square tri-state wildlife sanctuary. It is dedicated to conserving the Ganges River dolphins, gharial, and the red-crowned roof turtle.

Padam Talao

Named after lotus flowers, Padam Talao is the largest lake in the park and a favorite watering hole. It is home to a variety of migratory birds and a fantastic spot for wildlife photography. You can also visit the Jogi Mahal, a converted hunting lodge with epic views.

Trinetra Ganesh Temple

Dating back to 1299, the Trinetra Ganesh Temple is one of the oldest in Rajasthan. The forest retreat is the only ancient structure with Lord Ganesha's effigy with trinetra. There are five Aarti ceremonies daily, from sunrise until sunset.

PARK HOURS AND CLOSURES

PARK SAFARI TIMING	MORNING SAFARI	EVENING SAFARI
01 Oct - 31 Oct	6:30 am - 10:00 am	14:30 - 18:00
01 Nov - 31 Jan	7:00 am - 10:30 am	14:00 - 17:30
01 Feb - 31 Mar	6:30 am - 10:00 am	14:30 - 18:00
01 Apr - 15 May	6:00 am - 9:30 am	15:00 - 18:30
16 May - 30 Jun	6:00 am - 9:30 am	15:30 - 19:00
The core zones (gates 1 - 5) are closed from July 1st - September 30th.		

SAFARI COST

TYPE OF SAFARI	MORNING SAFARI	EVENING SAFARI
Shared Jeep Safari (1 to 4 pax)	INR 2390 Per Person	INR 2390 Per Person
Exclusive Jeep Safari (1 to 4 pax)	INR 13750	INR 13750
Half Day Jeep Safari (1 to 4 pax)	INR 37250	INR 37250
Full Day Jeep Safari (1 to 4 pax)	INR 66250	INR 66250
Shared Safari by Canter (1 to 14 pax)	INR 1762 Per Person	INR 1762 Per Person
Exclusive Safari by Canter (1 to 14 pax)	INR 35250 Net	INR 35250 Net
Costs include permits, gypsy (jeep), and a naturalist. Rates are subject to change by the forest department.		

The Half-day safari permits allow visitors to spend a maximum of six hours in the park either in the morning (sunrise to noon) or the afternoon (noon to sunset). The Full-day safari permits allow visitors to spend a maximum of 12 hours in the park, from dawn to dusk.

WHERE TO STAY

Ranthambore Regency
An affordable family-operated hotel located ten minutes from the park.
$$ / https://ranthamboreregency.com / +91 88 7502 0681

Khem Vilas
An exclusive jungle camp set on 30 acres that offers cottages and luxury tents.
$$$ / www.khemvillas.com / +91 94 1403 0262

Sawai Vilas
A rustic retreat tucked away in the rustic woodlands of Ranthambore.
$$$ / https://sawaivilas.com /+91 82 7864 0012

Vivanta Sawai Madhopur Lodge
An 80-year-old heritage hotel located near the railway station.
$$$ / https://www.vivantahotels.com / +91 74 6222 5155

Sujan Sherbagh
A private estate with exclusive tents and farm-to-table cuisine.
$$$$ / www.thesujanlife.com / +91 11 4617 2700

Oberoi Vanyavilas
An award-winning property with luxury tents inspired by the opulent caravans of royal families.
$$$$ / www.oberoihotels.com / +91 74 6222 3999

GIR NATIONAL PARK

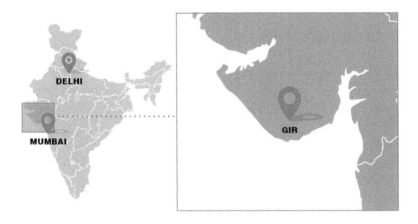

Gir National Park and Wildlife Sanctuary is the only place outside Africa to view lions in the wild. Also known as Sasan Gir, it was established to protect the once critically endangered Asiatic lions. The rulers of Indian princely states used to invite British colonists for hunting expeditions. At the end of the 19th century, only about a dozen Asiatic lions remained in the Gir Forest as part of the Nawab of Junagarh's private hunting grounds. With commanding conservation efforts, the most recent survey shows almost 700 lions in the park. Gir is currently considered one of the most important protected areas in Asia due to its supported species.

TRANSPORTATION HUBS

Gir is located in the state of Gujarat. The closest town, Junagadh, is a 1.5 hour drive (70 km).

By Train

Junagadh Junction (JND)
Joshipura, Junagadh, Gujarat

The nearest rail station is Junagadh Junction (JND); you can hire a taxi or private car from the station for the 1.5 hour drive to Gir. Trains operate regularly from both Rajkot and Ahmedabad to Junagadh.

By Air

The nearest airport is Diu (DIU) with limited domestic flights via Mumbai. From the airport you can hire a private car or taxi for the 2-hour drive (110 km). Rajkot, another domestic airport, is three hours away (168 km). The closest major airport is Ahmedabad (AMD) but it takes almost eight hours (354 km) to reach the park.

By Road

Gir is well connected to all major cities in Gujarat and there are state and private buses that travel frequently to the park. We recommend hiring a private car for the drive, but make sure to set the price in advance. You can also hire a private bus from Ahmedabad, but be prepared for an 8-hour drive.

WHEN TO VISIT

The park is open from mid-October until mid-June; the Gir Interpretation Zone is open year round. The heat makes the dry landscape more enticing for sightings and photography in April and May. However, for more favorable weather, visit from November - March.

Lions are the most active in the morning, so try and reserve the early safari. We reserved both a morning and afternoon safari and were lucky enough to spot two sparring males on the morning ride.

WILDLIFE AND ATTRACTIONS

With a habitat of open deciduous forest, the main attraction is the Asiatic lion. You can also view the Indian leopard, jungle cats, hyena, mongoose, and multiple deer species such as Nilgai Antelope and Chital Spotted Deer.

Gir's unique vegetation is home to 606 species of plants, 36 species of mammals, and 2000 insect breeds. With over 300 species of birds, the sanctuary is also designated as a significant birding location by the Indian Bird Conservation Network. During the winter months, you can catch a glimpse of uncommon migrating species including the Paradise Flycatcher and the Malabar Whistling Thrush.

Hiking is not permitted in the park.

Siddi Community, Zambur Village ("Little Africa" of India)

The Siddis, also known as Sidi or Habshi, are an Indian-African ethnic group. Brought as slaves over 500 years ago, the communities are primarily descendants of the Southeast African Bantu tribes. In and around Gir, the Siddi find work as guides, drivers, farmers, and merchants; others perform for tourists with fire breathing, traditional drumming, and gymnastics. Zambur Village offers a unique insight into the "Little Africa" of India.

Junagadh

From Buddhist caves to the unique blend of Indo-Islamic and Gothic architecture, history flows in the veins of Junagadh. (Fun fact: It's also the town where my brother-in-law was raised!) Visit the Uparkot Fort, founded in 300 BC.

Somnath Darshan

45 km from Gir is Somnath Temple, the first of 12 Jyotirlinga shrines devoted to Lord Shiva. It is an important pilgrimage site with legacies and legends dating back to 649 CE.

PARK HOURS AND CLOSURES

PARK SAFARI TIMING	MORNING SAFARI	EVENING SAFARI
16 Oct to 28/29 Feb	6:45 am - 9:45 am	15:00 - 18:00
01 Mar to 15 Jun	6:00 am - 9:00 am 8:30 am - 11:30 am	16:00 - 19:00

Gir is closed from mid-June until mid-October for the southwest monsoon. The Gir Interpretation Zone is open all year from Thursday - Tuesday (closed Wednesday).

SAFARI COST

The safari cost is per jeep (up to five guests) and includes a driver and guide:	
Weekdays (Mon - Fri)	INR 9700 per jeep
Weekend (Sat - Sun)	INR 10700 per jeep
Festival Season (X-mas, Diwali, and Navratri)	INR 11700 per jeep

The safari charges are non-refundable and non-amendable. Before reserving a jeep (gypsy), you must first buy a permit for either Gir National Park (Gir Jungle Trail) or the Gir Interpretation Zone (in neighboring Devalia Safari Park). Permits must be obtained in advance and presented at the safari entry gate.

Safari reservations are open up to three months in advance. Only 30 vehicles are allowed in Gir at one time and each is randomly assigned one of eight safari routes.

Though at a premium, upmarket Gir hotels also facilitate their own jeep safari, including securing park permits. (I utilized this service during my recent visit to Gir, and although it was more expensive, it was well worth it to avoid the guesswork with online reservations.)

WHERE TO STAY

The Wilds Villa Gir
A budget friendly (and pet friendly!) riverside resort with non A/C cottages and dormitories.
$ / www.thewildsvillagir.com / +91 99 7499 4271

Hotel Anil Farmhouse
A local, family-owned resort on the banks of Hiran River.
$$ / www.girjungleresort.com / +91 94 2699 5315

The Fern Gir Resort
A luxury family-friendly property set among gorgeous hills, green pastures, and magnificent groomed gardens.
$$$ / www.fernhotels.com / +91 90 9904 9264

Woods at Sasan
A boutique wellness retreat offering yoga and Ayurveda and set on eight acres of beautiful mango orchards.
$$$$ / www.woodsatsasan.com / +91 28 7728 1000

DO'S AND DON'TS IN GIR

DO's

- Ensure that you have valid permissions
- Attend the activities on time and observe silence
- Always respect the animals
- Dress in a way that blends with the surrounding environment
- Take photos without disturbing the wildlife
- Respect local norms and the dignity of holy locations
- Follow the designated route and time limit

DON'Ts

- Animals should not be fed
- Pets are not allowed
- Do not take samples, seeds, or roots from flora and fauna
- Plastic bags and littering of any kind are not permitted in the sanctuary
- Trespassing is prohibited in the forest
- Do not step out of the vehicle

KANHA
NATIONAL PARK

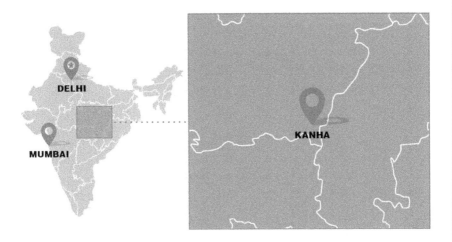

Kanha National Park is occupied by two protected sanctuaries, Hallon and Banjar. Also known as Kanha Tiger Reserve and Kanha-Kisli National Park, it was declared a national park in 1955. The lush sal and bamboo forests, grassy meadows, and ravines of Kanha inspired Rudyard Kipling when writing *The Jungle Book*. Considered one of Asia's best-administered parks, it is an abode of the Bengal tiger.

TRANSPORTATION HUBS

Kanha is located in the foothills of the Maikal range of Satpuras in the state of Madhya Pradesh. The closest city, Jabalpur, is a 4-hour drive (160 km).

By Road

Although Kanha has good road connectivity throughout Madhya Pradesh and with neighboring states, it is still fairly secluded and a long distance from other major cities. We recommend flying to Jabalpur and then hiring a private car for the 4-hour journey to the park.

By Train

The nearest railway station is Gondia Junction (G) in the neighboring state of Maharashtra (3 hours / 145 km); the next closest station is Jabalpur (JBP) at a distance of 160 km (four hours). Hire a private car in advance for the transfer from the station to the park.

By Air

The nearest airport is Jabalpur (JBP). Reserve a private car in advance for the transfer to Bandhavgarh (200 km / 4 hours). Jabalpur has daily connectivity to Delhi and Mumbai, with direct service via other major cities.

BEST TIME TO VISIT

Kanha is open from October 15th until June 30th. For favorable weather, the best time to visit is November - March but be prepared for cold mornings in December - January.

For tracking tigers, the best time to visit is April - May when the land is dry and wildlife congregates at waterholes; however, temperatures can soar above 42 degrees C.

WILDLIFE AND ATTRACTIONS

Kanha's wildlife includes Bengal tigers, leopards, sloth bears, jungle cats, hyenas, and 300 species of birds. One of its landmark achievements is the preservation of the rare hardground Swamp Deer (Barasingha). The park also has over 1000 flowering plants like the Shorea robusta and a notable Indian ghost tree (Davidia involucrata).

Reserve a guided nature walk that takes place in the buffer forest that adjoins Kipling Camp. The walk is aimed at experiencing the forest through all five senses and awakening the sixth sense - intuition or instinct. Being on foot allows the senses to be permeated by the jungle and opens a secret world that is normally missed when in a vehicle on safari. The focus of the walk will be on wildlife viewing but with an emphasis on interpretation of tracks and jungle signs. The length of walks can be tailored but typically last a couple of hours, stopping en-route for refreshments/picnics.

Local Villages

In addition to game drives and naturalist activities, take time to explore the neighboring villages inhabited by the Gond Tribe. Being forest dwellers, the tribals hold great respect for the land and its fauna. Mohgaon, Baihar, and Sarekha are three village marts - operating on different days of the week - offering a chance to experience the charming chaos of traditional markets. On offer you will find fresh farm produce, seeds and saplings, spices, bamboo wares, earthen pots, and ethnic jewelry.

Kanha Museum

Located inside the park near the Kisli Gate, the museum details the struggle of national park conservation. As you walk down the gallery, witness sculpted structures of wildlife remains.

Amarkantak

Also known as the Teerthraj, Amarkantak adds a religious touch to your Kanha experience. Located on the banks of the Narmada River, the temple is famous for its Dudh-Dhara waterfall with foaming water that resembles milk. Several neighboring temples are also renowned for their brilliant architecture.

Kawardha Palace

Built in the 1930's with imported Italian marble and stone, Kawardha offers panoramic views of the Maikal Hill Range. Located 91 km from Kanha, the palace has been converted to a heritage hotel. Reserve an overnight stay and enjoy the royal treatment in the bar and library.

Mandla and Ramnagar Fort

35 km from Kanha is Mandla, a town uniquely surrounded by the Narmada River on three sides. Mandla is known for forts and temples, including the Ramnagar Fort built in the late 17th century by the Gond Kings. There are also sulphur-rich hot springs 20 km from the town.

PARK HOURS AND CLOSURES

PARK SAFARI TIMING	MORNING SAFARI	AFTERNOON SAFARI
16 Oct - 15 Feb	7:00 am - 10:30 am	14:00 - 17:30
16 Feb - 31 Mar	6:00 am - 9:30 am	15:00 - 18:30
01 Apr - 30 Jun	6:00 am - 9:30 am	15:30 - 19:00

During operational months, Kanha is closed every Wednesday afternoon. Be sure to check park closures on national holidays and festivals, like Holi and Diwali.

SAFARI COST

There are three core zones in Kanha: Khatia, Mukki, and Sarhi. The buffer zones are Khatia, Motinala, Khapa, Sijhora, Samnapur, and Garhi. The safari cost depends on the location and zone that is available. Usually the park authorities only offer exclusive safaris, ranging from INR 7500 to INR 10000 per jeep (up to 4 guests). You can also reserve a shared jeep safari with your hotel and the price ranges from INR 3500 to INR 5000 per person per safari. The cost includes permits, gypsy (jeep) and naturalist. Rates are subject to change by the forest department.

You can reserve an elephant or jeep safari and reservations open 120 days in advance. Passport details are mandatory. You can also book a night safari from 7 pm - 10 pm in the Khatia buffer zone; tickets are available the same day at the park gate. Call ahead to check availability.

WHERE TO STAY

Tuli Tiger Resort
A budget friendly option with a picturesque wildlife setup.
$$ / www.tulihotels.com / +91 71 2665 3666

Kanha Earth Lodge
An eco-lux lodge and winner of the World Travel Awards bordering Kanha's buffer zone.
$$$ / www.kanhaearthlodge.com / +91 11 4014 6400

Kipling Camp
A jungle camp on the edge of Kanha that was established by a family of conservationists.
$$$ / www.kiplingcamp.com /+91 11 6519 6377

Shergarh Tented Camp
A rustic safari camp offering six tents and a camp house at the edge of the park.
$$$ / www.shergarh.com /+91 90 9818 7346

Banjaar Tola, A Taj Safari
An exclusive and ethereal lodge nestled on 90 acres in the private Sal Forest.
$$$$ / www.tajhotels.com / +91 22 6601 1825

Chitvan Jungle Lodge
An unassuming jungle retreat near Mukki Gate.
$$$$ / www.chitvan.com / +91 88 6051 8887

Flame of the Forest
An experiential jungle lodge offering an intimate safari experience.
$$$$ / https://flameoftheforest.in / +91 98 2602 1688

BANDHAVGARH
NATIONAL PARK

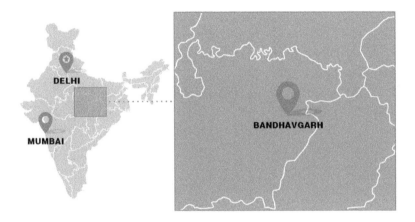

Wearing the Vindhya Hills like a crown, Bandhavgarh National Park was once the hunting preserve of the Maharaja of Rewa. Declared a national park in 1968 and a Tiger Reserve in 1993, Bandhavgarh has the highest density of tigers in India. The park shares a connection with ancient Hindu mythology, *Ramayana*. According to local folklore, Lord Rama gifted the most prominent hill of the area to his brother Laxman to keep watch over Lanka.

TRANSPORTATION HUBS

Bandhavgarh is located in the Umaria district of Madhya Pradesh. The closest town is Umaria (32 km).

By Air
The nearest airport is Jabalpur (JBL); Reserve a private car in advance for the transfer to Bandhavgarh (200 km / 4 hours). Jabalpur has daily connectivity to Delhi and Mumbai, with direct service via other major cities.

By Train
The nearest railway stations are Umaria (UMR) and Katni (KTE). Umaria is 32 km (45 minutes) and Katni is 100 km (two-hours). From the stations, hire a taxi for the drive to Bandhavgarh.

By Road
You can reach Bandhavgarh by state buses of Madhya Pradesh. The park is connected with national highways and easily commuted by road. However, due to its remote location, we highly recommend hiring a private car in advance from the JBL airport or a taxi from the UMR railway station.

BEST TIME TO VISIT

Bandhavgarh is open from October 15th until June 30th. Peak season is November - March for favorable weather; Although April and May see scorching temperatures, there are frequent tiger sightings.

WILDLIFE AND ATTRACTIONS

The park is divided into three different zones: Tala (Gate 1), Magdhi (Gate 2), and Khitauli (Gate 3). Tala is the richest zone in terms of flora and fauna. The park is known for its tiger population and has the highest density of Bengal tigers in the country. In 1951, Maharaja Martnad Singh of Rewa captured a white tiger in the region. It is now stuffed and displayed in the palace of Rewa.

Bandhavgarh is home to 22+ species of mammals, 250 species of birds, and 80 species of butterflies. The lush greenery and dense forest attract pairs of sarus cranes to breed in the park during monsoon season. The reserve is densely populated with animals like Indian bison, barking deer, and striped hyena. The park is also famous for its rich biodiversity and the favorable topography uniquely supports the growth of a wide variety of flora like Tendu, Arjun, Amla, and Kadam.

Trek to Bandhavgarh Fort
Believed to be 2000 years old, Bandhavgarh Fort is one of the oldest forts in India. The easy, one-hour trek starts from the Tala zone. Inside

stands a 35 ft Lord Vishu statue and several caves are adorned with ancient artifacts and paintings.

Explore Tala Village
One of the chief entrances of the reserve, Tala Village is a traditional community of modest, mud clustered homes. It offers visitors an insider view to the local lifestyle of Bandhavgarh.

Chenchpur Waterfall
Just 60 km from Bandhavgarh is the best kept secret of the area. Pack a picnic and enjoy an easy hike to the falls.

Jwalamukhi Temple
Located 10 km from Bandhavgarh on the Charan Ganga River, the temple is dedicated to Goddess Jwalamukhi. Devotees come to seek blessings from the deity of the flaming face.

PARK HOURS AND CLOSURES

PARK SAFARI TIMING	MORNING SAFARI	AFTERNOON SAFARI
16 Oct - 15 Feb	7:00 am - 10:30 am	14:00 - 17:30
16 Feb - 31 Mar	6:00 am - 9:30 am	15:00 - 18:30
01 Apr - 30 Jun	6:00 am - 9:30 am	15:30 - 19:00

During operational months (October 15th - June 30th), Bandhavgarh is closed every Wednesday afternoon. Be sure to check park closures on national holidays and festivals, like Holi and Diwali.

SAFARI COST

The safari cost depends on the location and zone that is available. Usually the park authorities only offer exclusive safaris, ranging from INR 7500 to INR 10000 per jeep (up to 4 guests). You can also reserve a shared jeep safari with your hotel and the price ranges from INR 3500 to INR 5000 per person per safari. The cost includes permits, gypsy (jeep) and naturalist. Note: There is a vehicle limit per safari block and rates are subject to change by the forest department.

You can reserve an elephant or jeep safari and reservations open 120 days in advance. Passport details are mandatory. You can also book a night safari from 7 - 10 pm in the buffer zone.

WHERE TO STAY

Pugdundee Safaris Tree House Hideaway
An elevated property with five treehouses and resident birds and reptiles.
$$$ / www.pugdundeesafaris.com / +91 11 4014 6400

Pugdundee Safaris Kings Lodge
A private lodge nestled in Sal forested hills of the buffer zone.
$$$ / www.pugdundeesafaris.com / +91 11 4014 6400

Mahua Kothi, a Taj Safari
A jungle safari resort with 12 luxury cottages and organic garden.
$$$$ / www.tajhotels.com / +91 22 6601 1825

Samode Safari Lodge
An exclusive lodge and spa with a well stocked library and jogging trails.
$$$$ / www.samode.com/safarilodge / +91 83 1957 6811

GO GREEN!

In the past five decades, the global population has doubled and the travel industry has evolved to accommodate the growing needs of mobility and recreation. The growth of these industries can be complex. International travel increases the awareness and tolerance of other cultures; it also provides tourism dollars to developing economies. However, the grim reality is that the travel industry substantially contributes to the carbon crisis. 10% of global carbon emissions are created by the travel industry, and 25% of that figure is just from the hotel industry. The push for sustainable travel is rooted in well-intentioned practices, but are we actually making a difference or just feeling better about our environmentally-friendly decisions?

The good news is that awareness creates solutions. Sustainability encompasses social and economic impacts - not just ecological. Many travelers are now seeking community-based projects or socially-conscious tours that aim to support local businesses and entrepreneurs. They are also becoming individual activists and using their voice to demand innovation. A traveler can make a difference as a consumer.

Here are eight GGG steps you can take toward becoming a more sustainable traveler:

Buy Local

One of the easiest ways to be a responsible traveler is to shop locally. Whether it is a quick snack or a souvenir, support local artisans and seek out items that have been regionally produced instead of imported in mass production. This cycle benefits small businesses and local communities.

Avoid Animal Tourism

Be mindful of unethical animal tourism. Many travelers can make a wrong choice with good intentions, not fully understanding how an animal is exploited for economic benefit. Avoid activities with any animal performance, rides, or wildlife selfies, as well as any experience where you hold or play with the wildlife. Often the animals are drugged or worse just to make a dollar.

Mindful Transportation

Most of a plane's carbon emissions are emitted during take-off and landing, so reserve direct and non-stop flights for international travel. Because a passenger's emissions are determined by the space they use, flying economy also lowers the carbon footprint. A business class seat occupies more space and has an even larger footprint. Once you arrive at your destination, walk, bike, or use local transportation when possible. Use rideshare services or take a train!

Hotel or No-tel

Research the properties you intend to reserve. Do they support sustainable practices like banning single use plastics and recycling waste? What percentage of the hotel's resources are local? Do they have a LEED certification or use renewable energy? Rather than staying at chain hotels, opt for heritage hotels or homestays. Not only do the tourism dollars stay in the community, but the experience can be more immersive and culturally authentic.

Reduce, Reuse, Recycle

Reusable water bottles, bags, and toiletry containers drastically cut down on damaging single-use plastics. Pack items for multi-purpose use and consider renting any bulky gear locally. This can include adventure equipment like skiis or even child strollers and car seats. When staying at your hotel, be mindful of energy consumption. Turn off electronics when leaving the room and use the heat/AC efficiently.

Responsible Touring

Research your travel company or tour operator. How are your tourism dollars directly benefiting a community? Even if local experiences are legal, are they ethical? Be aware of greenwashing, the false marketing of a service or product that appears eco-friendly or sustainable. This deceptive practice often convinces even savvy travelers that their financial contribution is environmentally friendly.

Limit Water Consumption

We all love our long, warm showers, but in India, water is a scarce commodity. Although you may have access to clean, fresh water, many don't, so limit your shower time and try to avoid baths. Don't leave the tap running when brushing your teeth or shaving. Reuse your towels instead of opting for daily laundry service; if washing your own clothes, fill the sink only once and select an eco-friendly laundry detergent.

Giving Back

Find ways to support a local cause or philanthropic organization. Across India, beggars are common. Fueled by compassion, travelers have good intentions to donate money. Unfortunately, many cities have homes that teach this craft as a scam, especially by manipulating children. If you feel compelled to give, we recommend donating money to a reputable charitable organization that will fairly and transparently disperse the funds to the community.

DON'T HATE. MEDITATE.

Because India is often considered the land of spirituality and philosophy, it is a popular destination for spiritual seekers. Several of the world's religions have roots in the country, including Hinduism, Buddhism, Sikhism, and Jainism. The diverse traditions provide a vibrant kaleidoscope of India's rich social composition where communities live in relative religious harmony.

From pilgrimage sites to holy rivers, check out these North India destinations for sacred spaces.

Varanasi

Varanasi, also known as Beneras, is often framed as the classic image of India's religiosity. According to ancient texts, the city was founded by the Hindu deity Shiva, making it one of the most important pilgrimage destinations in the country. It is Lord Shiva who is known for creation and destruction, perfectly exemplified by the pious Hindu's who are cremated along the banks of the holy Ganges River to break the cycle of rebirth and attain salvation. The evening Aarti ceremony is a Hindu ritual where light is offered to one or more deities. To the chant of Sanskrit mantras, and the clash of cymbals and drums, the river is worshipped with flowers, incense, sandalwood, milk, and vermilion. Also nearby is Sarnath, where Buddha gave his first sermon after attaining enlightenment.

Bodh Gaya

Bodh Gaya is where Siddhartha Gautama attained enlightenment, making it one of the most important Buddhist pilgrimage sites. During his travels to understand life, Siddhartha arrived in the Gaya district of

Bihar. Here he sat under a large fig tree and, upon meditation, achieved enlightenment. This is also where he discovered the Noble eight-fold path, known as the Middle Path or Middle Way, which demonstrates a balanced life. Travelers and pilgrims visit the monastic rural town for meditation, studies, and the Mahabodhi Temple.

Haridwar and Rishikesh

The twin holy cities of Haridwar and Rishikesh are located just 20 km from each other in the foothills of the Himalayas. Haridwar is not just one of the seven pilgrimage destinations of India, but also one of the four sites where the grand Hindu festival of Kumbh Mela takes place every 12 years. There are several sacred ghats, or bathing steps, with the largest hosting the evening Aarti ceremony. The Mansa Devi temple, perched on a hilltop, offers spectacular views of the Ganges and surrounding landscapes.

Rishikesh is considered the yoga capital of North India. It is believed that meditating at this earth energy vortex will help achieve moksha, or liberation from the cycle of rebirth. Rishikesh has been popular worldwide ever since famous artists, including The Beatles, traveled to ashrams for transcendence and inspiration. Because of the religious significance, non-vegetarian food and alcohol are prohibited in both towns.

Amritsar

Amritsar is an important seat of Sikh history and culture. Guru Ram Das, the fourth Sikh guru, is credited with founding the holy city. Located in the state of Punjab, Amritsar houses the Golden Temple, the most sacred shrine of Sikhism. Built around a man-made pool, the temple is an open house of worship for men and women of all faiths. Adjacent to the complex is Langar Hall, the world's largest community kitchen offering free meals to all pilgrims irrespective of caste, creed, and religion.

Dharamshala

Surrounded by cedar forests on the edge of the Himalayas, Dharamshala is home to the Dalai Lama and the Tibetan government-in-exile. The culture of Dharamshala is a perfect blend of serenity and spirituality. There are numerous temples and monasteries, as well as ashrams and retreat centers catering to the practice of meditation. The town has also become a refuge for several thousand Tibetan exiles who have settled in the area. Dharamshala also features the religion of nature, with spectacular views of the Kangra Valley and Dhauladhar Range.

Kedarnath

Kedarnath is part of the Char Dham Yatra in the northern state of Uttarakhand. The yatra, or pilgrimage, also includes Gangotri, Yamunotri, and Badrinath. The temple is dedicated to Lord Shiva and dates back over 1,200 years. At a height of 3,500 meters, Kedarnath remains covered by snow most of the year. The temple is closed during the winter season when the deity is brought down the mountain to a local village. When the weather improves during the summer, great fanfare and rituals accompany the return of the deity to the temple.

Ranakpur

Located just two hours from Udaipur and surrounded by tangled forests with monkeys abounding in the courtyard, Ranakpur is one of the five important pilgrimage centers for the Jain community. The temple, including the extraordinary array of 1144 pillars, is distinct in design with carved ceilings and arches depicting scenes from the lives of the Jain saints. Following a divine vision, a local Jain businessman started construction of the temple in the 15th century.

RECIPES

RECIPES FROM JAIPUR

Chandrika and Devika host dinners at Ikaki Niwas in Jaipur. Chandrika has a masters in computer science and loves teaching mathematics to children. She has traveled to many places but her favorite experience is trekking to the mighty Kailash Mansarovar. Her dishes are a fusion of North Indian cuisine and mostly non-vegetarian.

Devika is a housewife and looks after guests at the homestay. With a passion for traditional Rajasthani cuisine, she also loves to share the benefits of Ayurvedic cooking and enlighten guests on the culture of Rajput families.

Here they share two of their favorite recipes:

GATTA CURRY

Chickpea Dumpling Curry

Gatte ki sabzi or Gatta Curry (Gram flour dumpling curry) is a traditional and authentic recipe from Rajasthan. Gattas are simmered in spicy-zingy curd gravy, making it really irresistible. Serve the curry for lunch or dinner along with chapati, paratha, naan, or rice.

Because Rajasthan is a dry climate state with less availability of fresh vegetables, there is abundant use of flours, grains, and pulses. If there are no vegetables available in your kitchen then you can quickly make this delectable curry with chickpea flour, curd, and few aromatic Indian spices. The curry is a main course dish, but the steamed and fried dumplings can also be served as a snack or be used to make gatta pulao.

Ingredients / Serves 4

For Gatta:
- 1.5 cup gram flour
- 2 tablespoons yogurt
- 1 tablespoon cooking oil
- Pinch of asafoetida
- Pinch of baking soda
- 1 teaspoon fennel seeds
- 1 teaspoon coriander seeds
- 1/4 teaspoon carom seeds
- 1 teaspoon red chilli powder
- 1 teaspoon salt

For Gravy / Curry Sauce:
- 2 tablespoons mustard oil
- 1 teaspoon cumin seeds

- 1/4 teaspoon fenugreek seeds
- 2 cloves
- 1 bay leaves
- 2 dried red chilli, whole (optional)
- 1.5 cup yogurt
- 2 medium size onions
- 1/2 teaspoon ginger
- 1 teaspoon coriander powder
- 1/2 teaspoon turmeric powder
- 1/4 teaspoon garam masala powder
- Handful of fresh cilantro, finely chopped
- Salt to taste

Directions

For Gatta/Dumpling:

1. Coarsely crush coriander and fennel seeds (to add in the gatta dough).
2. In a bowl add gram flour, crushed seeds and all the ingredients listed for making gattas.
3. Mix and make a medium soft dough, add some more yoghurt if needed.
4. Make 6 balls from the dough and roll them to make long and medium thick rolls.
5. Boil 2.5 glasses of water in a pan, when it starts boiling then add the rolls in it. Boil for around 10 minutes, they will float on top of water when done.
6. Take out boiled gattas from the pan and let them cool down for 5 minutes. Do not throw the water; you will need this to add in the gravy.
7. Slice into medium size pieces and keep aside.

For the Gravy/Curry Sauce:

1. Heat oil in a pan and crackle cumin, fenugreek, cloves, bay leaves, and the dried whole chillies.
2. Add finely chopped onions and cook them till they turn golden.
3. Make a paste of turmeric, coriander and chilli powder with 1/2 a cup of yogurt and cook until the oil separates.
4. Add the remaining whisked yogurt and stir for a few minutes.
5. Now add water (in which you have boiled the gattas) and cook, stirring continuously.
6. When gravy starts boiling, add the sliced gattas.
7. Simmer for 3-5 minutes.
8. Add garam masala and fresh coriander.
9. Serve hot with millet or wheat flour breads, parathas, poori, steamed rice, or Khichdi.

Tips to Make the Perfect Gatta Curry

While kneading the dough, if the quantity of water is too much then the dough will become too thin and gatta prepared with this dough will splatter while frying.

If there is no boil in water and you drop the logs into it, then it will splatter.

If the dough is too firm then the gatta will also become hard as well. If you are preparing gravy using only curd then after adding all the spices add curd in small portions and keep stirring continuously until the gravy starts simmering then add the leftover water into it. Remember to stir the gravy continuously or the curd will coagulate.

For a vegan option, the gravy can be prepared using tomatoes (2 medium for this preparation).

Don't throw the leftover water in which you have boiled the gattas, as the cooked curry may thicken after some time so you can add this water to adjust the consistency.

You can add chopped fresh fenugreek leaves or Kasuri Methi in the gatta dough.

You can use the gatta's for making gatta pulao.

Gatta curry is made with gram flour dumplings boiled in water, sliced, and added in a spicy yogurt curry. Some like to fry the steamed gattas before adding in the curry, and this depends on personal choice.

Make a big batch of Gattas, far more than you would add to the gravy. Why? Because of all those invisible creatures (husband in my case) won't miss a chance to vanish a few Gattas every time you step out of the kitchen!

NARIYAL BURFI

A Coconut Sweet Prepared with Grated Coconut, Mawa, and Sugar Syrup

Burfi is an Indian sweet that is relished across the country on various celebratory occasions and festivities. It is a common dry sweet recipe commonly prepared during winter and during festivals like Diwali or Holi. Similar to any other barfi recipe, coconut barfi can also be prepared by topping it with dry fruits like pistachios, almonds, and cashews.

Our recipe is very simple and requires very basic ingredients - coconut, mawa, sugar, and clarified butter (ghee).

Ingredients

- 2 cups desiccated and grated coconut
- 1 cup sugar or add as required

- 1/2 cup mawa (whole dry milk)
- 1 tablespoon ghee (clarified butter)
- 1 teaspoon green cardamom powder
- A few pistachios (sliced) to decorate
- A pinch of saffron
- 1 - 2 teaspoon ghee to grease the tray

Directions

1. Grease the 7-8 inch tray using ghee and keep it aside.
2. Put ghee in a heavy pan, add mawa and continuously stir on low flame for 2-3 minutes or until it loosen up.
3. Add coconut and cardamom powder. Mix well and turn off the flame.
4. In another pan, add water and dissolve the sugar into the water over low heat.
5. Bring it to a boil. Keep a plate handy and test a few drops of sugar for 1 string consistency. (Take some between your fingers and pull apart, one thread should form).
6. Add the syrup to the coconut and mawa mixture and vigorously mix well. Pour the mixture into a greased tray. With the help of a spatula, even the layer.
7. Sprinkle it with sliced pistachios. Press it with spatula, so that they stick to the mixture.
8. Now let it set completely for a few hours. Once set, cut into cubes.
9. Gently remove the pieces and serve.

Tips

Cook on a low flame or it might burn and taste bitter.
Adjust the amount of sugar depending on your preferred sweetness.

RECIPES FROM DELHI

Neha Gupta, the founder of Saffron Palate, believes the secret ingredient to any recipe is love! The daughter of an Indian Air Force officer, Neha has been blessed to traverse the scenic landscapes and experience the vibrant cultures of India. After completing her MBA and working as a Corporate Trainer for over five years, Neha realized her passion was for cooking and making people experience the rich culture and cuisine of India. She believes that good company and delicious food brings a cheer to the heart and happiness on the face!

Neha started teaching in 2013 and has since hosted 8000+ guests in her studio and 5000+ virtually. She is the ONLY recommended Delhi cooking class in *Lonely Planet India* and Saffron Palate was featured in *Lonely Planet Food Trails of the World*, *DK Eyewitness Country Guides*, *New York Magazine*, and other local and international publications. Neha was also awarded the Times of India SheUnLTD Entrepreneur Award 2020 which honors successful women entrepreneurs.

CHICKEN KORMA

Chicken with Cashew Nuts

Ingredients

- 300 grams chicken (with bones or boneless cut into bite size pieces)
- 2 tsp ghee
- 1 tsp ginger garlic paste / 1 tsp grated ginger garlic
- 1 cup yogurt
- 1 cup onion (diced)
- 10 cashew nuts
- 5 Almonds
- 2 tbsp cilantro
- 1 Serrano pepper/ any hot pepper sliced in the middle into two
- ½ cup milk
- 2 tbsp heavy cream

- 1 tsp garam masala
- 1 tsp coriander powder
- 1 tsp smoked paprika
- 1 tsp turmeric powder
- 4 green cardamom
- 6 black peppercorns
- 1 inch cinnamon quill/bark/stick

Directions

1. Place chicken in a deep dish and mix with yogurt, spices, and salt.
2. Heat ghee and put in the chicken mix; fry until creamy and cooked.
3. Remove and keep aside.
4. Heat ghee in a dish and fry the onion, nuts, cilantro, and serrano pepper on medium flame for two minutes.
5. Transfer the above in a blender and make a fine paste.
6. Transfer the paste to a warm dish and add ½ cup water and get to boil.
7. Add the fried chicken and mix.
8. Add ½ cup milk.
9. Cover and simmer cook for 5 minutes.
10. Keep stirring occasionally.

GARLIC NAAN

White Flour Flatbread

Ingredients

- 2 cups all-purpose flour
- 2 tbsp melted butter

- 1 cup yogurt
- ½ tsp salt
- 2 tbsp powdered sugar
- ¼ lukewarm milk
- ¼ tbsp baking soda

Mix the above and make a dough. Keep aside outside for minimum 1 hour and maximum 8 hours.

In addition to the above, we you will also need:
- 2 tbsp butter
- 1 tbsp onion seeds
- 2 tbsp peeled and grated garlic
- 2 tbsp chopped cilantro

Directions

1. Take a small round portion and with the help of dry flour and a rolling pin roll it into a thin round shape.
2. Sprinkle 1/6 tsp onion seeds and roll further.
3. On the other side of the bread spread some water with a brush.
4. Heat a griddle and place the bread on it (water side down). Cook on moderate heat till you start to see bubbles and just a little puffing.
5. Turn the griddle upside down directly on the heat source and wait till it starts to burn in places.
6. Remove the bread from the griddle. It should be crunchy from the side placed with water.
7. Spread some butter, cilantro /coriander and garlic on it and serve hot.

RECIPES FROM GOA

Located in the picturesque town of Dabolim is Rita's Gourmet, a culinary school offering cooking classes and workshops. Rita Shinde, who started the venture in 2011, was born in Diu and brought up in Goa. She is very passionate about Goan cuisine and honed her skills from her mother. Rita was also one of twelve participants chosen by Maggi Nestle as women who are an inspiration through the power of cooking.

Rita's culinary tours and cooking classes have been featured in various publications, including Le Figaro, Spice Route, Jetwings, Travel Weekly UK, and The Chandigarh Tribune. She has created several culinary experiences - a one-day local farmer's market and cooking class, two seven-day comprehensive cooking workshops, a three-day culinary heritage tour, vegan cooking classes, and shore excursions for tourists visiting Goa by cruise ship. Rita's Gourmet Goa was also recognized as a TripAdvisor® Certificate of Excellence Hall of Fame winner.

GOAN PRAWN CURRY

A Tangy Curry Prepared with Shrimp, Spices, and Coconut Milk

Ingredients / Serves 4

- 3/4 cup (200 gr) prawns, cleaned and deveined
- 1 3/4 cup (400 ml) coconut milk
- 2 tsp red chili powder
- ½ tsp black pepper powder
- 1/2 tsp turmeric powder
- 1 tbsp tamarind pulp
- 1 small onion, sliced
- 3 tbsp oil
- 2 green chilies, slit
- 1 1/3 cup(200 ml) water
- Salt to taste

Directions

1. In a bowl marinate the prawns with 1/4 teaspoon salt and set aside.
2. Add the coconut milk, red chili powder, black peppercorn powder, turmeric powder, tamarind pulp to a bowl and mix well. Make sure there are no lumps.
3. Heat oil in a deep bottom pan and sauté the onions till pink.
4. To it add the coconut milk mixture, mix welSl and bring to boil.
5. Now keep the pan half covered, cooking on medium flame for 4 to 5 minutes. The consistency of curry should not be very thick, as it is served with steamed rice.
6. Add the marinated prawns, slit green chilies and salt to taste. Bring to a boil and cook for another 1 minute. Do not overcook the prawns.
7. Turn off the flame.
8. Best served hot with steamed rice.

CHICKEN CAFREAL

Chicken in Cilantro Sauce

Ingredients / Serves 4

- 400 grams chicken
- 1/2 teaspoon turmeric powder
- 6 cloves
- 1/4 tsp poppy seeds
- 1/2 tsp cumin seeds
- 2 green chilies
- 1/2-inch piece of cinnamon
- 5-6 garlic cloves
- 1 cup (50 gr) cilantro or coriander leaves
- Handful of mint leaves (optional, it adds aroma and flavor)
- 10 peppercorns
- 1/4-inch piece of ginger
- 1 tbsp sugar
- 3 tbsp lemon or lime juice
- 2 tbsp Worchester sauce
- 1 medium onion, finely chopped
- 2/3 cup (150 ml) chicken/vegetable stock or water
- 4 tbsp vegetable oil
- Salt to taste

Directions

1. Cut the chicken into 2-inch pieces, wash well. Leave it in the colander to let the water drain off completely.
2. In a blender, add turmeric powder, cloves, poppy seeds, cumin seeds, green chilies, cinnamon, garlic, cilantro leaves, mint leaves, peppercorns, ginger, sugar, lemon or lime juice and 3

tablespoons of water and grind to a smooth paste. The paste should have a thick consistency and should not be watery.

3. In a bowl, add the chicken pieces, ground paste, Worchester sauce and salt to taste. Give it a good mix and let the chicken marinate for at least 30 minutes.

4. Heat oil in a flat bottom pan and sauté the onions till golden brown.

5. Add the marinated chicken to the pan leaving the marinade behind.

6. Sear the chicken well on all the sides on medium to high flame for 2 to 3 minutes

7. Add the marinade, and the water or stock. Mix well and bring to a boil.

8. Check for seasoning and add salt if required.

9. Cover the pan and cook on medium flame for another 5 to 6 minutes. The sauce has to arrive at a semi dry consistency.

10. Turn off the flame and serve with French fries, mashed potatoes or sautéed veggies.

ACKNOWLEDGEMENTS

To my Parth: You and me together, we could do anything, baby; Thank you for loving me unconditionally and believing in the story of us.

To Alexander, Veer, and Amara: Thank you for being my greatest teachers and the best traveling companions. To Mom and Dad, for showing me the world.

To Karyn, for the laughs and worldly adventures. To Datri, for your content contribution, friendship, and adventurous spirit. To Dadi, for welcoming me with open arms.

To Kelly, for your support, inspiration, and telling the world SHE CAN.

To my incredible team in Delhi, for your dedication and passion to share the beauty of India with the world.

To Neha, for your resources, edits, and sense of humor with my Hindi translations.

To Abhishek Hajela, for your photography talents.

And to Mother India, for your raw, uncensored, and profound ability to always show the way.

With gratitude.

Milton Keynes UK
Ingram Content Group UK Ltd.
UKHW011824040923
428043UK00001B/113

9 780985 912253